Journalism and Truth in an Age
of Social Media

Journalism and Truth in an Age of Social Media

Edited by

JAMES E. KATZ AND KATE K. MAYS

OXFORD
UNIVERSITY PRESS

OXFORD
UNIVERSITY PRESS

Oxford University Press is a department of the University of Oxford. It furthers
the University's objective of excellence in research, scholarship, and education
by publishing worldwide. Oxford is a registered trade mark of Oxford University
Press in the UK and certain other countries.

Published in the United States of America by Oxford University Press
198 Madison Avenue, New York, NY 10016, United States of America.

© Oxford University Press 2019

CIP data is on file at the Library of Congress
ISBN 978-0-19-090026-7 (pbk.)
ISBN 978-0-19-090025-0 (hbk.)

Hardback printed by Bridgeport National Bindery, Inc., United States of America

Contents

Preface

There is an old story concerning squabbling umpires in the traditional American game of baseball. As many readers know, their job includes judging whether a baseball pitched to a hitter crosses through a certain specified zone, which is imaginary, called a strike zone, or outside of it, in which case the pitch is (confusingly) called a ball. Three strikes and the hitter is out, four balls and the hitter moves to first base. The three umpires take turns characterizing their judgmental process. The first umpire says, "I call them as best as I can see them." The second umpire says, "That's not good enough. I call them as what they really are." The third umpire says, "What they are is what I call them."

In a rudimentary way, this simple story of three umpires characterizes a view about the way journalists proceed. What is reality, and therefore what can be deemed true, is at least for the game of baseball in the hands of the umpires. For journalists, it's a bit more complicated. Yet this anecdote lays out the problem of what journalists perceive and reproduce for their audience in terms of the truth.

The situation is made all the more thorny by the advent of so-called fake news and other forms that depart from the legitimate and fair pursuit of facts in order to report the news. Although we will say more about this in Chapter 1, we can at this point add a fourth umpire to the hoary story, who would say, "I just call the pitch as anything I want, just as I feel at the moment; indeed, I can make up the whole game." This example is one form of fake news, which is itself an old game, reaching back into the mists of time long before baseball was invented. Another type of fake news is when perpetrators profoundly believe in the truth of their views and resist all evidence. ("All pitches made by that team are balls," would be an apt formulation.)

A variation on this theme of unfair perception is bias. Despite the fact that this form of perspective taking in journalism may be fully acknowledged, bias itself is more often subtle, and to the extent the possibility is acknowledged, tends to be downplayed. Yet it is far-reaching and pernicious, and may be formulated in our metaphor as, "While I think of myself as fair, I privately favor one team. But I am not biased; if my calls favor my preferred team, it's only because I know they are better." In such cases, the "team" may be a personality, ideology, country, or social class. While often unconscious, bias is not fake news in terms of the latter's qualities of pure fabrication and intentional misleading, yet it does cumulatively distort public perceptions, likely more strongly than any fake news onslaughts to date. Yet, like much of formal fake news, there is no easy fix for this problem.

These concerns over whether news is accurate and whether the press is a fair umpire are certainly long-standing. Yet, after the Brexit vote, and most especially since the unexpected election of Donald J. Trump as president of the United States in 2016, the intellectual world has been set alight by concerns over fake news. Opinions vary as to what fake news is, and multiple, often nuanced, definitions and distinctions have been proposed (Tandoc, Lim, and Ling 2018). Opinions also vary as to the import of fake news, which has been characterized across a range, from a manageable problem, to dangerously threatening, to already devastatingly consequential. According to a good many commentators, fake news has altered the trajectory of world history, including, as mentioned, the Brexit vote and the election of Mr. Trump, and, in the case of Emmanuel Macron, almost derailed the will of the electorate. Unsurprisingly and appropriately, there have been a flood of popular and academic publications addressing the fake news problem, and this volume adds to that discussion in several of our chapters.

But it also follows the trail in the opposite direction by asking how journalists pursue the truth in their work, and how audiences receive and perceive the truth value of what journalists produce. It's easy enough to outline the book's aim, which is to shed light on these issues, but questions of identifying, characterizing, and communicating the truth has been a nettlesome problem for millennia. Indeed, the definition of what is truth and the identification of what about the world is true is a vast society-wide enterprise encompassing religious and political institutions, not to mention scientific and judicial bodies. Here we focus on but one institution: the journalistic enterprise.

As complicated as the search for truth has been historically, the situation has become even more so with the onslaught of social media. As to its effects on journalism, many readers will be familiar with the major changes wrought by social media. These include

- dramatic changes in the economic model of revenue for newspapers in particular and the news industry in general;
- downsizing of newspaper staff and newsrooms generally—newsroom employment has dropped by about 25% in 1998 compared to a decade earlier (Grieco 2018);
- accessibility and use of undercover videos, bystander cell phone videos, angry tweets, and other sources of compelling documentation of questionable or improper behavior (Gordon 2018);
- increased accountability for reporters' activities, both in terms of management from above and public reception of their handiwork; this includes monitoring by click counts and reader responses as well as possible detection of plagiarism for instance;
- fragmentation of the media environment and personalization of distribution channels; this has the dual effect of both presenting content out of context and on the same "playing field," and giving consumers tailored lists of news that may only render a particular and narrow worldview;
- largely unknown algorithmic mechanisms that are potentially powerful gatekeepers, elevating some viewpoints while limiting others, depending on the (opaque) technological parameters of each platform. This in turn has raised pointed questions about bias, representation, and fairness.

Readers may recognize how some of the above technological advances have given rise to the widely discussed fake news phenomenon, which we argue is neither entirely new nor entirely old hat. Nevertheless, it is justifiably a hot topic.

As some of our contributors put forth, fake news can encompass everything from sarcastic or ironic humor (as in the case of stories being picked up from the Babylon Bee) all the way to bot-driven, made-up stories. Yet it also includes the use of incomplete or misleadingly selective framing of stories, adjectives used in the story, and photographs that editorially convey certain characteristics. In fact, fake news has come to encompass so much that a group at Harvard's Shorenstein Center has created an entire

"Information Disorder" toolkit that includes a glossary for all the terms relevant to today's information environment. Like the term "social media," which we discuss more in the introduction, we use the term "fake news" capaciously. If people would like an exhaustive definition that once and for all allows journalistic efforts to be judged true or not, we have to disappoint them. Rather than laser-focus on fake news as a current phenomenon, we address truth in journalism, as it has in the past and continues to operate in politics, and how technology may be complicating that relationship. In all aspects, journalism is a social enterprise, with many players and roles, which not only include creators but also audiences, and not only production but also assimilation and response.

A word is in order about the book's audience. Our contributors and we have written this book for the sophisticated general reader, those interested in the social consequences of emerging media on information and truth, as well as the community of journalism studies scholars, which range from active journalists to researchers, and most especially to students. The volume seeks to connect the worlds of practical journalism and philosophical inquiry, when both often proceed without the other. For students learning the craft, it is important to know how to not only practice it but also to be aware of the larger context and intellectual import of what they are doing. Likewise, for students who tend to look at abstract ethical issues and are focused on analytical philosophy, they might find their deliberations enriched by an understanding of the craft and practical constraints of journalism.

This collection should also be of interest to scholars working in fields related to emerging media, a relatively new field of study that is expanding rapidly and crisscrosses multiple disciplines. As such, the approach is inherently interdisciplinary in nature, encompassing philosophy, behavioral and social sciences, human interaction, and digital and communication studies, among others. In terms of its aim at journalists, the book provides a lens to study both the evolving craft of journalism and considers larger questions about the social effects of emerging technologies, such as the growing role of algorithms, big data, and automatic-content production regimes. Journalism scholars can look to this volume to keep pace with systemic technological advancements and their effects on the practices of journalistic production and information dissemination. Moreover, scholars working in varied disciplines such as computational studies, sociology, media and communication, philosophy, and political science, who study issues related to information diffusion and truth, may find the volume useful for under-standing emerging media's relevance to and implications for their respec-tive fields. While the book emphasizes what is new and novel, by drawing on historical perspectives it also considers what is enduring and consistent. We should also mention the international scope of our contributors and their coverage as it goes beyond exclusively US-centric concerns.

We assembled this collection of expert analyses in large part to serve as a tool for classroom instruction. As we developed the book, several jour-nalism instructors expressed enthusiasm for adopting such a book for their courses. If it sparks among our readers greater understanding of and in-terest in the topic of social media as part of the journalistic endeavor, our goal will have been achieved.

References

Grieco, Elizabeth. 2018. "Newsroom Employment Dropped Nearly a Quarter in Less than 10 Years, with Greatest Decline at Newspapers." Pew Research Center. July 30. http://www.pewresearch.org/fact-tank/2018/07/30/newsroom-employment-dropped-nearly-a-quarter-in-less-than-10-years-with-greatest-decline-at-newspapers/.

Gordon, Stephen. 2018. "An Unfair Game: Urban Meyer, a History of Abuse." Project Veritas. August 2. https://www.projectveritas.com/2018/08/02/an-unfair-game-urban-meyer-a-history-of-abuse/.

Tandoc, Edson C. Jr., Zheng Wei Lim, and Richard Ling. 2018. "Defining 'Fake News': A Typology of Scholarly Definitions." *Digital Journalism* 6, no. 2: 137–153.

Acknowledgments

Words of gratitude are in order. Hallie Stebbins, the commissioning editor at Oxford University Press, did a wonderful job helping refine the book's overarching structure, and editorial assistant Hannah Doyle managed all of the logistics handily. In its later stages, Angela Chapko and her assistant Alexcee Bechthold, guided our book project to the finished product presented here. Co-author and co-editor Kate Mays was an invaluable collaborator and was pitch-perfect in encouraging our contributors to stay on schedule. She is also co-author of the introductory chapter and the concluding chapter. Dean Tom Fiedler and Andrew Lack helped inspire the project and nurtured it in its early phases. Though new to this particular corner of the world, Boston University colleague and philosopher Juliet Floyd did much to stimulate our deeper thinking about the ethical and intellectual politics of these issues. Allison Keir helped organize the conference that proved to be the foundational event that catalyzed this book. The generosity of the Feld Family and Kenneth Feld in particular have helped create a rich intellectual environment at Boston University and have supported numerous worthy endeavors here.

Many colleagues were extremely helpful in the preparation of this volume. Their fine eye and discerning judgment have done much to assist us. Of particular note in this regard are Michelle Amazeen, Chris Daly, Jacob Groshek, Lei Guo, Bill McKeen, and Chris Wells.

A word of thanks is due to our peer reviewers. Every chapter was blind reviewed and passed by at least two field experts. Their care and critical engagement were vital in advancing the quality of the contributed chapters. In order to preserve the blind quality of the reviews, we will not identify the peer reviewers here but they should know they have our thanks.

Our colleague from Texas Tech, Erik P. Bucy, deserves special mention for his deft, sage, and timely critiquing the volume's contents and advice about its structure and direction. Over my years of professional experience, I've never encountered anyone who surpassed him in generosity of spirit, fine eye for detail, and supercomputer-like capacity for constructive criticism and analytical insight. To this encomium, I must add his incredible speed and facility in achieving such scholarly benchmarks. He is a remarkable colleague.

On behalf of co-editor Kate Mays, the chapter authors, and myself, I express heartfelt thanks to the colleagues who have done so much to help bring this volume to fruition.

James E. Katz

Kenmore Square, Boston

Thanksgiving, 2018

List of Contributors

Colin Agur is Assistant Professor at the Hubbard School of Journalism & Mass Communication at the University of Minnesota-Twin Cities. A former research fellow at Columbia University's Tow Center for Digital Journalism, he is also affiliated with Yale Law School's Information Society Project and was recently a resident faculty fellow at the Institute for Advanced Study (IAS) at the University of Minnesota.

Valerie Belair-Gagnon is a Media Sociologist, an Assistant Professor of Journalism Studies at the Hubbard School of Journalism & Mass Communication, and affiliated faculty in the Department of Sociology at the University of Minnesota. She directs the Minnesota Journalism Center and is affiliated with the Yale Information Society Project.

Erik P. Bucy is Marshall and Sharleen Formby Regents Professor of Strategic Communication in the College of Media and Communication at Texas Tech University. His research focuses on misinformation, nonverbal communication, and digital media and has been funded by the National Association of Broadcasters; C-SPAN Education Foundation; Social Science Research Council; and Harvard University's Shorenstein Center on Press, Politics, and Public Policy.

Juliet Floyd is Professor of Philosophy at Boston University. She has been a Visiting Professor of Philosophy at the University of Vienna, the University of Paris I Panthéon-Sorbonne, the University of Bordeaux 3, Université Michel de Montaigne, and a fellow of the Dibner Institute at MIT and the Lichtenberg-Kolleg, an institute of advanced study at the Georg August Universität, Göttingen.

R. Kelly Garrett is Associate Professor in the School of Communication at Ohio State University. His work has been supported by the National Science Foundation (NSF), and he was previously a senior research fellow at the Center for Research on Information Technology and Organizations (CRITO) at the University of California, Irvine.

Lucas Graves is Associate Professor in the School of Journalism and Mass Communication at the University of Wisconsin-Madison, where he is also a faculty affiliate of the Holtz Center for Science & Technology Studies and the Center for Communication and Democracy. From 2017 to 2019 he was Senior Research Fellow at the Reuters Institute for the Study of Journalism at the University of Oxford. His book *Deciding What's True: The Rise of Political Fact-Checking in American Journalism* came out in 2016 from Columbia University Press.

Yael de Haan is Professor of Applied Sciences for Journalism in Digital Transition at the University of Applied Sciences Utrecht in the Netherlands. She obtained her PhD at the Amsterdam School of Communication Research (ASCoR) at the University of Amsterdam.

John Maxwell Hamilton is Hopkins P. Breazeale Professor of Journalism at Louisiana State University's Manship School of Mass Communication and Senior Scholar at the Woodrow Wilson International Center. A longtime journalist, academic, and public servant, he was a founding dean of the Manship School and reported abroad for ABC Radio and *the Christian Science Monitor*, among other media. His most recent book, *Journalism's Roving Eye: A History of American Foreign Reporting*, won the Goldsmith Prize. He was a fellow at Harvard University's Shorenstein Center on the Press, Politics, and Public Policy.

James E. Katz is Feld Professor of Emerging Media at Boston University's College of Communication, where he directs the Center for Mobile Communication Studies and Division of Emerging Media, and Distinguished Professor at Peking University in Beijing. Before Boston University, he received the highest faculty honor at Rutgers University as its Board of Governors Professor of Communication, and he was twice Chair of the Department of Communication there. He has been awarded a Distinguished Fulbright Chair to Italy; fellowships at Princeton, Harvard, and MIT; and the Ogburn career achievement award from the American Sociological Association. He is also a fellow of the International Communication Association and the American Association for the Advancement Science (AAAS). Earlier he was a Distinguished Member of Staff and Director of the social science research unit at Bell Communications Research (Bellcore).

Nicole M. Krause is a doctoral candidate in Life Sciences Communication at the University of Wisconsin–Madison.

Sanne Kruikemeier is Assistant Professor of Political Communication and Journalism at the Amsterdam School of Communication Research (ASCoR) at the University of Amsterdam in the Netherlands. Her research focuses on the consequences and implications of online communication for individuals and society.

Sophie Lecheler is Professor of Political Communication at the University of Vienna in Austria. She was also a Marie Curie Research fellow at the London School of Economics and Political Science, and an Associate Professor at the Amsterdam School of Communication Research (ASCoR) at the University of Amsterdam in the Netherlands.

Kate K. Mays is a doctoral candidate in the Division of Emerging Media Studies at Boston University's College of Communication. She is also a graduate student fellow for computational and data-driven research at the Rafik B. Hariri Institute for Computing and Computational Science & Engineering at Boston University.

Maria D. Molina is a doctoral student (ABD) in the Donald P. Bellisario College of Communications at The Pennsylvania State University. Maria's research builds upon psychology and communication theory to advance interface design and user experience of digital media technologies. She is particularly interested in social and motivational technologies. Among her projects is the examination of the role of technological affordances in the consumption of false information and on tracking technologies in the health context. Her research on misinformation is supported by the US National Science Foundation, Rita Allen Foundation, and WhatsApp.

John E. Newhagen is Associate Professor Emeritus in the College of Journalism at the University of Maryland. Prior to his academic career he worked as a foreign correspondent in Central America and the Caribbean, serving as bureau chief in San Salvador, regional correspondent in Mexico City, and foreign editor in Washington, DC for United Press International.

Peppino Ortoleva has been Professor of Media History and Theory at the University of Torino, and for over 40 years has been a scholar, critic, and curator at the crossroads of history, media studies, TV and radio authoring, and museums and exhibitions. His most recent book is *Miti a bassa intensità. Racconti, media, vita quotidiana* ("Low Intensity Myths. Stories, Media, Daily Life), Einaudi, Torino, 2019.

Dietram A. Scheufele is the John E. Ross Professor in Science Communication and Vilas Distinguished Achievement Professor at the University of Wisconsin–Madison and in the Morgridge Institute for Research. He is an elected member of the German National Academy of Science and Engineering, and a fellow of the American Association for the Advancement of Science, the International Communication Association, and the Wisconsin Academy of Sciences, Arts & Letters.

Edward Schiappa is the John E. Burchard Professor of Humanities and Professor and Head of Comparative Media Studies/Writing at the Massachusetts Institute of Technology. He has been editor of *Argumentation and Advocacy* and received the Douglas W. Ehninger Distinguished Rhetorical and Rhetorical and Communication Theory Distinguished Scholar Awards. He has been named a National Communication Association Distinguished Scholar.

Michael Schudson is Professor of Journalism at the Columbia University Graduate School of Journalism. He is a MacArthur Foundation "genius" fellow, and has also been awarded honorary doctorates by the University of Groningen, The Netherlands in 2014 and by Hong Kong Baptist University in 2018.

Zeynep Soysal is Assistant Professor in Philosophy at the University of Rochester. She was formerly a postdoctoral associate on the Andrew W. Mellon Sawyer Seminar Grant, "Humanities and Technology at the Crossroads, 2016–2018" at Boston University after she received her doctorate in philosophy from Harvard University.

S. Shyam Sundar is James P. Jimirro Professor of Media Effects and Co-Director of the Media Effects Research Laboratory at the Donald P. Bellisario College of Communications in The Pennsylvania State University. His research has been supported by the National Science Foundation, Korea Science and Engineering Foundation, the MacArthur Foundation, Facebook Inc., and Lockheed Martin Information Systems and Global Services. He edited the first-ever *Handbook of the Psychology of Communication Technology* (Wiley Blackwell 2015) and served as Editor-in-Chief of the *Journal of Computer Mediated Communication* from 2013 to 2017.

David L. Swartz, following retirement from full-time teaching, is a Researcher in the Department of Sociology at Boston University, where he was previously Assistant Professor. He is a Senior Editor and Book Review Editor of *Theory and Society*. He is formerly Chair of the History of Sociology Section of the American Sociological Association and Co-Chair of the Political Sociology Standing Group in the European Consortium of Political Sociology.

Edson C. Tandoc Jr. is Associate Professor at the Wee Kim Wee School of Communication and Information at the Nanyang Technological University in Singapore, as well as the Director of the PhD and master's research programs there. He is an Associate Editor for *Digital Journalism*.

Heidi Tworek is Assistant Professor in the Department of History at the University of British Columbia in Vancouver, Canada, where she is also a member of the Science and Technology Studies program, the Language Science Initiative, and the Institute for European Studies at UBC. She is a visiting fellow at the Joint Center for History and Economics at Harvard University as well as a non-resident fellow at the German Marshall Fund of the United States and the Canadian Global Affairs Institute. She has held visiting fellowships at the Transatlantic Academy in Washington, DC; Birkbeck, University of London; and the Centre for Contemporary History, Potsdam, Germany. She was previously Assistant Director of Undergraduate Studies and Lecturer in the History Department at Harvard University. She is a term member of the Council on Foreign Relations.

Brian E. Weeks is Assistant Professor in the Department of Communication Studies and a faculty associate in the Center for Political Studies at the University of Michigan.

Chris Wells is Assistant Professor in the Division of Emerging Media Studies and Department of Journalism at Boston University's College of Communication, where he studies political communication and digital media. His book *The Civic Organization and the Digital Citizen: Communicating Engagement in a Networked Age* was published by Oxford University Press in 2015.

Christopher D. Wirz is a doctoral candidate in Life Sciences Communication at the University of Wisconsin–Madison.

Michael A. Xenos is Professor of Communication Science in the Department of Communication Arts at the University of Wisconsin–Madison, where he is also an affiliate faculty member in the Department of Life Sciences Communication and the School of Journalism and Mass Communication. He is also (with Paul R. Brewer) Co-Editor-in-Chief of *International Journal of Public Opinion Research* and has previously served as Editor-in-Chief of the *Journal of Information Technology and Politics*.

1

Introduction

James E. Katz and Kate K. Mays

In 1998, at the beginning of the Internet era, the senior editor of this volume wrote an article discussing challenges to truth in the emerging online arena. Entitled "Struggle in Cyberspace: Fact and Friction on the World Wide Web" (Katz 1998), he predicted that the Internet would lead to challenges to the received societal wisdom and lead to the proliferation of false information, including news. He held: "Among the consequences for the facts of our time, and for those of the future, are that equal time is given to any viewpoint; false information spreads quickly; true information spreads quickly; and facts more easily escape from their creator's or owner's control." The role of compelling but false rumors was highlighted. Rather than fears of Russian influence over elections, the early concerns about fake and misleading information on the Internet revolved around warnings to the unwary of gang initiation attack rituals and kidney thefts from unwary business travelers (both of which were urban legends).

In the more than two decades since that article was written, problems of correctly perceiving reality have been exacerbated by the increasing polarization of society. It seems beyond question that the Internet and the growth of social media have played important roles in this process.

The journalism profession is under unprecedented pressure to respond to both the business and the procedural challenges precipitated by these communication technologies. The accuracy and fairness of news justifiably occupies a central place in the pantheon of public concerns. For most people the news they receive allows them to understand the world beyond their immediate sensory experience and come to conclusions about the organization of the world and their place in it. After all, "fake news" and biased news are said to affect matters of war and peace and even the destinies of nations.

This book explores how the relationship between journalism and the pursuit of truth is changing due to the growth of social media and ancillary computer systems. The volume's chapters include inquiries into how news is perceived and identified, how news is presented to the public, and how the public responds to news. They also consider social media's effect on the craft of journalism, as well as the growing role of algorithms, big data, and automatic-content production regimes. The volume is interdisciplinary— encompassing philosophy, behavioral science, human-computer interaction, and digital and communication studies. This volume's aim is to focus insightfully and articulately on these issues in a way that will be of enduring relevance; the discussions about journalism now will be able to stand the test of time to inform current and future scholars. Each chapter addresses a different component of journalism in today's digital age and reflects on questions such as: What is different and what remains the same in terms of journalism's pursuit of truth now that social media has become such a prominent force in news gathering, dissemination, reinterpretation, and reader participation/responses? What are the implications for journalistic information gathering and truth claims? What are the implications for the social role of journalists and their media institutions? How have algorithms and other digital formats affected what is perceived and produced as news? In what ways does the interaction between journalists and social media affect democratic practices? The chapters offer a mix of critical and empirical work that considers journalism's past, present, and future roles in our lives and in society. Within its capacious umbrella, this book assembles leading scholars in the fields of journalism and communication studies, philosophy, and the social sciences to address critical questions of how we should understand journalism's changing landscape as it relates to fundamental questions about the role of truth and information in society.

The contributors and we are building on a foundation laid over decades. The founding figures of the United States recognized the value of a free press in the Constitution's Bill of Rights, a view that societies and governments in many parts of the world have adopted to varying degrees (and, equally, resisted by authoritarian governments everywhere else). It is now enshrined in the International Declaration of Human Rights and many constitutions and laws (including article 125 of the USSR's 1936 Constitution, thus exemplifying the distressing gap between word and practice when it comes to press freedom).

Complementing the legal framework of acknowledgment of the press's pivotal role in society has been the work of social scientists. In terms of outstanding analytical figures in the United States, Walter Lippmann might be considered the field's founder. He has been followed by an array of thinkers from Herbert Gans a half-century ago to today's scholars such as Esther Thorson and Michael Schudson. Parallel and intersecting work has been carried out in other countries, most notably in France, through the work of Pierre Bourdieu. Our book seeks to build on the shoulders of these giants. We have chapters by Schudson and a collaborator of Thorson, as well as a brief analysis of Bourdieu's contribution by David Swartz. Peppino Ortoleva presents a historical analysis of news from an earlier era of France, while Nicole Krause and colleagues draw on Lippmann in their chapter.

Vast is the topic of truth in journalism; in this book we selectively inquire about the topic by seeking to bridge discussions of digital disruption in journalism precipitated by social media technologies with deeper inquiries about truth and objectivity in journalism. Detailed critiques of objectivity in journalism have been laid out elsewhere (e.g., Maras 2013; Ward 2004; Hearns-Branaman 2016), and we do not need to repeat their work in this volume. Although we do not focus exhaustively on ethical and philosophical perspectives of truth in journalism, these considerations foreground much of the discussion in the coming chapters. We therefore briefly review some of these fundamental concepts.

As Ward (2004) lays out in his comprehensive history of how media ethics emerged and evolved, the epistemological norms for journalists have changed over time. Indeed, journalism began as a mere hobby for people in the 17th century, which gradually shifted from a social activity to a social practice in the next century. As new governments formed (e.g., in America and France) in the 18th to 19th centuries, the "press" became more formalized and recognized as a "fourth estate" vital to democracy and thus the public interest. In response to the increasing professionalism of journalism in the 1900s, particularly as power consolidated in a mass media system, professional associations sprung up to establish norms and standards that journalists would have to follow—a "professional ethic" (Ward 2004, 360)—in order to cement and justify their role in serving the public interest. As such, journalists' views of truth and their roles in conveying truth have not remained static.

Ward argues that, in the digital age, we are in a "fifth revolution in journalism ethics" (2004, 342), not only because technology has altered journalistic practices, but also because it has created a global form of journalism. No longer are the media in one country isolated by regional or even national boundaries—media now have far-reaching cultural and so-cial reach on a global scale. In terms of journalists' responsibilities, this has critical implications because journalists' "publics" are becoming radi-cally different from earlier eras. Further, the norms and market structures may differ across countries, such that the different cultural values and sys-tems of organization result in conflicting media standards and practices. (These varying conditions are visible in contrasting press laws and practices among the United States, the UK, and China, for instance. They have widely varying policies on journalistic reporting on political party mis-deeds and court proceedings, among many other areas.) Beyond Ward (2013), who writes about global media ethics, including in the Global South, and Hargreaves (2003), who gives an international perspective on the problems that plague journalists, we can recommend McBride and Rosenstiel's (2014) useful primer on journalism ethics in the digital age, emphasizing as they do the principles of truth, transparency, and community.

A detailed discussion of media ethics is outside the scope of this book, however, and while our chapter authors touch on facets of epistemology and truth in journalism, we do not give a thorough treatment of the topic. For those interested, Hearns-Branaman's (2016) book applies various philosophical approaches of truth to journalistic practices. In particular, he explicates four major epistemological approaches to journalistic prac-tice, all of which take a more nuanced angle than do those who see objec-tivity as the primary goal of journalism. Of these four approaches, the first two—realism and pragmatism—are both normative theories of journalism, prescribing as they do specific aims for how journalists should perform their role.

The realist approach is predicated on Enlightenment and positivist ideas that reality is accessible to the human mind; therefore, journalists can convey reality to their audiences through the news media. In the 19th cen-tury, this view emphasized collecting the most "objective" physical evidence. At the turn of the 20th century, the focus shifted to language as the "sub-stance" between people and reality. From this assumption, the focus in a journalist's practice is to gather and transmit evidence that can most closely approximate reality—the journalist's goal is to provide the most valid infor-mation that corresponds to the reality.

In contrast, the pragmatic approach shifts the emphasis from presenting the "most valid information" to the "most diverse information." The conten-tion in pragmatism is that "[r]eality is out of the bounds of our perception,

[but] it is the best explanation we have at this moment to explain the world" (Hearns-Branaman 2016, 64). Pragmatist truth, then, is socially and culturally "contingent" in that it is whatever opinions and knowledge "win out" to prove themselves as useful to society. This "marketplace of ideas" approach privileges the airing of as many ideas and knowledge sources as possible; in journalism, this manifests as making stories "balanced" by offering as many diverse perspectives as possible. The danger of the pragmatic approach is projecting an appearance of balance of *all* ideas when, in fact, only a few ideas are presented: while journalists may purport to have a balance of truth and debate in their stories, "instead, we get a narrow discussion and journalists disempowered by an obsessive need to balance certain topics in which powerful people have a different view" (Hearns-Branaman 2016, 64).

Despite their contradictory nature, Hearns-Branaman (2016) sees both realism and pragmatism as necessary poles between which journalists operate, and whether they reside more in the pragmatist or realist end depends on context. There may be certain stories or topics that call more for a pragmatic approach, and others that are better served by realism. Both approaches, however, are based on the idea that information about reality can be conveyed; in contrast, "antirealism"—a third approach to journalistic practice—takes an entirely social constructivist view of reality and truth. The "reproductions of reality" that journalists create can never actually correspond to reality, and thus the focus here is on *how* journalists construct reality, given various influences of language, politics, and society. As opposed to the realists, who aim to use language in a way that corresponds most closely to reality, antirealists contend that there will always be an unbridgeable gap between language and reality. In this, reality comes about "through the structure of a society and its specific culture," and, as such, media are influential in constructing (rather than representing) reality (e.g., facts and events do not come into existence without their human interpretation of them).

The antirealist approach is based on the notion that reality does not exist but for that which is constructed by humans, which is a useful notion for journalists to keep in mind—they are not mere stenographers or recorders, and may contribute to a certain version of reality. (Readers may recognize glimmers of this notion in the classic communication theory of "agenda setting," wherein the news has a tangible effect on what consumers consider important.)

However, antirealism "brackets out discussion of reality," which is certainly less helpful if the aim is to discern some kind of truth from journalistic reports. From these three differing perspectives, Hearns-Branaman (2016) suggests "hyperrealism" as a solution because it incorporates the "uncertainty of reality," while still grounded in a sense that conveying reality is a journalist's goal. However, considering the social constructivist nature of reality—as a construct created from language and other influences—in the hyperrealist framework, "journalists give signs of Reality, relying on the self-referential codes of media logic" (Hearns-Branaman 2016, 133). Realism had pursued the merging of signs and reality, pragmatism could only provide many "signs from different positions" (134), and antirealism focused on the process of choosing and presenting signs. On the other hand:

> Hyperrealism . . . forces us to consider that the "Something" from which journalists and the public get the information they need to construct news is largely self-referring signifiers, bits of information that only signify other bits of information and have become too highly abstracted from real life . . . news media is "beyond true and false," and any Realism that we think is out there is, in fact, Hyperreal, forced to be more real than the real in order to reinject Reality in an otherwise Antirealist world. (Hearns-Branaman 2016, 134).

There are practical considerations of a journalist's role that ground these ideas. Ward reminds us that "journalism ethics belongs to the public" (2004, 360), and therefore journalists should establish the "media needs" of their audience conceptualized as

> citizens in self-governing democracies. There are at least six such needs: (1) informational needs—wide and deep; (2) explanatory needs; (3) "perspective enrichment" needs; (4) advocational and reform needs; (5) participatory needs; and (6) dialogic needs. (Ward 2004, 360)

These needs may be more or less salient depending on the context, and so it is important to have in the mind the various roles that journalism and news play in our society. In a similar fashion, Erik Bucy has formulated a six-fold definition of news, which he developed for us and that we present here.

"Six Definitions": Spotlight on Defining News, by Erik P. Bucy

Typically, and without much reflection, news is casually defined as those events in the past 24 hours that are new and important. *Hard news*, according to Jamieson and Campbell, "is the report of an event that happened or that was disclosed within the previous 24 hours and treats an issue of ongoing concern" (2001, 40). From this perspective, news is described as having several enduring characteristics, including a personalized focus on individuals; dramatic, conflict-filled, and violent content; an identifiable occurrence or event; information that is novel, deviant, or out of the ordinary; and linkages to issues prevalent in society at the time of reporting (see also Bennett 2016; Iyengar and Westwood 2015). These practical criteria allow editors to make news decisions in newsrooms under real-time pressures.

However functional these criteria are for news production purposes, practitioner definitions of news do not explain why audiences attend to novel, threatening, or offbeat stimuli and why so much news on traditional and social media platforms is intended to attract attention first and inform second. Therefore, it is important to consider the other perspectives on news that may also inform, beyond the *practitioner* view of news, why journalism seems to be losing its way: the democratic, sociological, psychological, economic, and political.

The *democratic* view of news holds the press accountable for delivering information important to political decision-making to the mass electorate. Analysis of the news media from this perspective frequently focuses attention on the quality of political news coverage and is critical toward the press for being overly interpretive and intrusive as well as playing an inflated arbitrative role in public life (see Bucy and D'Angelo 1999; 2004). In the democratic view, audiences are regarded first and foremost as *citizens*.

From the *sociological* perspective, news performs a variety of important social functions, including the classic surveillance function of "disclosing threats and opportunities affecting the value position of the community and of the component parts within it" (Lasswell [1948] 1972, 98). Another particularly important function of the news is the social coordination of individuals and groups through shared symbols and meanings (Schudson 2003, 11), which Lasswell labeled correlation. Of course, any particular account of the day's events is selective by definition, and some important items are inevitably ignored while others are given substantial coverage. Journalists, in this sense, have broad discretion in deciding what is news and thereby construct a picture of reality driven by certain values and professional practices rather than conveying a wholly neutral version of reality (Gans 1979; Schudson 2003). From the sociological perspective, news audiences are regarded first and foremost as *members of a social system.*

Important to any systematic discussion about news is the difference between routine, everyday information and warnings about threats, dangers, and attacks (Fox 2003, 56). Because of its nonthreatening nature, routine information is easily overlooked or ignored; on the other hand, negative information about events is much more likely to compel attention because survival depends on it (Newhagen 1998; Reeves and Nass 1996). "The unique character of news," Newhagen and Levy (2013, 10) observe, "has to do with a basic need common to all living things for information about novel or threatening events in their surroundings."

The September 11 terrorist attacks and subsequent US military interventions in Afghanistan and Iraq brought this point home in dramatic, and enduring, fashion. Since 9/11, the news emphasis on terrorism and national security has focused public attention on survival-relevant topics to a degree probably unseen since the height of the Cold War. The value of national crisis coverage thus stems from its survival relevance—and psychological significance. From the *psychological* view of news, members of the news audience are positioned as active information processors who employ cognitive and emotional heuristics, including routine scanning of the information environment, in the daily assessment of risk.

In the *economic* view, news is regarded as an information product tasked with attracting the widest possible audience to generate the largest amount of revenue possible. From this perspective, criticism has been leveled at media organizations for debasing public discourse for the sake of putting the profit motive first, for instance, linking to viral videos or "click bait" ads designed to attract eyeballs but little else (see Deuze 2007). News audiences, in the economic view, are regarded first and foremost as *consumers.*

Finally, in the *political* view of news, information is regarded as a strategic resource, typically by a political campaign or administration already in office, to be wielded for moving public opinion and galvanizing support. When the goal is to rattle an opponent or obfuscate controversial details of a piece of legislation or justify a highly unpopular administrative action, like war, sometimes false information is leaked with the intention to mislead the public and misinform the press. Here, information serves the needs of power rather than the needs of citizens.

Given the various perspectives Erik Bucy presents, it is clear that journalism should be studied and critiqued from a number of angles, which is what this book aims to do. In particular, we seek to examine the craft and reception of the news process in order to see the way in which the idea of truth is created, propagated, received, and distorted. We hope the chapters in this book, to a certain degree, bridge the two worlds of the practical and philosophical, as both often proceed without the other. For students learning the craft, it is important they not only know how to practice journalism but also are aware of the larger context and intellectual import of what they're doing. Likewise, for students who tend to look at abstract ethical issues, and are focused on analytical philosophy, they may find their deliberations enriched by an understanding of the craft and practical constraints of journalists, particularly in today's social media environment. At a high level, our chapters covered the following ground arranged in several parts and a concluding chapter.

Democracy, News, and Society

We start with a broader, sociological view of journalism's role as it intersects with truth, politics, and power. **Michael Schudson** opens his chapter with an apt observation that runs throughout this book: the rocky relationship between truth and politics (or news) is not a new phenomenon—certainly not with Donald Trump, and not with the advent of the Internet and digital technology. Rather, following Hannah Arendt, power has always threatened truth, and so we cannot say that we live in a post-truth age now as opposed to any other time. This threat is possible because truth is a "social consensus," though it is one that is, nevertheless, constrained by reality. In framing truth this way, he identifies the "4 P's" that can threaten truth: propaganda, profit, prejudice, and pranks. This framework nicely foregrounds the subsequent chapters, as others' investigations tackle facets of the 4 P's to varying degrees. **Lucas Graves and Chris Wells** consider the implications of political speech that has become unmoored from institutional norms and practices in a media environment driven by the attention economy—within Schudson's 4 P's framework, for example, this may be seen as propaganda unwittingly enabled by profit motives. They distinguish between notions of information availability (facts are reachable) and factual accountability (facts matter). Typically, truthful political speech and behavior are buoyed by institutional norms, which the media could reliably assume. Now, however, we seem to be in an environment where politicians and democratic institutions do not necessarily adhere to truth-telling norms: the question is less about whether facts are reachable, but that politicians hold themselves and are held by the public to factual accountability.

In one of two special sections, called "spotlight," **David Swartz** revisits the relationship between truth and power through the lens of Pierre Bourdieu. Journalism may be viewed as a "field of struggle for truth" related to power because fundamentally journalism is a struggle to impose a certain viewpoint as legitimate, against other fields like politics and economics. His analysis reveals the struggle within journalism, as well, between competing economic and cultural "poles."

Nicole Krause and colleagues address more directly, as Schudson alludes to in his chapter, the people who choose to ignore that the emperor walking down the street has no clothes. They establish first that fake news is not a new phenomenon; it has manifested in tabloids, satirical news, paid content as news, as well as journalists' own fallibility. Crucially, these types of fake news can be traced to individual tendencies of information processing that Lippmann identified as selectively attuning to and incorporating information so it fits our belief systems. Thus, in tackling the contemporary issues of fake news, they argue that attention also should be paid to people's motivations in consuming information. In the contemporary debate about fake news, the emphases have been on creating systems for identifying the offending, misleading content. But the issue runs deeper than any platform's content and should be centered on people's motivated reasoning for consuming the news that they do.

Pillars of Truth in Journalism

The next part continues with an exploration of how to conceive of truth and its role in journalism. As **Edward Schiappa** highlights in his spotlight minichapter, there are a variety of decisions journalists must make in the process of publishing a news story: not just how to cover a story, but whether to cover it at all. In this sense, the journalist has in mind the potentially competing views of journalism—economic, sociological, democratic—and must negotiate and weigh them against one another when making decisions. **Zeynep Soysal** raises the trade-offs and balances journalists may face to reconcile conflicting goals. She offers the solution of transparency: journalists pull back the curtain for their readers, and, in the course of reporting a story, also report the trade-offs they made while constructing the story.

Juliet Floyd explores in her chapter the concept of "The True" in journalism. She shows how the concept can be pursued but in the sense of interpretation and that meaningfulness can only be approximated. She also offers some guidance for the profession of journalism and its responsibility toward "The True."

Craft of Journalism and Truth

The previous two parts identify the broader social implications and truth (or "Truth") concerns in journalism. This part brings the analysis to the more practical questions of journalism's craft. It begins by looking at false information through a historical lens. **Peppino Ortoleva** places today's "fake news" moment in the context of three historical time periods, each representing different threads of false information that arose during the time: (1) as a "professional inclination" in Balzac's 19th-century Paris; (2) as part of a psycho-social crisis, identified by Bloch in the emergence of profound military power at the start of 20th century; and (3) as the product of a paranoid worldview, characterized by Hofstadter's description of the "paranoid style" exemplified in America's McCarthy and Cold War era. He argues that social media and fake news should not be evaluated as a single peculiar blip in time, but rather as a convergence of processes, some of which have historical roots.

John Maxwell Hamilton and Heidi Tworek continue with a historical analysis of foreign correspondence. A niche area of journalism, they argue that foreign correspondence has always been accomplished through the technology of the day. This technology has bolstered the practice, but also complicated its reliability, as the particular situation of foreign correspondents—far from home with little oversight, in a strange land with incomplete knowledge—strain their resources for truthful reporting, defined as "accuracy, balance, completeness." They argue that the trade-offs from foreign correspondence reporting can be recalibrated to understand our current moment with social media: independence (versus managed news), speed (versus superficiality), and abundant sources (versus reliability). Citizen and freelance journalists, enabled by social media, have created new ways in which independence, speed, and reliability are sacrificed; they consider how foreign correspondence should respond to these threats, in part based on how they were tackled a century ago when misinformation and hoaxes from abroad were rampant.

For example, a lot of foreign correspondents would just look at the home country's newspapers to get stories—**Sophie Lecheler, Sanne Kruikemeier, and Yael de Haan** track how, in a similarly lazy fashion, journalists today rely heavily on Google as a mode of information gathering. Given the murky workings and capriciousness of search algorithms, this is an inherently risky dependence. Their chapter offers a practitioner's view on source selection and verification in an online newsgathering environment that is increasingly unmoored from offline realities and consistently changing. One example of this is the algorithms that drive the architecture of information searching—journalists do not have much choice but to trust that returned search results on a topic are indeed the most relevant, but given the black-box nature of algorithms, they cannot know the mechanisms behind what produces the results (and algorithms are always being tweaked). It is important, therefore, that journalists are both judicious in their selection of online sources and have ways to verify those sources.

Colin Agur and Valerie Belair-Gagnon explore how journalists verify sources and information in social media in one type of social communication technology, chat apps. A hybrid of public and private communication, chat apps represent a challenge to traditional journalistic sourcing and reporting practices because they are fragmented online spaces, but they also present opportunities for innovative reporting, offering access to more private conversations within social groups. The chapter presents a case study for how journalists navigate the perennial problems of verification on social media, which are no less an issue on chat apps, and also how the chat apps' features may be optimized for new reporting methods.

Zooming out from one particular technology, **Maria Molina** and **S. Shyam Sundar** review online technological affordances that may aid or impede a journalist's news coverage. Applying a psychological approach to the practitioner's view, they categorize various actions and cues online that may trigger certain cognitive heuristics in individuals. These heuristics may potentially short-circuit a journalist's news judgment and therefore are important for any journalist in today's media environment to be aware of.

Reception and Perception

The final part turns the lens from journalistic producers to their audiences. These are not separate entities that operate independently of one another—it has always been the case that journalists and the newspapers, radio stations, and TV networks that employ them have an eye toward what will catch a news consumer's attention and lead to higher reader-, listener-, or viewership. "If it bleeds, it leads," would need to be updated to reflect the nature of social media, but the principle still holds. **Erik Bucy and John Newhagen** reframe the "fake news" problem as one that has arisen in large part due to social media feedback mechanisms (likes, shares) that drive online news. This process is part of a larger big data phenomenon online, wherein unprecedented volumes of information are processed at such speeds that can outstrip thoughtful human intervention and judgment. These social media feedback mechanisms become a "proxy for [a post's] truth value," and, as a result, popularity, rather than expertise, is the "currency" in online information sharing. The growth of fake news is buoyed not only by the emphases on social media to share information without verifying it but also by humans' cognitive propensities when discerning whether something is true. People are "cognitive misers," who prefer to reserve their cognitive expenditures whenever possible. As a result of this tendency, people are prone to initially accept any piece of information as true, and only in the process of evaluating it do we discount some information as false. With the volume of information bombarding us online, there are too many demands on people's cognitive reasoning, creating fertile ground for misinformation campaigns.

Edson Tandoc continues this thread of how feedback mechanisms affect content creation. Social media's affordances enable journalists to better generate, tailor, and disseminate their content, and then they constantly track their content's performance through these feedback mechanisms and metrics. Thus, there are tensions between speed (getting news out as quickly as possible for maximum impact) versus verification (of the news' contents), as well as weighing what audiences *want* to consume compared to what they may need to consume. In this way, the chapter balances an economic view of news—updated for the social media context—against the democratic view of news.

Finally, **Brian Weeks and Kelly Garrett** consider the implications for journalists in creating for audiences who are not just consumers of news but also potential creators and disseminators of news. Social media have enabled a new kind of audience with expanded capacities beyond just voting with their eyeballs, that is, choosing which news sources to watch, read or listen to: they can share news items; add commentary to news items; and, through their personal accounts, "break" news. Applying a psychological view of news, the authors examine how emotions may play into individuals' information processing and ultimate decisions for believing and/ or passing on news to others via social media channels. These emotionally driven decisions also influence the extent to which people believe political misinformation, which has implications for both the political view of news (e.g., these emotional drivers may be exploited for political gain) and the democratic view.

We conclude the book by summarizing "practitioner lessons" that we can draw from various chapters, as well as the trends we see for journalists in the age of social media. We consider what is old and what is new with social media and journalism through the three lenses that have guided the book's contents: politics, truth, and technology. We finish our conclusion with some forward-looking thoughts on how technology may evolve and adapt for people's needs to be civically and politically engaged online, but not consumed by the ever-growing mountain of causes and outrages that necessarily proliferate given the nature of the technological environment, but perhaps needlessly overwhelm, excite, and enrage to the point of distraction and cognitive overload.

Concluding Thoughts

A Word About Truth and Its Use in Journalism

Of course certain "facts" that are empirically demonstrable, such as the height of Mount Everest above mean sea level, can be truthfully answered within the parameters of available instrumentation. Other truths, such as the number of grains of sand on planet earth at a particular moment in time, are theoretically obtainable, but not practically so. On the other hand, we might believe we could know the truth about, for example, why someone did something, that too is practically unknowable. All this, of course, does not mean that truth is unimportant and completely arbitrary or relative, although there is certainly an arbitrariness to its attempted formulation.

The approach to the meaning of truth we favor is derived from the pragmatist tradition espoused by William James as supplemented by John Dewey and Ludwig Wittgenstein.

The Jamesian viewpoint is less concerned about some platonic ideal of absolute truth and more concerned about what works effectively. He said, "Truth in our ideas means their power to work" (James [1907] 1995, 34), and "True ideas are those that we can assimilate, validate, corroborate, and verify. False ideas are those that we cannot" (97). Over time, truth works like a credit system: we invest belief in those ideas that pay off by successfully achieving validation and corroboration with external reality as best we can perceive it.

Moving beyond the specific philosophical context, Ludwig Wittgenstein emphasized word games and the role they play in the way we make meaning. (He presumably used word games in both the sense of constrained interaction, often with the goal, and as a form of competitive and collaborative engagement.) Indeed, he goes so far as to describe meaning making of word games as a form of life: "It is what human beings *say* that is true and false, and they agree in the *language* they use. That is not agreement in opinions but in form of life" (Wittgenstein, cited in Hunter 1968, 233). In the journalistic context, this asserts agreement about the meaning of the words we share and use with one another; through this interaction and deliberation, individuals and groups end up making contextualized judgments about matters of truth and falsehood.

A Word About Social Media Technology

We use the term social media capaciously in this volume. For us it includes not only more recent forms of computer-mediated interpersonal communication, such as Facebook, Twitter, Instagram, and Skype, but also the technologies that enable social media. Here for example we include the Internet, email, worldwide and various proprietary and dark webs, data compression and encryption technologies that allow vast amounts of data to move quickly and even surreptitiously, and mobile phones. It also includes recording technologies such as camera phones and audio-recording apps. Geo-locational and tracking technologies are also included.

For our purposes, it makes little sense to try to neatly carve away older forms of "new media" (e.g., the Internet) from "emerging media" (Instagram and Twitter). Given that the journalistic enterprise is the focus of our interest here, we look holistically at the mediated communication technologies and data resources transforming the creation, distribution, and consumption of journalistic products. Our scope includes databases, online searches, one-to-one and one-to-many computerized systems, once again, including mobile and location-sensitive technologies.

A Word About Politics

Perhaps there was a time when politics played only a small part of people's discussions and concerns about the world. An interesting study would be to look at how much of the news produced has been focused on politics; it may well be the case that historically people's concerns (or at least the journalism that was produced) focused more topics other than politics. It does certainly appear to be the case that science previously occupied a much more prominent place in newspapers and news magazines. Nonetheless, whether it was previously of great importance, political topics certainly occupy a major part of people's concerns as reflected in newspapers, news magazines, television and radio programming, blogs, and other journalistic outlets. Therefore it's only fitting and proper that we also engage heavily with the topic of politics. This is reflected in the content of many of the chapters.

Nonetheless, it is important to bear in mind that there are many other forms of news besides politics. These include business, science, health, culture, arts, community activities, sports, and hobbies. For some of these, the question of truth is more important and may also be more difficult to discern than in others. (For example, the significance of surprising research findings in the realm of health versus surprising outcomes of sports teams.)

In closing, we invite the reader to explore the topics of social media and journalism as they play out in the chapters that follow. We asked each contributor to include analyses of the role of politics, technology, and social media within their specific topics of concern. We pull together and compare these points in the concluding chapter.

References

Bennett, W. Lance. 2016. *News: The Politics of Illusion*. Chicago: University of Chicago Press.

Bucy, Erik P., and Paul D'Angelo. 1999. "The Crisis of Political Communication: Normative Critiques of News and Democratic Processes." *Annals of the International Communication Association* 22, no. 1: 301–339.

Bucy, Erik P., and Paul D'Angelo. 2004. "Democratic Realism, Neoconservatism, and the Normative Underpinnings of Political Communication Research. " *Mass Communication & Society* 7, no. 1: 3–28.

Deuze, Mark. 2007. *Media Work*. Cambridge: Polity Press.

Fox, Julia R. 2003. "The Alarm Function of Mass Media: A Critical Study of 'The Plot Against America,' a Special Edition of *NBC Nightly News* with Tom Brokaw." In *Studies in Terrorism: Media Scholarship and the Enigma of Terror*, edited by Naren Chitty. 55–71. Penang, Malaysia: Southbound (in association with the *Journal of International Communication*).

Gans, Herbert J. 1979. *Deciding What's News: A Study of* CBS Evening News, NBC Nightly News, Newsweek, *and* Time. New York: Pantheon Books.

Hargreaves, Ian. 2003. *Journalism*. USA: Oxford University Press.

Hearns-Branaman, Jesse Owens. 2016. *Journalism and the Philosophy of Truth: Beyond Objectivity and Balance*. New York: Routledge.

Hunter, John F. M. 1968. "'Forms of Life' in Wittgenstein's 'Philosophical Investigations.'" *American Philosophical Quarterly* 5, no. 4: 233–243.

Iyengar, Shanto, and Sean J. Westwood. 2015. "Fear and Loathing Across Party Lines: New Evidence on Group Polarization." *American Journal of Political Science* 59, no. 3: 690–707.

James, William. (1907) 1995. *Pragmatism: A New Name for Some Old Ways of Thinking*. New York: Longmans, Green, New York. Reprint Dover Press.

Jamieson, Kathleen Hall, and Campbell, Karlyn Kohrs. 2001. *The Interplay of Influence: News, Advertising, Politics, and the Mass Media*. 5th ed. Belmont, CA; London: Wadsworth/Thomson Learning.

Katz, James E. 1998. "Struggle in Cyberspace: Fact and Friction on the World Wide Web." *Annals of the American Academy of Political and Social Science* 556, 194–200.

Lasswell, Harold D. 1948. "The Structure and Function of Communication in Society." *Communication of Ideas* 37: 215–228.

Lasswell, Harold D. 1972. "Communications Research and Public Policy." *Public Opinion Quarterly* 36, no. 3: 301–310.

Maras, Steven. 2013. *Objectivity in Journalism (Key Concepts in Journalism)*. Malden, MA: Polity Press.

McBride, Kelly, and Tom Rosenstiel. 2014. *The New Ethics of Journalism*. Washington, DC: Sage.

Newhagen, John E. 1998. "TV News Images That Induce Anger, Fear, and Disgust: Effects on Approach-Avoidance and Memory." *Journal of Broadcasting & Electronic Media* 42, no. 2: 265–276.

Newhagen, John E., and Mark R. Levy. 2013. "The Future of Journalism in a Distributed Communication Architecture." In *The Electronic Grapevine*, edited by Diane L. Borden and Kerric Harvey, 14–28. New York: Taylor & Francis.

Reeves, Byron, and Clifford Ivar Nass. 1996. *The Media Equation: How People Treat Computers, Television, and New Media Like Real People and Places*. Cambridge: Cambridge University Press.

Schudson, Michael. 2003. *The Sociology of News, Contemporary Societies*. New York: W. W. Norton.

Ward, Stephen J. A. 2004. *The Invention of Journalism Ethics: The Path to Objectivity and Beyond*. McGill-Queen's Studies in the History of Ideas, 38. Montreal; Ithaca: McGill-Queen's University Press.

Ward, Stephen J. A. 2013. *Global Media Ethics Problems and Perspectives*. Chichester, West Sussex, UK: Wiley-Blackwell.

PART I
DEMOCRACY, NEWS, AND SOCIETY

2

Belgium Invades Germany

Can Facts Survive Politics?

Michael Schudson

Donald Trump: I will mention his name only a few times here. He cannot be omitted, but he did not invent the fretful and bitter relations between truth and politics. Nor did George W. Bush, although his peculiar relationship to truth inspired Stephen Colbert in 2005 to develop the notion of "truthiness" to describe how President Bush accepted as true what "felt" true to him, what he wanted to be true. This was before Facebook took off, so Facebook gets no credit either for beginning the war between politics and truth.

Serious commentary about the truth-politics relationship goes back centuries. One landmark in truth-politics criticism is philosopher Hannah Arendt's simply titled "Truth and Politics." This was published not in a philosophical journal but in *The New Yorker* in February 1967.[1] At that time, Donald Trump was a college student. Stephen Colbert was three years old. There was no Mark Zuckerberg. But truth and politics were not on good terms.

Arendt's essay is a starting point for understanding how complicated ascertaining the truth is, how difficult it is to assess what is or is not truthful, how dangerous it is that people make things up, and how profoundly troubling it is today that lies, as well as truths, now circulate at speeds we can't comprehend, often advanced by agents called "bots" that are lies themselves from top to bottom, millions of online devices programmed to comment on, praise, attack, forward, retweet, and recirculate online items while posing as humans (Confessore et al. 2018). I will try to connect Arendt's observations specifically to journalism.

Power, Arendt held, threatened truth, especially factual truth rather than formal truths like "two plus two equals four." Factual truth is more vulnerable because "facts and events—the invariable outcome of men living and acting together—constitute the very text of the political realm."

But she realized that facts were under assault. "Do facts independent of opinion and interpretation, exist at all? Have not generations of historians and philosophers of history demonstrated the impossibility of ascertaining facts without interpretation, since they must first be picked out of a chaos of sheer happenings (and the principles of choice are surely not factual data) and then be fitted into a story that can be told only in a certain perspective, which has nothing to do with the original occurrence?" (Arendt 1968, 238).

But for Arendt, the complexity of sorting out fact from interpretation is not an argument against the existence of facts. She tells a little story, of Georges Clemenceau, prime minister of France during World War I. A few years after the war, he was discussing the question of which country was responsible for initiating that horrendous, world-shattering, and pointless conflict. Clemenceau was asked what future historians would conclude. He responded, "This I don't know. But I know for certain that they will not say Belgium invaded Germany" (Arendt 1968, 239).

For those whose World War I history is a little rusty: on August 4, 1914, German troops crossed into neutral Belgium. Germans recognized this. Belgians recognized this. Declarations of war had been flying across Europe for a week at that point, but this was the opening act of blood-spilling aggression, when the German army attacked Belgium en route to France, the country they were at war with.

Some things, Clemenceau asserts, are just simply facts. And Arendt at first seems to agree, despite having acknowledged the social construction of reality. But then, she backs away. She adds that this fact—German troops moved into Belgium August 4, 1914—like any other fact is vulnerable to power. However, it would take "a power monopoly over the entire civilized world" to erase the recognition that German troops invaded Belgium, not Belgian troops Germany (Arendt 1968, 239).

Ahh, then truth is safe? No. Arendt writes that "such a power monopoly is far from being inconceivable, and it is not difficult to imagine what the fate of factual truth would be if power interests, national or social, had the last say in these matters" (Arendt 1968, 239).

Truth

That is my text for this chapter's sermon. *Time* magazine asked on a cover in 2017, "Is Truth Dead?" (April 3, 2017). The correct answer to *Time*'s question is "no." Or, following Arendt, no, not so long as "power interests" can be prevented from having the last say. We live in a real world where men and women living and acting together produce facts and events that even the powerful must reckon with. In the 2017 (April 22) "March for Science," one person held up a sign that read, "I Can't Believe I'm Marching For Facts." My sentiments exactly. I can't believe that what I want to communicate in this essay is that we do not live in a post-truth age and that we never will.

Of course, as Arendt makes clear, politics inspires lying. There have been plenty of earlier objections that presidents and presidential candidates in the United States have lied. It is widely accepted that John F. Kennedy's attacks on the Eisenhower administration in 1960 for letting the Soviet Union forge ahead in building a nuclear stockpile—the so-called "missile gap"—were false and that he and his aides most likely knew them to be false. Kennedy is credited with first using the term "missile gap" in his 1958 re-election campaign for the Senate. He pushed the argument that the Republicans were weak on defense. If Kennedy did not know the truth then, he certainly knew it when he and Lyndon Johnson were briefed in the summer of 1960 after their nomination in the presidential campaign. Yet Kennedy continued to press the "missile gap" charge on the campaign trail.

When the Russians shot down an American spy plane and captured pilot Francis Gary Powers, President Eisenhower responded by asserting, falsely, that the spy plane was not spying. Soon an embarrassed Eisenhower administration had to back down from the lie. What a US spy plane was doing in Soviet air space was—surprise, surprise!—spying. Strategic misdirection or outright lies are standard in politics to gain a strategic advantage internationally or to sway voters domestically. And there are many opportunities that politicians regularly take advantage of for hyperbole.

There is lots of precedent for presidential exaggeration, partial and intentionally misleading truths, and lying. There is, likewise, precedent for pervasive falsehoods circulating widely and influencing public opinion. One need look no further than the influential belief in an international Jewish conspiracy—but there are many others. Some even fit under the rubric of "fake news." Among the most powerful fake news stories ever was the widely circulated tales of German atrocities in the invasion of Belgium that influenced public opinion for decades to come. There were indeed German atrocities in many unprovoked attacks on Belgian civilians, but many of the most widely circulated instances of alleged atrocities were sheer propagandistic inventions. That these especially sensational and hor-rifying presumed atrocities were never tracked down and seemed clearly to have emerged and circulated as anti-German propaganda even con-tributed to the reluctance in the American press to give credence to early reports of the authentic atrocities committed by Germany in World War II (Lipstadt 1986).

For Arendt, the guarantor of facts is what she calls "the standpoint out-side the political realm" or what she also calls "one of the various modes of being alone" (Arendt 1968, 259). People standing alone have the inde-pendence to be truth-tellers, and she listed the following categories of truth-telling: "the solitude of the philosopher, the isolation of the scientist and the artist, the impartiality of the historian and the judge, and the independence of the fact-finder, the witness, and the reporter" (Arendt 1968, 260).

But this is an entirely unrealistic portrait of independent thinkers. Philosophers can work alone in their studies because they have salaries and libraries, students and colleagues. Judges have a legal education—which is also a moral education, and they are constrained by laws, legal ethics, and social support within their professional group that prizes independent judg-ment. What conditions must be preserved to permit people to take these standpoints outside the political? And what are the conditions of reality that must be acknowledged that power cannot overcome?

Consider how truth-seeking operates in science. Science, like journalism, is not like Mount Everest. It is not the natural world itself but a human con-struction about the natural world. It is much more like Mount Rushmore—it is carved from natural materials, but it is made by humans working together. And are its conclusions absolutely true?

Certainly not. After all, they change quite often. They change for sci-ence and scientists. They may change because new information turns up that invalidates old verities. They may also change because the framework assumptions or "paradigms" that guide scientists about what data to look at and what questions to ask change, too. And how does this happen? How does one paradigm replace another? The famous atomic physicist, Max Planck, gave a simple and distressing answer: they change because an older generation committed to the old paradigm dies out and a new generation rises to power: "A new scientific truth does not triumph by convincing its opponents and making them see the light, but rather because its opponents eventually die, and a new generation grows up that is familiar with it" (Planck, quoted in Kuhn 1970, 150).

Truth is a set of agreements. It is a social consensus, but it is a consensus constrained by conditions of reality. The distinguishing feature of the agreements we think of as "truth" is that they correspond to what we know or think we know about an external world. How can realities act as a brake on consensus gone mad? You may or may not believe your life is one moment in a cycle of rebirths. But you will not disagree with my proposition that in this part of the cycle you were born from the womb of a woman. No exceptions. You do not know when or how you will die but you are 100% confident that, in this moment of your eternal cycle, if that is your belief, or in your only lifetime on earth, if that is your belief, you will die. No exceptions. Reality does not necessarily limit our imaginations or our wishes, but it constrains our theorizing about what the real world is. We cannot posit as true just any propositions that please us.

A poignant and comic sign held up by a child at the San Francisco Women's March in January 2017 (and visible again many times over in April's March for Science) read as follows: "What do we want? Evidence-based science. When do we want it? After peer review." Just so! That is how science works. That is what science is: a community of scholars that collectively determines what counts as evidence and what passes as evidence based. Science is less one of "the various modes of being alone" than it is a distinctive mode of being together. This community falters when scientists make up their data, and we know that scientific fraud happens. We know that journalistic fraud happens, too. It has happened in recent memory at both the *New York Times* (reporter Jayson Blair was forced to resign in 2003 for plagiarism and fabrication) and the *New Republic* (Stephen Glass was fired in 1998 for fabricating all or parts of most of his published work in the magazine). These were not cases of bias but of total fabrication. Science, too, is vulnerable to total fabrication.

In everyday life, people readily believe exaggerations and lies and even wild fabrications. That is why scam artists, confidence operators, rip-off artists who prey on the elderly, Wells Fargo bank executives who invent financial products to defraud their own customers, and mortgage brokers who sell people homes they know their clients will quickly lose abide with us. The facts constrain but people believe what they wish to, what accords with preconceptions, what flatters the communities they identify with, what pleases the state that governs them, and what helps explain and assuage their fears, or gives them hopes for health, wealth, security, or love where reason and experience counsel that there is no hope.

Truth has formidable enemies. It suffers under an onslaught from what we may call the 4 P's: (1) propaganda—propositions that states, parties, and politicians promote to gain or extend power; (2) profit—propositions that individuals or organizations circulate to sell products, services, or false hopes in order to make money; (3) prejudices—prejudgments that many individuals routinely place ahead of actually seeking truth; and (4) pranks—propositions or practices designed to mislead for the sake of a sick joke.

We should not discount pranks as a factor, least of all in an era of easily circulated fake news. In 2001, while I served as acting provost of Thurgood Marshall College, one of several undergraduate units of the University of California, San Diego (UCSD), I received a package addressed to the Thurgood Marshall College provost. The college office staff and I learned upon opening it, that it contained nothing except a small plastic baggie full of white powder. Similar packages with white powder had been sent to a number of news outlets and politicians soon after 9/11. In some of these cases, the white powder was deadly anthrax, and it sickened some 20 people and killed several. We handed the package over to campus police, the police handed it over to hazmat personnel, and hazmat took it to the FBI who promptly discarded it without examining it. Why examine it? It was almost surely talcum powder, not anthrax, because hundreds of similar packages were mailed all over the country, a sick joke indeed. In this case, it was likely also a sick racist joke, since Thurgood Marshall College, named after the first African American justice of the Supreme Court, was the only administrative unit at the university targeted.

People will fall prey to untruths because they know no better, because their knowledge is limited, because they do not think through how ridiculously unlikely it is that Pope Francis endorsed Donald Trump for president (or any other candidate, for that matter) or that high-level Democratic Party officials and aides to Hillary Clinton were key figures in a child pornography and satanic ritual conspiracy operating out of the Comet Pizza chain of pizza parlors. But people's divorce from reality need not be large, and they may be led to give credit to ridiculous claims for no greater reason than not wanting to appear a fool. Remember the story of the emperor's new clothes, published by Danish writer Hans Christian Andersen in 1837. It is difficult for most of us to stand alone, even when the penalty for dissent is trivial, and even when our eyes tell us that the king is parading down the street naked.

How do we know what's true? We are no more in a post-truth era than Hans Christian Andersen was 180 years ago, but the conditions under which we learn and can confirm truths or disconfirm falsehoods has grown complicated in ways we have not yet socially and politically assimilated. Knowing the truth is harder because propaganda, profits, prejudices, and pranks travel more quickly and are empowered by new means of cloaking themselves in the garb of truthfulness. Keeping tabs on the truth has indeed become more difficult today at the same time and by the same mechanism that it is also less difficult than ever. Indeed, the emphasis on the snarky, the quick-witted remark, and the joke in the transmission of words and photos and videos online moves communication quickly in style from frank to prank.

The philosopher Michael Patrick Lynch has argued that we have today a whole new way of knowing he calls "Google-knowing" and that he defines simply as "knowledge acquired online." And he holds, "Most knowing now is Google-knowing" (Lynch 2016, 23). He contrasts this to experiential knowledge, that is, knowledge derived by "being receptive to the facts outside of ourselves." He also writes of this as knowledge anchored "by the objective world itself" (Lynch 2016, 131).

Lynch is right that there is a fresh sort of knowing in the world, thanks to digital technology, that we can call Google-knowledge. It is in many ways transformative. Still, even with Google-knowing, a great deal of our knowledge remains experiential and remains something that even a unified power structure cannot talk us out of. If I am tortured, can I be convinced by the torturer that it does not hurt? If a woman is in labor, can anything convince her she is not giving birth? These are the powerful realities of bodily experience. There is also memory of bodily experience. If I attend a conference and stay at the conference hotel for several days and get to the conference itself the first day by walking in a certain direction, when the conference continues the next day, I can assume that walking in the same direction past the same landmarks and on the same streets will get me to the same place. That is also experiential knowledge but stored, more or less faithfully, in memory. If my mother tells me over and over that I should never accept a ride in a car from a stranger, I will accept this as a trustworthy guide to living—at least until I become a teenager—because I trust that my mother (a) has my best welfare at heart and (b) knows what she is talking about. This is a kind of mediated experiential knowledge. I may be misled by books or by Google or by news in the media, but I trust my mother. And

I have learned also by my own experience or by the recommendations of others I trust to trust some sources more than others. I trust on this basis the *New York Times* that I have been reading for decades. It has not been perfect. It has admitted to errors and corrected them. It has considered and sometimes accepted, sometimes rejected public criticism (notably in its "public editor" column, discontinued in 2017), but it has been broadly, in my experience, reliable. We have friends and acquaintances we know from experience who are very reliable in relating a story or giving directions or recalling who said what when—and there are others we have learned are quite unreliable, even if we love them. We judge—perhaps with more difficulty—news outlets similarly.

Pain, experience, the memory of one's own experience, and the mediated experience we may summarize as "track record" or "reputation": none of these agents of provisional verification are perfect sources of knowledge, but all of them are powerful. They are powerful enough with a modicum of social support to overcome determined efforts to promote lies. An additional resource underlies all of these and is a kind of preface to them: skepticism. We should know that finding truth is complicated, not simple; that it is a cumulative, social activity, not a flash of inspiration even if it incorporates flashes of inspiration; and that it requires vigilant bullshit-detection. As the saying goes in journalism, "If your mother says she loves you, check it out!"

Knowledge, of course, is not reducible to irrefutable facts. Historian Richard Hofstadter half a century ago wrote about conspiracy-minded thinkers (again, if it needs to be said, neither Facebook nor Google was ever required for the proliferation of conspiracy-centered fantasies). Hofstadter (1965) noted that conspiracy theorists do not ignore facts. They typically are obsessed with facts. What is distinctive is that they marshal their facts toward an overwhelming "proof" of the conspiracy they mean to confirm. "It is nothing if not coherent," Hofstadter writes, "in fact the paranoid mentality is far more coherent than the real world, since it leaves no room for mistakes, failures, or ambiguities." It is not that the conspiracy-minded have no facts but that they use them as scaffolding toward a "curious leap in imagination that is always made at some critical point in the recital of events." They make a "big leap from the undeniable to the unbelievable" (Hofstadter 1965, 36–38). We must have trust in our bodily experience, trust in our memories, trust in reputations established over time, and beyond that an abiding skepticism.

Professional Journalism

The first newspaper, as far as we know, was published in Strasbourg, Germany, in 1605. The first English-language newspaper was published in Amsterdam in 1620. The first newspaper in the American colonies (apart from one in 1690 that survived for only a single issue) was published in 1704—our Pilgrim fathers and mothers apparently survived the cold New England winters without any printed news media at all. And for the most part there would be no local news in colonial newspapers until around the 1750s. Most news Americans read when Benjamin Franklin first started publishing the *Pennsylvania Gazette* in 1729 concerned European political and economic affairs. From the latter part of the 18th century on, newspapers in England and in the American colonies expressed criticism of politicians and accused politicians of lying or worse. But this was easily discounted because the large majority of newspapers from that point into the first half of the 20th century were partisan newspapers. The Democratic papers believed the Whig (and later the Republican) presidents and governors and mayors were liars; the Whig and later the Republican papers thought only the Democratic presidents and governors and mayors lied.

How that changed is a long story that historians of journalism have told elsewhere.[2] It is a story of journalism becoming a self-conscious and proud occupational group relatively—not fully, but relatively—independent of the views and values of the newspaper publisher. Once publishers figured out that they could make a lot of money running a newspaper, they began to care less about whether news stories favored one political side or another and to care more about whether news stories attracted readers. If the news could attract readers, newspaper circulation could attract advertisers, and the publisher could get rich. This commercialization of the press provided relative freedom for the reporters to write independent-minded news.

Despite some 300 years of journalism history, a fact-checking movement in journalism has been formally organized only in the past 20 years, beginning with Factcheck.org in 2003 (for an illuminating account of the rise of fact-checking organizations, see Graves 2016). What began in 2003 is now an international movement (see Graves 2018, and Graves and Cherubini 2017). And fact-checking has been made possible by two relatively new features in journalism. The first was the rise of investigative reporting, contextual reporting, and critical reporting. In a variety of studies of US journalism and Swedish public broadcasting and German and French and

Dutch news media over time, it is clear that the 1960s and 1970s was a watershed era that brought a new skepticism and critical instinct to journalism (Schudson 2018). The most misleading word in all of US journalism history is "muckraking" because it makes us believe that we have had a strong tradition of fearless investigative work in journalism since the days of Teddy Roosevelt. But the muckrakers Teddy Roosevelt criticized produced their work for a handful of new middle-class magazines, the vogue for muckraking lasted not quite a decade, and it never spread into the general circulation daily newspapers that were responsible for the lion's share of reporting and reached by far the largest number of readers.

The second factor that made fact-checking organizations possible is Google-knowing. True, diligent fact-checkers do not rely exclusively on Google-knowledge. They also interview experts and examine documents, although often they find the experts and the documents through links on Google. And then they try to make judgments about whether politicians' assertions are fact or fiction. We know that nonsense and bullshit and lies circulate rapidly online. We all know people who say without blushing that the source of their knowledge about this or that is "the Internet." That's not an answer. "Facebook" is not an answer. "The newspaper" is not an answer. But "Wikipedia" is an answer. "The *New York Times*" is an answer. "Fox News" is an answer. These are all news institutions, very different ones, with enough of a track record that gives us enough context to approximate how and how much to believe what they report.

The whole project of organized, independent fact-checking in journalism is rooted in a belief that one can stand outside politics, that facts exist, and that facts in the end matter. On the other hand, the fact-checkers recognize a certain comedy in their exercise and so they present their work in a self-mocking vein. The *Washington Post* FactChecker does not make a binary judgment between true and false but awards from one to four "Pinocchio's" for the degree to which a politician's assertions stray from solid truth. Or take PolitiFact's measurement of five degrees of factuality from "True" to "Pants on Fire." Its signature symbol is the Truth-O-Meter, a machine for judging the truth of assertions whose chief feature is, of course, that it does not exist. There is no way around the realization that the journalists at fact-checking organizations make consensual judgments among themselves that they expect others to take as honest and fact-based and as authoritative as they know how to make them, even when they themselves know that their authority is inevitably a little fuzzy around the edges.

What my Columbia Journalism School colleagues tell their students, over and over again, as I understand it, seems to emphasize at least these three rules, among others, that should govern what reporters do. First, be accurate. Facts are not everything, but they are necessary, and they are often ascertainable. There's no room for relativism here. The name is either Smith or Jones. The address is either 10 Main Street or 20 Main Street. Taking the average and reporting it as 15 Main Street won't do.

Second, report against your own assumptions. Don't deny that you have views and values and preconceptions. But know what they are, especially if they are strong and well-formed (usually they are not), and in your reporting look for what might invalidate them and include this in what you write.

Third, follow the story. Even if you find out things that contradict the preferences of you, your publisher, your editor, or the general set of preconceptions in your newsroom, follow the story wherever it takes you. The *New York Times* regularly endorsed former New York Governor Eliot Spitzer for office. But in 2006 it also ran the story about his relations with prostitutes that forced him to resign. No one told the reporter to abandon the story certain to embarrass a potential presidential candidate the paper's editorial staff admired. The reporter was told to follow the story wherever it would lead. In 2016 the *Times* broke the story of Hillary Clinton's use of a private server for State Department communications while she was secretary of state. The *Times* endorsed Clinton on the editorial page, but the news story about her e-mail practices may have been as damaging to her chances of being elected as any other news item of the campaign. The *Times* is not without leanings of its own, but in general the model that the *Times* and other leading mainstream news organizations try to adhere to is: follow a story, don't follow a political line.

That's what it means to be a professional journalist working for a professional news organization: it requires a mastery of professional practices and professional ideals that place truth-seeking and truth-telling above profit, above partisanship, above chummy getting-along-with politicians and other powerful groups and individuals. Obviously, it is not always achieved. What is particularly distressing today in the wild territory of the Internet is how regularly it is abandoned altogether and scorned. Also regrettable is that on the left as well as the right, the fallibility of human truth-seeking has led critics to argue that there is no such thing as independent judgment in truth-seeking.

Democracy

Given enough resources and enough effort, Belgium invaded Germany.

The chance that people will accept that Belgium invaded Germany is greatly enhanced when the most powerful force for persuasion in the world—the views of the president of the United States—are indifferent to or even fiercely hostile to facts when they do not flatter him. Google is powerful. Facebook is powerful. But neither has the power to dominate the public agenda the way American presidents have been doing at least since Franklin D. Roosevelt's fireside chats.

When President Trump went from circulating lies with no sense of obligation to check them out, to accusing the mainstream media of publishing fake news and being the enemies of the people, he turned "fake news" into an applause line for his supporters instead of a plausible description of intentional lies circulated to deceive. President Trump's reckless use of Twitter may seem original with him, but it follows a familiar pattern set by Latin American left-wing populist leaders who, for years before Trump became president, used Twitter to provide a new top-down channel of presidential communication, to keep presidential communications focused on breaking events of the day rather than on policy, and to attack enemies or purported enemies, notably the news media (Waisbord and Amado 2017). For all of Trump's originality, and however freakish he seems in the long line of American presidents, he takes up a populist style in a recognizable way.

Populism is a kind of political auto-immune disorder in which the agent of a vital democracy itself—popular participation—attacks the very organs that make democratic self-governance possible. Democracy is not the best system of government because it puts faith in ordinary people but because it puts faith in no one. C. S. Lewis wrote in the midst of World War II that he was a democrat because, as he put it, "I believe in the Fall of Man. I think most people are democrats for the opposite reason. A great deal of democratic enthusiasm descends from the ideas of people . . . who believed in a democracy because they thought mankind so wise and good that everyone deserved a share in the government. The danger of defending democracy on those grounds is that they're not true. . . . The real reason for democracy is . . . Mankind is so fallen that no man can be trusted with unchecked power over his fellows" (quoted in Keane 2009, 865). E. M. Forster said the same thing when he offered two cheers for democracy—"One because it admits variety and two because it permits criticism. Two cheers are quite enough: there is no occasion to give three" (quoted in Keane 2009, 867). We can add that democracy, operating as it should, does not just permit criticism but also encourages it, nurtures it, requires it.

The American founding fathers were very close to these views. They did not believe mankind wise and good. They did not even think they were establishing a democracy, which meant to them mob rule open to exploitation by demagogues. They were establishing republican government in which white men who owned property would vote for the accepted social leaders of their communities. And they would serve in a government where one branch could prevent another branch from exercising its will, even during a short term of office. The people should be involved, yes, and over time it would come to include men without property, and then men who were not white, and then women, too. America became democratic, it was not born democratic. But it did not leave behind a fear of unchecked power, the need for deliberation, and the opportunity for revision, repeal, and constant criticism. And this is exactly where the news media come in.

It is a hard lesson to learn—that reality is socially constructed, and that facts are hard to hold steadily in view when we approach them through paradigms and perspectives and prior knowledge and prior ignorance and prior interpretations and presuppositions as we all, always, inevitably do, And—this is the important "and"—at the same time: we can nonetheless affirm that facts exist. Given facts can and will be knocked off their pedestals but, unless truth-seeking is crushed by the weight of power, the facts can be disposed of only by the legitimate array of evidence and reasoning of the sort we would willingly credit as they are employed by the physicians, meteorologists, air traffic controllers, engineers, and a variety of other evidence-reliant classes of people we daily entrust to put facts above wishes and dreams while screening out, as best as we can, claims about reality driven by propaganda, profit, prejudice, and pranks. Because most of us recognize that our very lives depend on this, we are not now and will not likely be ever in a "post-truth" age.

Yes, truth is arrived at by social consensus. Yes, our grasp of facts is often shaky because we approach them through various faulty prisms. But the conclusion is not that we live without reliable truths. The conclusion is not that our senses routinely betray us. We know that they normally get us safely across the street.

I can't believe that I am marching for facts, but I do not think there is any other choice.[3]

Notes

1. Reprinted in Hannah Arendt, *Between Past and Future: Eight Exercises in Political Thought* (New York: Viking Press, 1968), 227–264. All page references to Arendt's "Truth and Politics" are to this book.

2. My own contribution is particularly in *Discovering the News: A Social History of American Newspapers* (New York: Basic Books, 1978). Other relevant work includes Richard Kaplan (2002), *Politics and the American Press: The Rise of Objectivity, 1865–1920* rightly does much more than I did to integrate the changing character of late 19th-century politics into the story. Borrowing from the important work of Michael McGerr (1986), *The Decline of Popular Politics: The American North, 1865–1928,* on changes in "political style"—changing beliefs and practices concerning how electoral politics should be done—I paid greater attention to changing popular attitudes toward politics as a contributing factor to professionalization than I had done originally, in *The Good Citizen: A History of American Civic Life* (1998). I recognized in later work that the era that introduced significantly more analysis, interpretation, and investigation into US journalism—the late 1960s and the 1970s—had a lasting impact on journalistic norms and values. See Katherine Fink and Michael Schudson (2014), "The Rise of Contextual Journalism, 1950s–2000s," the chapter on the news media in Michael Schudson (2015), *The Rise of the Right to Know: Politics and the Culture of Transparency, 1945–1975,* and Michael Schudson (2018), *Why Journalism Still Matters.*

3. This paper was originally presented at the 2017 conference organized by James E. Katz for the Boston University Division of Emerging Media. In a revised form it has been published in a collection of essays—Michael Schudson (2018), *Why Journalism Still Matters.* With a different set of revisions, it appears here with the permission of Polity Press and with thanks to Jim Katz for putting together the original conference so brilliantly.

References

Arendt, Hannah. 1968. *Between Past and Future; Eight Exercises in Political Thought.* Enl. ed. New York: Viking Press.

Confessore, Nicholas, Gabriel J. X. Dance, Richard Harris, and Mark Hansen. 2018. "Buying Online Influence from a Shadowy Market." *New York Times,* January 28.

Fink, Katherine, and Michael Schudson. 2014. "The Rise of Contextual Journalism, 1950s–2000s." *Journalism* 15, no. 1: 3–20.

Graves, Lucas. 2016. *Deciding What's True: The Rise of Political Fact-Checking in American Journalism.* New York: Columbia University Press.

Graves, Lucas. 2018. "Boundaries Not Drawn: Mapping the Institutional Roots of the Global Fact-Checking Movement." *Journalism Studies* 19, no. 5: 613–631.

Graves, Lucas, and Federica Cherubini. 2017. *The Rise of Fact-Checking Sites in Europe.* Oxford: Reuters Institute for the Study of Journalism.

Hofstadter, Richard. 1965. *The Paranoid Style in American Politics, and Other Essays*. New York: Knopf.

Kaplan, Richard L. 2002. *Politics and the American Press: The Rise of Objectivity, 1865–1920*. Cambridge, UK; New York: Cambridge University Press.

Keane, John. 2009. *The Life and Death of Democracy*. New York: W. W. Norton.

Kuhn, Thomas S. 1970. *The Structure of Scientific Revolutions*. 2nd enl. ed. International Encyclopedia of Unified Science, v. 2, no. 2. Chicago: University of Chicago Press.

Lipstadt, Deborah E. 1986. *Beyond Belief: The American Press and the Coming of the Holocaust, 1933–1945*. New York: Free Press.

Lynch, Michael P. 2016. *The Internet of Us: Knowing More and Understanding Less in the Age of Big Data*. New York: Liveright, a Division of W. W. Norton.

McGerr, Michael E. 1986. *The Decline of Popular Politics: The American North, 1865–1928*. New York: Oxford University Press.

Schudson, Michael. 1998. *The Good Citizen: A History of American Civic Life*. New York: Martin Kessler Books

Schudson, Michael. 2015. *The Rise of the Right to Know: Politics and the Culture of Transparency, 1945–1975*. Cambridge, MA: Belknap Press of Harvard University Press.

Schudson, Michael. 2018. *Why Journalism Still Matters*. Cambridge: Polity Press.

Waisbord, Silvio, and Adriana Amado. 2017. "Populist Communication by Digital Means: Presidential Twitter in Latin America." *Information, Communication, & Society* 20, no. 9: 1330–1346.

Spotlight

Pierre Bourdieu and the Journalistic Field

David L. Swartz

Power is a central organizing feature of journalism and should be analyzed as a field of struggle for truth, or more precisely, for the legitimate right to impose particular viewpoints as newsworthy. Journalism is a struggle for symbolic power, that is, the capacity to impose a viewpoint as the legitimate one, the true one. So argues Pierre Bourdieu (1930–2002), one of the greatest post–World War II sociologists and globally the most cited one today.

To understand journalism, Bourdieu argues, one should not focus on single factors, such as technology, or class, corporate, national, or organizational interests, or even individual styles. The media includes all of these and more, which Bourdieu contends is best understood sociologically as a microcosm of intersections of various power resources. Bourdieu's sociology offers conceptual tools for analyzing three types of power in the media; power vested in particular resources (capitals), power concentrated in specific spheres of struggle over forms of capital (fields), and power to impose perceptions of the social world as legitimate (symbolic power).

Rejecting both Marxist and non-Marxist forms of economic reductionism, Bourdieu identifies a wide variety of valued resources, such as cultural capital (knowledge, skills, credentials), social capital (networks), and symbolic capital (honor and prestige), that also function as resources of power. In the journalistic field, individuals and media outlets struggle over the very definition and distribution of media capital that can be measured by indicators linked to the production of news itself, such as number of "exclusives," rate of articles "picked up" by other media outlets, size of audience, and editorial space allocated to a topic. They struggle also for symbolic capital, usually correlated with media capital, that signals the amount of authority and prestige they enjoy within the journalistic field. Thus journalists and media outlets are unequally distributed across field positions defined by amounts and types of capital.

Journalists also struggle against other fields, particularly the economic and political fields, for the power to define what is legitimate knowledge for the society as a whole. What is the economic truth or the political truth of any period? Politicians offer their views, economists offer theirs. Journalists try to sort through the competing viewpoints to say what is the most credible. In this they affirm their professional autonomy. Unfortunately, journalism has become increasingly beholden to political leaders for access to the latest insider information. And media organizations are increasingly subservient to the bottom line.

Journalists also compete to self-define relative to other journalists. Relationality is important Bourdieu argues: "To think in terms of field is to think relationally" (quoted in Swartz 1997, 119)—by which Bourdieu means that field positions and their occupants obtain significance only in comparison to others in the field. Journalists read other journalists and adjust their output relative to the competition from other journalists more than to their respective readerships. They become locked into a differentiating configuration of relations that creates a relatively autonomous microcosm that can insulate them from the demands of democratic society.

Journalists bring to their field positions pre-existing dispositions (*habitus*) acquired through socialization in family, schooling, and later professional experience. These formative dispositions guide individuals in navigating social hierarchies, pointing them to where they belong or do not belong in the social world. These dispositions in combination with the demands of field positions shape journalistic behavior. Hence social class and educational background are influential but mediated through the differentiating dynamics of media fields.

Like other power fields, the journalistic field is bifurcated between two opposing poles: an economic pole in the form of circulation and advertising revenues and audience ratings, and a cultural pole in the form of reasoned commentary, in-depth reporting, the kind of journalism rewarded by the US Pulitzer Prizes. Bourdieu sees the journalistic field increasingly dominated by its economic side; that is, by commercial interests particularly in the form of what he calls the "audience ratings mentality." Its autonomous pole represented by cultural capital specific to journalism, such as writing, interviewing skills, and investigative techniques, is being compromised by economic interests. Negative effects of this increasing domination by commercial interests include uniformity in coverage, censorship, and conservatism in limiting the scope of coverage. But these negative effects extend beyond the journalistic field itself as media culture becomes pervasive in modern societies; media visibility has become a key and constraining standard for modern cultural and political life. It thereby contributes to a degradation of public discourse by offering up media hype and "cultural fast food" rather than probing and reasoned analyses of contemporary issues.

Bourdieu makes these arguments in *On Television* (1988), his most widely known critique of an advertising-saturated, audience-ratings-driven media culture. That book became a national bestseller and provoked sharp critical debate in France on the constraining social and intellectual effects of media visibility.

References

Bourdieu, Pierre. 1998. *On Television*. New York: New Press.
Swartz, David. 1997. *Culture & Power: The Sociology of Pierre Bourdieu*. Chicago: University of Chicago Press.

3

From Information Availability
to Factual Accountability

Reconsidering How Truth Matters for Politicians, Publics, and the News Media

Lucas Graves and Chris Wells

Introduction

Concern about what Arendt (1967) called "lying in politics" is nothing new, but it does seem to be especially salient today. The United States and other established democracies have recently seen the rise of a strain of populist political rhetoric that is openly hostile to the press and to expert institutions (Waisbord 2018). We know more than ever about the psychological mechanisms that help people maintain convenient misperceptions (Flynn, Nyhan, and Reifler 2017). Such beliefs may be supported and sustained by a fragmented media system with few effective gatekeepers, in which rumors and falsehoods often circulate unchecked (Timberg et al. 2017; Faris et al. 2017).

The standard approach, among both academics and journalists, has been to view the problem of truth in politics in terms that might be described as primarily *informational*. Thus, news organizations count falsehoods and publicize them for readers (e.g., Kessler and Kelly 2018); a growing class of professional political fact-checkers identify and correct misleading claims (Graves 2016); and scholars try to measure the reach and influence of misinformation (e.g., Allcott and Gentzkow 2017; Guess, Nyhan, and Reifler 2018) and the extent of mistaken beliefs (e.g., Thorson 2016; Vosoughi, Roy, and Aral, 2018). These efforts reflect a common but also particular understanding of political information and journalism, one that emphasizes the cognitive and rational components of discourse and citizenship (see Kreiss 2016). This framing invites the assumption that correcting falsehoods is primarily a matter of containing the spread of bad information and replacing it with facts.

Without detracting from the value of this informational perspective, in this chapter we highlight a different approach to the problem. Rather than focus on the spread of misinformation, we argue that an account of truth's role in political society must investigate the institutions, formal and informal, that uphold norms of truth-telling and evidence-based discourse in the public sphere. Attention to what we call the domain of *factual accountability* shifts the focus from whether facts are *available* to citizens, or being espoused by politicians, to the conditions under which they *make a difference* for public life; we are interested in understanding the mechanisms and incentives that exist to promote fact-based discourse and to hold public figures accountable for false or misleading statements.

This approach views truth as an inherently political object. We mean this not in the sense that truth is arbitrary or that power alone defines what is true in a society, but nearly the opposite: that for truth to play the regulative function it is assumed to play in both academic and folk theories of democracy, it must be embedded in and supported by institutions that enable—and sometimes require—political actors, the news media, civil society, and citizens to evaluate and respond in good faith to public truth claims. When the norms and institutions that sustain factual exchange are degraded, other dimensions of political discourse—foremost partisanship and power itself—fill the gap; the degradation of factual accountability yields what Rosen has called "a political style in which power gets to write its own story" (2018).

To develop our account of factual accountability, we begin by reviewing how communications research has approached the question of truth. We suggest that the traditional emphasis on the availability and effects of information and misinformation has largely neglected accountability as a quality of the civil sphere that exists to the degree political speech and behavior are governed by truth-telling norms. This leads us to consider the institutions, formal and informal, that support those norms, a discussion that connects to a larger literature on changing political norms among elites and the broader public. After considering the relation of these shifts to the changing structure of the media system, we conclude with a discussion of how these changes affect journalism as an essentially "fact-based discourse" (Chalaby 1996) and how they fit into the wider crisis in journalism.

Information Availability and Factual Accountability

Research on media and politics has long emphasized the role of news and other public information in the formation of public opinion. Many studies measure what citizens know and don't know about politics (Delli Carpini and Keeter 1996) or how new information affects existing beliefs or attitudes (e.g., Eveland 2001). Research on news production has been concerned above all with explaining systematic influences on and biases of journalism as public information—which sources and stories make it into the news, how news narratives encode certain interpretations, and so on (see Shoemaker and Reese 1996). Some of the most successful concepts in communication research, like framing and agenda setting, bridge the concern with the supply of information and its impact on individual members of the public.

For social scientists, the question of truth has largely been subsumed within this informational paradigm. This has come into sharp relief in the clamor over "fake news" and post-truth politics. These terms speak to a litany of concerns about political communication in a digital world: among others, that serious journalism is losing ground while sensationalist and partisan reporting thrive, that rumors and conspiracy theories spread unchecked in a networked media environment with no gatekeepers, and that people increasingly inhabit informational universes in which false beliefs are never challenged (Friedland and Hove 2016).

The focus on truth as an information problem reflects a commonsense picture of how democracy works, or should work, in which citizens express preferences based on what they learn from the press and other sources (Achen and Bartels 2016). It aligns with notions of informed citizenship as a virtue, and with journalists' views of their own role in making democratic self-government possible (Delli Carpini and Keeter 1996; Schudson 1999). In deliberative theory, facts provide the foundation upon which public opinions and public discourse rest; citizens must be prepared "to subject public opinions to a process of rational-critical debate" (Friedland and Hove 2016, 24).

What this understanding of factual information implicitly presumes is that those unwilling to abide by the core discursive norms of the liberal public sphere will be censured and eventually excluded from it. This is at the core of the ideal of the press as democratic "watchdog." As Downie and Schudson (2009) put it, at its best reporting "is aggressive and reliable enough to instill fear of public embarrassment, loss of employment, economic sanctions, or even criminal prosecution in those with political and economic power" (9). In Alexander's formulation of the civil sphere (2006), one of the core constituent elements of the discourse of liberty is honesty (60).

We call this often overlooked element of democratic society—the regulating functions binding actors in the public sphere to truth-telling—the feature of *factual accountability*. It is factual accountability, at least as much as the availability or relative prevalence of accurate information, that appears to be under threat today. As many observers have noted, the most worrying cases occur when falsehoods are widely known, and thoroughly reported, and yet *it does not seem to matter* (Roberts 2017). The corrective mechanisms presumed to punish repeated and unrepentant falsehood-telling appear not to be operative. This signals a breakdown of something larger than the provision of accurate civic information.

Working with Alexander's (2006) framework, Kreiss (2017) locates the breakdown in a portion of the civil sphere itself. Alexander's work (e.g., 2010) emphasizes that political success within a healthy civil sphere is achieved through politicians' adherence to and successful performance of *civil* norms, such as treating opponents with respect and speaking for a broad cross-section of the electorate. This is because a healthy civil sphere is dependent, in part, on citizens being more committed to shared norms of civil behavior than to partisan identification. But Kreiss's interpretation of the 2016 election shows the failure of this optimistic model, detailing the severity and impunity of Trump's violation of numerous civil norms—including repeated violations of norms of truth-telling. Kreiss's conclusion is that partisanship has annexed the role of civil norms in critical domains of moral evaluation and the interpretation of information, representing the "weakening of democratic social solidarity" (13).

The urgent question is how to understand this shift, and how repair of core elements of the civil sphere might take place. Focusing on factual accountability as the feature of the civil sphere perhaps most important to journalism, we argue that we can gain purchase on this question by observing that facts matter democratically to the extent they can compel some form of acknowledgment, whether in public exchange or official action. Facts matter when actors of the civil sphere are constrained, by social norms, legal sanctions, or some other mechanism, to respond to them. Our primary concern is in articulating the domain of factual accountability and tracking its potential degradation.

Formal and Informal Institutions of Factual Accountability

To illustrate the difference between information availability and factual accountability as approaches to truth in politics, consider the problem of meaningful policy responses to the scientific consensus on anthropogenic climate change. The United States has an unusually high proportion of climate-science skeptics; even more striking, it is alone among developed nations in having a major political party that questions climate science and rejects the need for action to mitigate the effects of climate change (Erickson 2017; Nuccitelli 2015).

If you want to understand the unusual politics of climate change in the United States or to explain different policy outcomes in the United States and Europe, focusing on truth as an information problem leads to the important question of what people know and how much they care about the issue. (The news here may surprise: surveys suggest Americans and Europeans are equally concerned about the issue.)[1] This leads naturally to further questions having to do with information and popular belief: How and how often do news outlets report on the issue? Where do climate skeptics get their information? How is climate science taught in schools? How does partisanship affect what people believe (e.g., Bolsen, Druckman, and Cook 2014)? (Of course, it is also possible to accept climate science while disagreeing about the appropriate policy response; the origins of this view can also be studied as an information problem.)

An approach focused on factual accountability, on the other hand, might begin by asking what allows public officials and other elites to *act as if* the facts of anthropogenic climate change remain in doubt. This leads to a different set of questions. For instance, how often are American politicians actually asked to state a clear position on the overwhelming scientific consensus? Why does global warming come up so rarely in presidential debates or interviews with major candidates? A comparative account of US and European environmental policy might consider the very different kinds of settings in which political leaders answer direct questions in parliamentary versus strong presidential systems. Equally important are unwritten codes that govern public talk among political actors. What prevents officials who accept climate science from breaking ranks to challenge misrepresentations about the topic, such as Donald Trump's famous tweet claiming that global warming is a Chinese hoax—one of more than 100 times he has challenged climate science on Twitter (Matthews 2017)? Which politicians are willing to challenge such a statement, and what circumstances tend to make that more common?

To treat the issue more systematically, we might draw the connection here between factual accountability and Azari and Smith's (2012) observation that the functioning of democratic societies relies on rules upheld by institutions of varying levels of formality: some are highly formalized, for example by encoding in statutes, while others are relatively informal and rely on regular voluntary adherence. The subset of democratic norms concerned with factual accountability are similarly embodied in both formal and informal institutions. On the formal side are legal and regulatory frameworks for producing authoritative information and compelling adherence to that information. Perjury is a statutory offense with corresponding penalties for making false statements in particular legal contexts. Environmental impact statements are the product of legally enforceable guidelines for producing information that must be publicly distributed and taken into account in certain public works projects. The Congressional Budget Office's (CBO) reports and cost estimates are required by law, though politicians' acceptance and interpretations of the information they produce are more informally institutionalized. That is, whereas the CBO is legally mandated to produce reports (Congressional Budget Office 2017), norms of adherence to those reports, in rhetoric and policy, are more informal, and as we have recently seen can be changed by the actions of elected officials (Elis 2018).

Or, to continue with the example of climate policy, a vital question concerns the rules and norms that govern selecting witnesses for congressional hearings, staffing federal and state agencies, appointing experts to advisory boards, and so on. A rich vein of administrative law deals with the principles that inform how scientific evidence and expertise is taken into account in public rule-making and other regulatory contexts (see Seifter 2016). Depending on how administrative rules are interpreted (a question sometimes settled by the courts) specific facts about anthropogenic climate change may have to be officially reckoned with in areas from drawing up budget forecasts to setting utility rates to siting schools and hospitals. For instance, the Trump administration has moved to prohibit the Environmental

Protection Agency (EPA) from considering evidence from health studies involving confidential research subjects, sharply restricting which scientific facts EPA scientists can take into account in rule-making (Eilperin and Dennis 2018).

Of course, the domain in which factual accountability is practiced and enforced is broader than government agencies and public officials; it also includes a wider network of "professional communicators" (Page 1996) at the center of the daily public conversation about politics and policy. Here the institutions of factual accountability are less formal, involving, for example, the circumstances that might lead a politician to call out someone from their own party over untruthful statements. And a vital question is what kind of factual accountability exists in the various venues—Sunday shows, call-in programs, policy journals, and so forth—that make up the "space of opinion" in which elites debate politics and policy (Jacobs and Townsley 2011). Finally, the court of public opinion is a further source of factual accountability for officials, though often this form of accountability operates as much indirectly as directly: congressional climate skeptics might be more likely to bend to the popular view if polls showed they would suffer defeat on Election Day, and a leader may be more likely to make a bold denouncement of untruths if she believes it matters to constituents (or the risks were small).

Public Truth and the Degradation
of Democratic Norms

Having sketched factual accountability as a quality of public discourse grounded in a range of norms and institutional mechanisms, our next task is to highlight what appear to be signs of its degradation. After all, norms are made to be broken—and then enforced; indeed, the enforcement is an important socially consolidating act. That is what makes them norms. It is only when they are *not* enforced that they are degraded. Unfortunately, there is evidence of substantial degradation of factual accountability practices within each of the major spheres of factual accountability just described: the general public, political elites, and the news media. We consider the former two in this section, and the latter in the next.

One of the great surprises of Trump's presidential candidacy was how unconcerned his supporters were with his manifest untruths and other norm violations, and how unconcerned rank-and-file Republicans were when party elites declined to oppose him or offer more than tepid censure (Sykes 2017b). But here Trump is as much exemplar as prime suspect; the phenomenon of detachment from strongly held truth norms is something we see in contexts beyond the presidency and across multiple Western democracies (Waisbord 2018). To be sure, his opponent had her share of misleading statements and obfuscations, though it is striking the degree to which Clinton was, in fact, held accountable for this reputation, which was both earned and manufactured: by the middle of the campaign, survey respondents reported seeing more news coverage of her email scandal than any other topic, while much of Trump's coverage focused on subjects he promoted, such as immigration (Newport et al. 2016).

Waisbord (2018) has called these conditions "post-truth communication," characterized by "the absence of conditions in the public sphere for citizens to concur on objectives and processual norms to determine the truth as verifiable statements about reality" (4). This raises the question of how the conditions leading the general public and political elites to adhere to such norms have been undermined.

Here, once again, it is helpful to recognize factual accountability as a category of the wider set of norms governing democratic practice (Azari and Smith 2012; Nyhan 2017). The origins of that decay are complex, but its features may be coming into focus. It is inescapable that mounting disillusionment with social and governing institutions within the public reflect the reality that for many citizens the political system is unresponsive and distant (Achen and Bartels 2016), especially in the eyes of increasingly actualized "critical citizens" (Norris 1999). Some scholars see the expression of these circumstances in the rise of explicitly anti-democratic attitudes (Foa and Mounk 2016). However, the linkage between anti-democratic attitudes and disillusionment with existing institutions is not as strong as some might like, since that linkage would imply that improved institutional performance may revive commitments to democracy. Rather, as Howe (2017) shows, anti-democratic views appear to be more strongly connected to deeper and growing anti-*social* attitudes such as acceptance of the practice of casual lying, overt selfishness, or dishonestly claiming a government benefit.

Social fragmentation and political polarization are also undermining social solidarity as political, social, gender, and racial cleavages become sharper (Mason and Wronski 2018). Not only have common experiences declined, but levels of inter-party animosity now supersede that of nearly all other cultural differences (Iyengar, Sood, and Lelkes 2012). Within the media system, partisan outlets on both sides of the divide have proliferated in response to the possibility of engaging audiences interested in self-reinforcing views, even as audiences for established outlets have differentiated on partisan lines. This polarization is asymmetric in the United States: the left does not have outlets with influence comparable to that of Fox News or Breitbart News on the right. Rather, liberal audiences continue to rely to a great extent on what we once referred to as the "mainstream" press (the *New York Times, Washington Post*, the major television news networks; Faris et al. 2017). For their part, many conservatives distrust establishment outlets commonly referred to as the "liberal" press (Mitchell et al. 2014). This is a situation decades in the making: newsrooms have also become more polarized, with only a fraction of mainstream reporters now identifying as Republican (Willnat and Weaver 2014). At the same time, conservative figures on talk radio and other ideologically driven formats have long made demonization of the mainstream press a major feature of their content (Ladd 2011; Sykes 2017a). The continued significance of talk radio is an important part of the explanation of conservative politicians' behavior: talk radio hosts continue to hold enormous sway, especially among the many Republican members of Congress who politically fear only a challenge from the right, not left (Calmes 2015). All of this is to say that greater degrees of social and political difference, and communication subsystems that serve those subgroups, provide the groundwork for divergent impressions of reality.

On top of all this, despite a strong professional core in American journalism (discussed below), the economics of the news industry have shifted toward the logics of an "attention economy" (Webster 2014). The ability to closely monitor audience attention and interest has led to a sea change in how news is made, as reporters and editors are increasingly mandated to be aware of how particular stories are being received on timescales of days or even hours (Chadwick 2010; Parmelee 2014). This has affected news outlets of all varieties, introducing a news-making logic that is not always consistent with traditional norms of accuracy and news value. And it fosters an environment in which the calculations of politicians and others in the public eye lean more toward attracting attention (witness President Trump's own vocal obsession with ratings) than other qualities such as truthfulness (Karpf 2016).

At the culmination of these trends, is a breakdown in the epistemic solidarity that provides the basis for the establishment of shared facts (Kreiss 2017). Lacking a shared epistemic orientation, strongly party-identified leaders have greater leeway for defining their own representations of truth. In a revealing and discomfiting study, Hahl and colleagues (2018) demonstrate experimentally that under certain conditions, a political leader can lie *with his supporters' full knowledge* and be perceived more favorably, and as more authentic, *because of the lie*. This rejection of common epistemological commitments occurs when supporters view the political and media systems as so illegitimate that lying represents a just violation of unjust norms. It may help explain the instances in which President Trump lies about easily falsifiable facts—that he won a "landslide" victory, or that his inauguration crowd size was larger than Obama's—that Hahl et al. (2018) refer to as "fragrant violations of the norm of truth-telling."

These findings are both comforting and disturbing: comforting because it may not be the case that individuals are unable to perceive obvious untruths from a favored politician (the primary concern of the informational paradigm), but disturbing because some supporters may not care when leaders lie. To the extent that is the case, adherence to truth is no longer a strong criterion for evaluating the behavior of public officials, or in Kreiss's (2017) terms, partisanship has overcome adherence to civil norms as the basis of solidarity. This latter attitude is what is distressingly anti-democratic, as it signals willingness to forgo baseline levels of factual accountability in favor of a potential authoritarian (Levy 2016).

Factual Accountability and the News

The limits of the information availability paradigm become clearest when considering the role of the elite press in an environment of weakening institutions and fragmenting media. Notwithstanding concerns about widespread online misinformation, leading US news organizations have been extraordinarily vigilant both in covering the new administration and in advocating more generally for democratic norms. But professional journalism's ability to hold power to account, rather than simply provide information, depends on a multi-institutional framework—what Ananny (2018) calls a "system of separations and dependencies" that establish autonomy and authority through relations to other public and private actors.

If institutional structures that promote factual accountability are in decline, there is not a lot that journalists, by themselves, can do about it.

Trump's presidential campaign and unexpected victory provoked waves of doubt and self-examination in the elite US press, as well as vocal commitments to shine a light on dishonesty and undemocratic impulses in the new administration (Jacobs 2019). "If we fail to pursue the truth and to tell it unflinchingly . . . the public will not forgive us," wrote the editor of the *Washington Post* (Baron 2016). But as essential as such affirmations may be to preserve professional culture, it is unclear that vigorous "accountability journalism" actually improves the public standing of the press. One recent poll found nearly half of Americans believe the media "makes up stories about Trump," compared with just 37% who disagree (Edsall 2017). As Margaret Sullivan (2017) observed a year into the new administration, the pace of revelations and counter-attacks can leave people confused: "There's a lot of he said/she said, so I believe maybe half of what I hear," one reader told her.

Anxiety over journalism in the "post-truth" era marks only the latest stage in the prolonged, global industry crisis brought on by the shift to a digital media environment—a crisis that has been especially severe in the United States both economically and professionally (Nielsen 2016). Given such wrenching changes, professional news culture—its core values and norms, its public orientation—can seem remarkably resilient, sustained by an institutional center that includes legacy newsrooms but also new sources of serious public-affairs reporting like investigative nonprofits and political fact-checkers (Alexander 2016; Schudson 2015). However, attacks on the press appear to have reached a new pitch in the United States, reflecting and reinforcing longer term trends of rising political polarization and declining trust in the press and other institutions (Hanitzsch, Van Dalen, and Steindl 2018). Some warn that this amounts to the potential "deinstitutionalization" of the press, as the "celebratory anti-institutionalism" of bloggers and digital evangelists gives way to a harsher populist critique that directly challenges the legitimacy of the press as a public institution (Reese 2018, 11; Kreiss 2016). In the United States and elsewhere, the rhetoric of populist outsider politicians like Trump takes direct aim at anchors of journalism's professional project, such as the claim to observe ethical standards and to serve the public (van Dalen 2017). In some respect the United States appears to be moving gradually toward "polarized pluralist" media systems characterized by partisan news sources, polarized news audiences, and highly uneven levels of news consumption and political awareness (Nechushtai 2018).

What would it mean for American journalism if this diagnosis is true, and the United States increasingly takes on features of "polarized pluralist" environments? The challenge in environments characterized by weak institutions and low political trust is not just the circulation of rising quantities of misinformation. Rather, the threat of "deinstitutionalization" directly challenges journalism's tenuous professional status; it limits the ability of journalists to keep politicians accountable by eroding the presumed authority of journalists and the information sources they rely on. In this way it threatens to erode the vital institutional layer of public and private actors—state agencies, civil society groups, think tanks, and so forth—that augment and enable journalism's watchdog function in contemporary democracies (Schudson 2015).

The genre of political fact-checking offers a good illustration. To evaluate the truth of political speech, fact-checkers seek out independent, widely trusted, preferably credentialed sources. Their authority in debunking misleading rhetoric—for instance, Trump's wildly inaccurate claims about who would benefit from the Republican tax overhaul backed by the White House, or, on the campaign trail, Hillary Clinton's claim that tax cuts caused the Great Recession—rests most often on official statistics produced by public agencies like the Bureau of Labor Statistics, the Congressional Budget Office, and the Government Accountability Office. In the United States, these sources retain their institutional authority, despite some worrying signs of politicization (such as recent attacks by the White House and some Republican lawmakers on the legitimacy of the CBO; see Ehrenfreund 2017).

In contrast, political fact-checkers in many parts of the world lack these regularly produced, publicly available, academically vetted sources of data about the public world, and thus offer a view of what "deinstitutionalization" might look like. For example, as an alternative to unreliable and frequently missing government figures, Argentina's Chequeado operates a public-sector data portal where it verifies and publishes documents and data sets leaked to it or uncovered during its own reporting (Graves 2016). To challenge dubious economic statistics, the independent Venezuelan news outlet Efecto Cocuyo, founded in 2015 amid concerns that censorship was inhibiting coverage of the country's financial crisis, maintains its own price index by regularly visiting stores to check for a typical basket of goods used by the hypothetical Quiroz family. Meanwhile, NGO-based fact-checkers in the Balkans and former Soviet states report similar difficulty obtaining public data and regularly file freedom-of-information requests in the effort to obtain routine economic data (Graves and Cherubini 2016). These challenges give a muckraking ethos to routine political fact-checking, and outside of North America and Western Europe fact-checkers are often attached to alternative media and investigative journalism projects.

These examples highlight that the challenge of checking facts authoritatively in weakly institutionalized environments is of a piece with a marginal position in public affairs. Reporters for American outlets like PolitiFact and FactCheck.org often joke that politicians ignore them. But US fact-checkers remain part of a media-political establishment. They strike up partnerships with news organizations and platform companies; public officials and political campaigns typically return their calls; and their work is widely cited in Congress, by major candidates, and across the news media (Graves 2016). In contrast, fact-checking organizations in environments with weaker democratic institutions don't enjoy professional relationships with the politicians they cover: when they receive attention it often comes in the form of threats or accusations of being agents of foreign powers (Graves and Cherubini 2016). Similarly, forming media partnerships is much thornier when leading news outlets are tied to political parties or powerful oligarchs; instead, fact-checkers often ally with smaller, activist media. In such environments the work of fact-checkers and other independent journalists is always already political: it lacks both the common universe of public information to establish institutionally sanctioned facts, and the mediated spaces or contexts to make those facts publicly relevant as part of routine political life.

Considering the challenges journalists face in weakly institutionalized environments underscores the tenuous political balance involved in sustaining contexts for factual accountability. One way to understand this balance is through what Hallin (1989) calls the spheres of consensus and legitimate controversy—that range of acceptable opinions and arguments that make up political debate day in and day out. This sphere may exclude inconvenient facts (for instance, about darker episodes in American foreign policy) but also encompasses much of the institutional fabric that sustains factual discourse in public: the mainstream press, public agencies, universities, think tanks, established NGOs, and other state and civic actors. Precisely because it depends on overarching political consensus, it defines a space for factual accountability—for facts which political actors cannot easily ignore, like an expose in the *New York Times* or the CBO's scoring of a piece of legislation. In an environment of shrinking consensus and eroding norms—one in which the White House openly attacks the credibility of government agencies like the CBO, calling their work "fake news" (Rattner 2018)—the possibilities for factual accountability and thus factual discourse diminish.

For News Practitioners and Consumers

- Considerable attention has been paid to the role of fake news and misinformation in influencing politics. While these are pressing issues, we also must consider the wider problem of factual accountability—the expectations that political leaders respect the truth and pay a price when they don't. However, as we have shown, there is evidence that factual accountability is suffering from degradation on multiple fronts; without it, the democratic value of information availability is greatly diminished.

- Journalists play an integral role in both providing quality information and preserving factual accountability. However, many journalists now operate in an environment in which some political elites, news outlets, and even the general public have wavered in their commitment to the norms of factual accountability. This makes good journalism harder and can blunt its impact, as it may today more often be ignored by publics and those in power. Journalists should be realistic about these new challenges, yet maintain their commitment to the norms that make the profession an essential democratic institution. Further, being sensitive to the importance of factual accountability, and calling out both breaches and reinforcements of this critical norm, may be one of the most important roles for journalists today.

- Citizens should become attuned to factual accountability and take steps to support institutions and individuals who are upholding its standards.

Note

1. For instance, in a 2015 survey, an equal share of European and American respondents (42%) were very concerned about climate change (Carle 2015). Recent surveys find strong majorities of Americans believe global warming is happening and caused by human activity, though concern varies by region and by party (e.g., Saad 2017).

References

Achen, Christopher H., and Larry M. Bartels. 2016. *Democracy for Realists: Why Elections Do Not Produce Responsive Government*. Princeton, NJ: Princeton University Press.

Alexander, Jeffrey C. 2006. *The Civil Sphere*. New York: Oxford University Press.

Alexander, Jeffrey C. 2010. *The Performance of Politics: Obama's Victory and the Democratic Struggle for Power*. New York: Oxford University Press.

Alexander, Jeffrey C. 2016. "Introduction: Journalism, Democratic Culture, and Creative Reconstruction." In *The Crisis of Journalism Reconsidered: Democratic Culture, Professional Codes, Digital Future*, edited by Jeffrey C. Alexander, Elizabeth Butler Breese, and Maria Luengo, 1–28. Cambridge: Cambridge University Press.

Allcott, Hunt, and Matthew Gentzkow. 2017. "Social Media and Fake News in the 2016 Election. *Journal of Economic Perspectives* 31, no. 2: 211–236.

Ananny, Michael. 2018. *Networked Press Freedom: Creating Infrastructures for a Public Right to Hear*. Cambridge, MA: MIT Press.

Arendt, Hannah. 1967. "Truth and Politics." *The New Yorker*, February 18. https://www.newyorker.com/magazine/1967/02/25/truth-and-politics.

Azari, Julia R., and Jennifer K. Smith. 2012. "Unwritten Rules: Informal Institutions in Established Democracies." *Perspectives on Politics* 10, no. 1: 37–55. https://doi.org/10.1017/S1537592711004890.

Baron, Martin. 2016. "Marty Baron's Message to Journalists in the Trump Era." *Vanity Fair* (blog). November 30, 2016. https://www.vanityfair.com/news/2016/11/washington-post-editor-marty-baron-message-to-journalists.

Bolsen, Toby, James N. Druckman, and Fay Lomax Cook. 2014. "The Influence of Partisan Motivated Reasoning on Public Opinion." *Political Behavior* 36, no. 2: 235–262. https://doi.org/10.1007/s11109-013-9238-0.

Calmes, Jackie. 2015. "'They Don't Give a Damn about Governing' Conservative Media's Influence on the Republican Party." Harvard Kennedy School, Shorenstein Center. https://shorensteincenter.org/conservative-media-influence-on-republican-party-jackie-calmes/.

Carle, Jill. 2015. "Climate Change Seen as Top Global Threat." Pew Research, July 14. http://www.pewglobal.org/2015/07/14/climate-change-seen-as-top-global-threat/.

Chadwick, Andrew. 2010. "Britain's First Live Televised Party Leaders' Debate: From the News Cycle to the Political Information Cycle." *Parliamentary Affairs* 64, no. 1 (Jan.): 24–44. https://doi.org/10.1093/pa/gsq045.

Chalaby, Jean K. 1996. "Journalism as an Anglo-American Invention: A Comparison of the Development of French and Anglo-American Journalism, 1830s–1920s." *European Journal of Communication* 11, no. 3: 303–326.

Delli Carpini, Michael X., and Scott Keeter. 1996. *What Americans Know about Politics and Why It Matters*. New Haven, CT: Yale University Press.

Downie, Leonard Jr., and Michael Schudson. 2009. *The Reconstruction of American Journalism*. New York: Columbia School of Journalism.

Edsall, Thomas B. 2017. "The Trump Voter Paradox." *New York Times*, September 28. https://www.nytimes.com/2017/09/28/opinion/trump-republicans-authoritarian.html.

Ehrenfreund, Max. 2017. "The Trump Administration Says CBO Can't Be Trusted Because Its Obamacare Predictions Were Wrong. Are They Right?" *Washington Post*,

June 26. https://www.washingtonpost.com/news/wonk/wp/2017/06/26/heres-how-well-the-cbo-did-at-forecasting-the-last-big-health-care-bill/.

Eilperin, Juliet, and Brady Dennis. 2018. "Pruitt Unveils Controversial 'Transparency' Rule Limiting What Research EPA Can Use." *Washington Post*, April 24. Retrieved from https://www.washingtonpost.com/news/energy-environment/wp/2018/04/24/pruitt-to-unveil-controversial-transparency-rule-limiting-what-research-epa-can-use/.

Elis, Niv. 2018. "GOP Dismisses Report That Tax Law Will Add $1.9 Trillion to Debt." *The Hill*, April 10. http://thehill.com/policy/finance/382493-gop-dismisses-report-that-tax-law-will-add-19-trillion-to-debt.

Erickson, Amanda. 2017. "The U.S. Has More Climate Skeptics Than Anywhere Else on Earth. Blame the GOP." *Washington Post*, November 17. https://www.washingtonpost.com/news/worldviews/wp/2017/11/17/the-u-s-has-more-climate-skeptics-than-anywhere-else-on-earth-blame-the-gop/.

Eveland, William P. 2001. "The Cognitive Mediation Model of Learning from the News: Evidence from Nonelection, Off-Year Election, and Presidential Election Contexts." *Communication Research* 28, no. 5: 571–601. https://doi.org/10.1177/009365001028005001.

Faris, Robert, Hal Roberts, Bruc Etling, Nikki Bourassa, Ethan Zuckerman, and Yochai Benkler. 2017. "Partisanship, Propaganda and Disinformation: Online Media and the 2016 Presidential Election." Berkman Klein Center for Internet and Society, Cambridge, MA. https://cyber.harvard.edu/publications/2017/08/mediacloud.

Flynn, D. J., Brendan Nyhan, and Jason Reifler. 2017. "The Nature and Origins of Misperceptions: Understanding False and Unsupported Beliefs about Politics." *Political Psychology* 38: 127–150. https://doi.org/10.1111/pops.12394.

Foa, Roberto Stefan, and Yascha Mounk. 2016. "The Danger of Deconsolidation: The Democratic Disconnect." *Journal of Democracy* 27, no. 3: 5–17.

Friedland, Lewis A., and Thomas. B. Hove. 2016. "Habermas' Account of Truth in Political Communication." In *Truth in the Public Sphere*, edited by Jason Hannan, 23–39. Lanham, MD: Lexington Books.

Graves, Lucas. 2016. *Deciding What's True: The Rise of Political Fact-Checking in American Journalism.* New York: Columbia University Press.

Graves, Lucas, and Federica Cherubini. 2016. "The Rise of Fact-Checking Sites in Europe." Oxford, UK: Reuters Institute. https://reutersinstitute.politics.ox.ac.uk/our-research/rise-fact-checking-sites-europe.

Guess, Andrew, Brendan Nyhan, and Jason Reifler. 2018. "Selective Exposure to Misinformation: Evidence from the Consumption of Fake News During the 2016 US Presidential Campaign." European Research Council. http://www.dartmouth.edu/~nyhan/fake-news-2016.pdf

Hahl, Oliver, Minjae Kim, and Ezra W. Zuckerman Sivan. 2018. "The Authentic Appeal of the Lying Demagogue: Proclaiming the Deeper Truth About Political Illegitimacy." *American Sociological Review* 83, no. 1: 1–33. https://doi.org/10.1177/0003122417749632.

Hallin, Daniel C. 1989. *The Uncensored War: The Media and Vietnam.* Berkeley, CA: University of California Press.

Hanitzsch, Thomas, Arlen Van Dalen, and Nina Steindl. 2018. "Caught in the Nexus: A Comparative and Longitudinal Analysis of Public Trust in the Press." *International Journal of Press/Politics* 23, no. 1, 3–23. https://doi.org/10.1177/1940161217740695.

Howe, Paul. 2017. "Eroding Norms and Democratic Deconsolidation." *Journal of Democracy* 28, no. 4: 15–29.

Iyengar, Shanto, Gaurav Sood, and Yphtach Lelkes. 2012. "Affect, Not Ideology: A Social Identity Perspective on Polarization." *Public Opinion Quarterly* 76, no. 3: 405–431. https://doi.org/10.1093/poq/nfs038.

Jacobs, Ronald N. 2019. "Journalism After Trump." In *Politics of Meaning/Meaning of Politics: Cultural Sociology of the 2016 U.S. Presidential Election*, edited by Jason L. Mast and Jeffrey C. Alexander, 75–93. Cultural Sociology. Cham: Springer International Publishing. https://doi.org/10.1007/978-3-319-95945-0_5.

Jacobs, Ronald N., and Eleanor Townsley. 2011. *The Space of Opinion: Media Intellectuals and the Public Sphere*. Oxford, New York: Oxford University Press.

Karpf, David. 2016. "The Clickbait Candidate." *The Chronicle of Higher Education*, June 19. http://chronicle.com/article/The-Clickbait-Candidate/236815?cid=rc_right.

Kessler, Glenn, and Meg Kelly. 2018. *Washington Post*, January 10. https://www.washingtonpost.com/news/fact-checker/wp/2018/01/10/president-trump-has-made-more-than-2000-false-or-misleading-claims-over-355-days/

Kreiss, Daniel. 2016. "Beyond Administrative Journalism: Civic Skepticism and the Crisis in Journalism." In *The Crisis of Journalism Reconsidered: Democratic Culture, Professional Codes, Digital Future*, edited by Jeffrey C. Alexander, Elizabeth Butler Breese, and Maria Luengo, 59–76. Cambridge: Cambridge University Press.

Kreiss, Daniel. 2017. "The Fragmenting of the Civil Sphere: How Partisan Identity Shapes the Moral Evaluation of Candidates and Epistemology." *American Journal of Cultural Sociology* 5, no. 3: 443–459. https://doi.org/10.1057/s41290-017-0039-5.

Ladd, Jonathan. M. 2011. *Why Americans Hate the Media and How It Matters*. Princeton, NJ: Princeton University Press.

Levy, Jacob T. 2016. "Authoritarianism and Post-Truth Politics." Niskanen Center, November 30. https://niskanencenter.org/blog/authoritarianism-post-truth-politics/.

Mason, Lilliana, and Julie Wronski. 2018. "One Tribe to Bind Them All: How Our Social Group Attachments Strengthen Partisanship." *Political Psychology* 39, no. S1: 257–277. https://doi.org/10.1111/pops.12485.

Matthews, Dylan. 2017. "Donald Trump has Tweeted Climate Change Skepticism 115 Times." *Vox*, June 1. https://www.vox.com/policy-and-politics/2017/6/1/15726472/trump-tweets-global-warming-paris-climate-agreement

Mitchell, Amy, Jeffre Gottfried, Jocelyn Kiley, and Katerina E. Matsa. 2014. "Political Polarization & Media Habits." Pew Research Center. http://www.journalism.org/2014/10/21/section-3-talking-politics-leaders-vs-listeners-and-the-views-people-hear/.

Nechushtai, Efrat. 2018. "From Liberal to Polarized Liberal? Contemporary U.S. News in Hallin and Mancini's Typology of News Systems." *International Journal of Press/Politics*, 23, no. 2: 183–201. https://doi.org/10.1177/1940161218771902.

Newport, Frank, Lisa Singh, Stuart Soroka, Michael Traugott, and Andrew Dugan. 2016. "'Email' Dominates What Americans Have Heard About Clinton." Gallup, September 19. https://news.gallup.com/poll/195596/email-dominates-americans-heard-clinton.aspx.

Nielsen, Rasmus Kleis. 2016. "The Many Crises of Western Journalism: A Comparative Analysis of Economic Crises, Professional Crises, and Crises of Confidence." In *The Crisis of Journalism Reconsidered: Democratic Culture, Professional Codes, Digital Future*, edited by Jeffrey C. Alexander, Elizabeth Butler Breese, and Maria Luengo, 77–97. Cambridge: Cambridge University Press.

Norris, Pippa. 1999. *Critical Citizens: Global Support for Democratic Government.* Oxford; New York: Oxford University Press.

Nuccitelli, Dana. 2015. "The Republican Party Stands Alone in Climate Denial." *The Guardian*, October 5. https://www.theguardian.com/environment/climate-consensus-97-per-cent/2015/oct/05/the-republican-party-stands-alone-in-climate-denial.

Nyhan, Brendan. 2017. "Norms Matter." *POLITICO*, September/October. https://www.politico.com/magazine/story/2017/09/05/why-norms-matter-politics-trump-215535.

Page, Benjamin. I. 1996. *Who Deliberates? Mass Media in Modern Democracy.* Chicago: University of Chicago Press.

Parmelee, John. H. 2014. "The Agenda-building Function of Political Tweets." *New Media & Society* 16, no. 3: 434–450. https://doi.org/10.1177/1461444813487955.

Rattner, Steven. 2018. "Opinion | The Boring Little Budget Office That Trump Hates." *The New York Times*, January 20, 2018, sec. Opinion. https://www.nytimes.com/2017/08/22/opinion/trump-cbo-republicans-hate.html.

Reese, Stephen D. 2018. "Does the Institutional Press Still Matter? Exploring the Hybrid Infrastructure in the New Media Ecosystem." Presented at the Annual Conference of the International Communication Association, Prague.

Roberts, David. 2017. "America Is Facing an Epistemic Crisis." *Vox*, November 2. https://www.vox.com/policy-and-politics/2017/11/2/16588964/america-epistemic-crisis.

Rosen, Jay. 2018. "Why Trump is Winning and the Press is Losing." *New York Review of Books*, April 25. https://www.nybooks.com/daily/2018/04/25/why-trump-is-winning-and-the-press-is-losing/

Saad, Lydia. 2017. "Global Warming Concern at Three-Decade High in U.S." Gallup, March 14. http://news.gallup.com/poll/206030/global-warming-concern-three-decade-high.aspx.

Schudson, Michael. 1999. *The Good Citizen: A History of American Civic Life.* New York: Martin Kessler Books.

Schudson, Michael. 2015. *The Rise of the Right to Know: Politics and the Culture of Transparency, 1945–1975.* Cambridge, MA: Harvard University Press.

Seifter, Miriam. 2016. "Second-Order Participation in Administrative Law." *UCLA Law Review* 63: 1300–1365.

Shoemaker, Pamela. J., and Stephen D. Reese. 1996. *Mediating the Message: Theories of Influences on Mass Media Content.* 2nd ed. White Plains, NY: Longman.

Sullivan, Margaret. 2017. "Trump's Message of Mistrust Is Sinking in, Even in Journalism's New 'Golden Age.'" *Washington Post*, November 5. https://www.washingtonpost.com/lifestyle/style/trumps-message-of-mistrust-is-sinking-in-even-in-journalisms-new-golden-age/2017/11/02/8b968730-ba5f-11e7-be94-fabb0f1e9ffb_story.html.

Sykes, Charlie J. 2017a. *How the Right Lost Its Mind.* New York: St. Martin's Press.

Sykes, Charlie J. 2017b. "Year One: The Mad King." *New York Review of Books*, November 10. http://www.nybooks.com/daily/2017/11/10/year-one-the-mad-king/.

Thorson, Emily. 2016. "Belief Echoes: The Persistent Effects of Corrected Misinformation." *Political Communication* 33, no. 3: 460–480. https://doi.org/10.1080/10584609.2015.1102187.

Timberg, Craig, Elizabeth Dwoskin, Adam Entous, and Karoun Demirjian. 2017. "Russian Ads, Now Publicly Released, Show Sophistication of Influence Campaign." *Washington Post*, November 1. https://www.washingtonpost.com/business/technology/russian-ads-now-publicly-released-show-sophistication-of-influence-campaign/2017/11/01/d26aead2-bf1b-11e7-8444-a0d4f04b89eb_story.html.

Van Dalen, Arlen. 2017. "Rethinking Journalist-Politician Relations in the Age of Post-truth Politics: Strategies of Delegitimization." Presented at the International Journal of Press/Politics Conference, Oxford, UK.

Vosoughi, Soroush, Deb Roy, and Sinan Aral. 2018. "The Spread of True and False News Online." *Science* 359, no. 6380 (Mar. 9): 1146–1151. https://doi.org/10.1126/science. aap9559.

Waisbord, Silvio. 2018. "The Elective Affinity Between Post-truth Communication and Populist Politics." *Communication Research and Practice* 4, no. 1: 17–34. https://doi. org/10.1080/22041451.2018.1428928.

Webster, James G. 2014. *The Marketplace of Attention: How Audiences Take Shape in a Digital Age*. Cambridge, MA: MIT Press.

Willnat, Lars, and David H. Weaver. "The American Journalist in the Digital Age." Bloomington, Indiana University, 2014. http://archive.news.indiana.edu/releases/iu/ 2014/05/2013-american-journalist-key-findings.pdf.

4

Fake News

A New Obsession with an Old Phenomenon?

Nicole M. Krause, Christopher D. Wirz, Dietram A. Scheufele,
and Michael A. Xenos

"Fake news" seems to be the term du jour since Donald Trump's surprise victory in the 2016 US presidential election. Media organizations, pundits, and technology leaders are sounding the alarm about a surge of misinformation attributed largely to the misuse of Internet-based media technologies like Facebook and Google. In response to public outcry over their role in the "rise" of fake news, technology companies have been rapidly churning through changes to their platforms, with an emphasis on fact-checking algorithms and interface solutions for "flagging" stories as fake (Oremus 2016; Mosseri 2016; Zuckerberg 2016; Hern 2017; Calfas 2017). Such solutions are aimed at improving Americans' *ability* to spot fake news, but is that really the only (or even the main) problem related to the production, dissemination, and consumption of misinformation in our current media environment?

In this chapter, we will argue that cycling through technical solutions that flag fake news for consumers will do little to curb the spread of misinformation because the "fake news problem" extends beyond and predates social media technologies. While we recognize that new media are particularly conducive to the spread of fake news, we offer two main clarifications: First, social media technology has been shaped by older economic trends, and, unless those trends are explicitly altered, they will continue to influence Americans' encounters with (mis)information. Second, Americans' limited factual understanding of civic matters goes beyond an *inability* to spot fake news—it is also a consequence of *unwillingness* among audiences to expose themselves to information that is inconsistent with firmly held prior values or beliefs.

Consider, for example, that although Americans generally believe fake news is problematic, 84% of them have said they are "somewhat" or "very" confident in their *own* ability to spot fake news, and they are similarly confident that they know which news is "trustworthy" (Pew Research Center 2016a; 2016b). Although Americans are confident, there is little evidence to suggest that their confidence is grounded in the necessary skills or abilities to spot false information. Meanwhile, close to seven in ten (67%) Americans turn to social media for news, despite expressing very low trust in information on social media (Pew Research Center 2017a). Furthermore, a small (but still unsettling) number of Americans (14%) have admitted to sharing news on social media when they knew it was false (Pew Research Center 2016b). These data raise questions about ability-centric solutions; even if we could improve Americans' ability to spot fake news, would they be motivated to reject it?

Beyond this, we know that Americans are most engaged with news they encounter through friends and family (Pew Research Center 2017a). When it comes to politics, however, there is reason to believe that Americans' closest contacts are like-minded. Americans are becoming polarized, and a deep animosity toward out-group partisans is developing, with cross-party friendships and marriages declining (Pew Research Center 2016c). Thus, as partisan "fake news" stories circulate online, the polarized climate raises concerns about Americans' information-related goals: Are we seeking "the truth" or reinforcing and defending partisan views? Moreover, amid recent reports that falsehoods have spread across the Internet "significantly farther, faster, deeper, and more broadly than the truth," and that *humans* (not robots) are the likely culprits (Vosoughi, Roy, and Aral 2018), we ask: How are well-known psychological tendencies interacting with new media capabilities to exacerbate the spread of misinformation?

As we address these questions in the arguments below, we do not mean to underappreciate efforts to devise technological solutions that can fact-check falsehoods or encourage Americans to think critically about news sources. Rather, we argue that if the broader goal is to improve Americans' encounters with politically relevant information, then we must *also* consider other systemic and psychological factors—including commercial pressures on the media system and people's personal motivations—that contribute to the spread of fake news.

Abstract Notions of Truth: "Fake News" Is Not Quite New

The question of what constitutes journalistic "truth" or "news" is an old one. By definition, news can only present a narrow slice of reality to its readers and viewers. What is selected as news by any given news outlet depends on a wide variety of influences, including journalists' professional norms (Tuchman 1978), news values—i.e., characteristics of news items that compete for space on the agenda (Galtung and Ruge 1965)—and, increasingly, audience demands (Rutenberg 2016). As a result, news content is "the result of practical, purposive, and creative activities on the part of news promoters, news assemblers and news consumers" (Molotch and Lester 1974, 101). Moreover, journalists routinely emphasize certain aspects of issues over others, or frame information in different ways, in order to provide readers with relevant context (Scheufele 1999). What gets covered, which aspects of issues get highlighted, and how evidence supporting factual claims is being interpreted are all determined by a complex interplay of numerous social, commercial, and political actors.

Therefore, with the exception of very narrow, directly verifiable claims, the idea that there is an objective "truth" against which the nature and content of coverage can be verified is often unrealistic. Given these complexities, journalistic search for truth is defined less by specific outcomes than by the processes through which news is gathered, sources are verified, and how errors in reporting get corrected and documented (e.g., (Shoemaker and Reese 1996). Consequently, for our purposes, "fake news" is defined not as news that deviates from some notion of objective reality, but rather as news that deviates from those journalistic conventions that have governed the presentation of truth claims as "news."

As we will demonstrate below, fake news of this kind has long existed in various forms, and it has ignited concern about the role of misinformation in American democratic life since well before the emergence of Internet-based media. For example, perhaps the most well-known form of fake news is political propaganda, which has existed for centuries, and which became particularly salient in America during and after World Wars I and II (Sproule 1987; Gary 1996). However, we would also argue that the (in)famous *War of the Worlds* radio broadcast, which claimed that Martians had invaded New York City (Campbell 2010), can be considered fake news, as can decades-old supermarket tabloids like *Globe* and the *National*

Enquirer. Consequently, to better articulate the extent to which fake news has appeared historically—including outside of Internet-based media—we offer the following.

Fake News That Was Never Meant to Be News

Some research pertaining to fake news has focused on the blurry line between entertainment and "news," exemplified by satirical television shows like *Saturday Night Live (SNL)* or late night comedies that resemble news broadcasts such as *The Daily Show* (Holbert 2005; Amarasingam 2011; Balmas 2014). There is some evidence that the satirical remarks made on these "fake news" shows can become conflated with reality. For example, when Tina Fey impersonated Republican vice presidential candidate Sarah Palin on *SNL,* she said "I can see Russia from my house." Although the real Palin never made this statement, almost seven out of ten Americans were convinced that she did—especially heavy viewers of traditional media (Cacciatore et al. 2014).

Paid Content as News

Another (quite different) way of thinking about fake news would be sponsored news—for example, when the Department of Education under President George W. Bush paid Armstrong Williams to promote the "No Child Left Behind Act" on radio and television shows, or the more recent appearance of "The Daily Telegraph," a self-described "Media/News" website created by the Republican Governors Association to promote its members' achievements and criticize Democrats in social media and elsewhere (Kurtz 2005; Barrow 2017).

In addition, in both online and print media, news outlets are displaying "native advertisements," or sponsored messages designed to look like news. For example, *Time, The New Yorker,* and *Rolling* Stone all recently tailored their print covers to act as advertisements for the NBC TV show *Blacklist* (Steinberg 2014). Other examples of these ads can be found in the *New York Times* and the *Atlantic,* where they often receive only mild acknowledgement as "sponsored content," arguably making it hard to distinguish them from real news (Carlson 2015; Shell 2014).

Journalistic Mistakes as Fake News

Yet another form of fake news might be instances of sloppy journalism. For example, on September 8, 2004, CBS news anchor Dan Rather falsely reported in an episode of *60 Minutes* that he was in possession of six authenticated documents claiming that President George W. Bush had disobeyed orders during military service (CBS News 2004). This report was disputed as fake in online blogs, prompting attention from other traditional media outlets (Memmott 2004). Consider also the recent scandal in which the cable outlet Fox News allegedly fabricated a story, claiming that the leak of Democratic National Committee (DNC) members' emails during the 2016 election was not caused by Russian hackers, but rather by a DNC insider, who they claimed was murdered as part of a cover-up (Seitz-Wald and Siemaszko 2017; Folkenflik 2017). Along the same lines, Donald Trump has used journalistic mistakes by news organizations to perpetuate his otherwise unfounded claims that sources such as CNN and ABC produce fake news (Shelbourne 2017).

Intentionally Fake "News"

Finally, we have examples of fake news that seem unique to modern times, in that they are driven by Internet-based information publishers who may consider themselves sources of "news," but who do not strictly adhere to journalistic norms. Examples of these non-traditional news sources can include blogs or opinion pages that have turned into news websites, such as Breitbart or Huffpost. Other sources include partisan Facebook pages that function solely to produce and circulate information that advances a partisan cause, such as Occupy Democrats or Eagle Rising (Herrman 2016; Silvermanet al. 2016).

These non-mainstream sources garnered increased attention in the popular press in the wake of Trump's presidential victory as people questioned the role of fake news in the election outcome. For example, a fake news story falsely claimed Pope Francis endorsed Donald Trump for president, although the pope had made no such endorsement and had criticized Trump's statements about a border wall between the United States and Mexico (Ritchie 2016). Heightened concern about this kind of fake news leading up to the election has prompted empirical evaluations of its impact on US political processes (Allcott and Gentzkow 2017).

The purpose of the preceding discussion has not been to offer a comprehensive typology of fake news. Rather, we have endeavored to show that fake news has a long history in non-Internet media, and that its older forms continue to exist even as new technologies gain traction and new problems emerge. In order to develop a more nuanced and helpful understanding of the fake news problem, we contend that it is vitally important to recognize that there are multiple, distinct dimensions of what is often subsumed under the broad umbrella of "fake news" in current social debates.

This raises the question of what, if anything, has changed about human behavior, the media system, and technology that distinguishes older fake news from "new" fake news. In the following discussion, we will argue that some of the same non-technological factors—including commercial pressures on the media system and people's psychological tendencies—have long influenced fake news, both online and off. In making this point, we present our concerns about narrow, technology-centric solutions that neglect important social and political dimensions of the problem, thereby limiting their ability to combat fake news. We then advocate for a more inclusive solution set that balances technical changes and improved news literacy with solutions aimed at addressing problems of *motivation*.

Technology: New Media, Shaped by Old Trends

The current design of popular social media technologies is not inevitable or accidental. Instead, it is another chapter in the long history of America's commercial media system. For example, in the late 19th century, publishers printed and reprinted fake, sensational stories because they were widely circulated and economically lucrative (Jordan 2018). However, by the late 20th century, commercial media relied more on tailoring content to certain segments of readers or viewers. Segmenting audiences for advertisers and then delivering content tailored to their interests only intensified as cable television emerged and brought an explosion of niche channels (Prior 2007; Turow 1997). Internet-based media technologies like Facebook and Google are merely continuing these existing trends with new tools and affordances made possible by online modes of information delivery and exchange.

However, what *is* new is that new technologies are taking these old trends to new levels of precision and sophistication. Enabled by dramatic increases in capacity for real-time data storage and analysis, technology companies have devised ways to collect, combine, and analyze complex data sets about their users' characteristics, preferences, and behaviors. These new tools for storage and real-time analysis allow technology companies to deliver content and advertising specifically targeted toward individual consumers. In other words, content is no longer tailored only to broad audience segments. Instead, advertising and other forms of communication are also microtargeted toward individual consumers.

This technical infrastructure is specifically designed to provide users with "relevant" content that will hold their attention and motivate them to regularly return to the platform. This maximizes profits along a wide variety of dimensions, including targeted advertising services, collection and commercialization of user data, distribution agreements with legacy media, and research consulting, such as A/B testing services for corporate partners. Unintentionally, however, narrowcasting information based on personal preferences also contributes to the formation of "filter bubbles" in which people are exposed to a subset of products, people, and information that align with their pre-existing beliefs and preferences (Pariser 2011; Sunstein 2007). Ultimately, there is a real danger of audiences developing ultra-tailored media diets, created both by the platforms and by the audiences themselves, in a process of preference-based reinforcement (Cacciatore, Scheufele, and Iyengar 2016). Legacy media, especially in commercial media systems like the United States, are increasingly faced with similar economic pressures. This point was recently emphasized by Jim VandeHei, a former *Washington Post* editor and Politico co-founder, when he said that news outlets' survival "depends on giving readers what they really want, how they want it, when they want it, and on not spending too much money producing what they don't want" (Rutenberg 2016).

Notably, a growing body of communications research has evaluated the prevalence and spread of political misperceptions in a media ecology beset by such pressures and new technologies. Examples of this work include the previously mentioned findings about the misattribution of Tina Fey's quip "I can see Russia from my house" to Sarah Palin, as well as other more high-profile examples like erroneous beliefs about President Obama's religion and/or birthplace, and the existence of weapons of mass destruction in Iraq (Cacciatore et al. 2014; Del Vicario et al. 2016; Garrett, Weeks, and Neo 2016).

Is Our *Inability* to Spot Fake News Really the Only Problem?

Faced with these new challenges, a plethora of technical and social solutions have emerged in the last decade to enhance Americans' ability to spot lies and fake stories while browsing the Internet. For example, various fact-checking organizations, such as PolitiFact.com and Factcheck.org, have engaged in a new kind of "newswork" that focuses not on presenting "balanced," newsworthy stories, but rather on evaluating the accuracy of statements made by American political elites (Graves 2016). Some of these fact-checking groups have also compiled lists of websites that are known purveyors of fake news, in order to help the public assess the credibility of news they encounter online (Schaedel 2017).

Beyond this, researchers in the field of computer science are continuing their efforts toward computer-assisted journalism with ongoing work on "automatic fake news detection" and "news verification" solutions that hope to algorithmically assess the veracity of claims made in digital media (Conroy, Rubin, and Chen 2015; Hassan et al. 2015). Similarly, members of the programming community have offered browser plugins to combat the problem: "Fake News Alert" and "B.S. Detector" both notify users that a given information source is questionable (Chrome Web Store 2016). Similar browser extensions have even been created to specifically assess the veracity of President Trump's statements on Twitter (Bump 2016).

These technical solutions have been supplemented by studies exposing Americans' lack of news literacy, along with calls to correct their ability to identify credible vs. dubious sources. One such report, conducted by the Stanford History Education Group, explained that an assessment of news literacy among 7,804 American students produced dismal results: (a) more than 80% of the students believed that a native advertisement was a real story, despite its label as "sponsored content," (b) less than a third of the students could satisfactorily discuss how tweets from politically charged groups might be biased, and (c) students were captivated by compelling visual content of online media while ignoring "key details, such as the source of the photo" (2016, 17).

While news literacy and fact-checking solutions offer an intuitive strategy, we see them as limited in their focus on improving Americans' *ability* to recognize fake news, unless they are paired with solutions that address *motivational* barriers to resisting fake news. Social science has taught us that people often rely on their prior beliefs and values as they select, process, and use information. Moreover, research has also suggested that a lack of familiarity with "the facts" does not actually explain the lion's share of political misperceptions; rather, a non-trivial proportion of those holding political misperceptions likely do so *in spite of* knowledge to the contrary (Garrett, Weeks, and Neo 2016). Dynamics like these have led a number of researchers to call for moving beyond ability-centric solutions to the problem of fake news (Lazer et al. 2017). Based on these considerations, we argue that enhancing people's *ability* to identify falsehoods in new media environments—through solutions such as automated fact-checking or "flagging" buttons—will not necessarily mean that Americans will resist or reject fake news.

The question of whether everyday people have the ability or the desire to carefully evaluate information pertinent to democratic life is an old one. Even if we focus narrowly on social science research in the United States, we can look back over 100 years and find debate about this very idea. People like Charles Cooley and John Dewey asserted long ago that the new communication technology of their era would help Americans become informed, rational citizens who could advance social progress (Cooley [1897] 2004; Dewey 1927). By contrast, people like Harold Lasswell [1927] (2004), Robert Lynd ([1940] 2004), and Walter Lippmann (1922) pointed to successful wartime propaganda as a disturbing indication of the media's ability to manipulate public opinion. In fact, Lippmann intuitively understood the tendency of people to filter perceptions of reality through the "pictures in our heads," rather than adjusting those pictures to new (and potentially belief-inconsistent) information. "We are told about the world before we see it," he wrote, "[w]e imagine most things before we experience them. And those preconceptions . . . govern deeply the whole process of perception" (1922, 59).

Selecting Our Own Reality

The behavior Lippmann described is partly due to the human tendency to select information that fits pre-existing beliefs or values, which is driven to some extent by "cognitive dissonance," or the psychological discomfort of encountering attitude-discrepant information (Festinger 1962). When given a choice of media messages to peruse, people are likely to select belief-consistent information in a process of "selective exposure." Notably, selective exposure can be triggered not only by agreeable and disagreeable content but also by labels or other contextual cues that signal the possible congruency of a message with a person's political views. Multiple studies have documented that *source cues*—regardless of content—are powerful predictors of exposure to news about politics, as well as seemingly "nonpolitical" scientific issues (Iyengar and Hahn 2009; Yeo et al. 2015).

Again, the algorithms underlying online media outlets are designed to profile audiences based on their past preferences and to deliver them similar information in the future, thus creating a "reinforcement" effect (Cacciatore, Scheufele, and Iyengar 2016). Consequently, as new media technology enhances selective exposure tendencies, people encounter increasingly agreeable media—as well as more and more content from like-minded social contacts—resulting in a homogeneous information diet that lowers the chance of experiencing disagreement (Messing and Westwood 2012). Unfortunately, if some news outlets (online or off) are more willing to produce or to spread misinformation, then selective exposure can exacerbate false beliefs among the people who select and rely almost entirely on those sources (Kull, Ramsay, and Lewis 2003).

In this way, algorithm-driven "filter bubbles" have been connected to rising political polarization, on the grounds that exposure to attitude-consistent (mis)information and a lack of exposure to countervailing or corrective news can lead to starkly divergent (and potentially false) perceptions of reality among strong partisans. However, some have challenged the notion that algorithms alone could wield such polarizing power. For example, a study funded by Facebook found that "compared to algorithmic ranking, individuals' choices about what to consume had a stronger effect limiting exposure to cross-cutting content" (Bakshy, Messing, and Adamic 2015, 1130). Importantly, this study quickly received criticism not only for its sponsorship but also for rhetorically downplaying its findings, which revealed that Facebook's "news feed curation algorithm acts to modestly accelerate selectivity and polarization" (Sandvig 2015). Still, arguably less controversial findings from a recent working paper suggest that the most pronounced political divergence in recent years (1996 to 2012) occurred among the oldest Americans, many of whom were not (or were barely) social media users (Boxell, Gentzkow, and Shapiro 2017). Instead, heavily polarized demographics have apparently used traditional media—a point which is especially interesting given Pew Research Center's (2017b) report that *television* functioned as Americans' dominant source for political information in the 2016 presidential election (Oremus 2017).

This debate about whether—and to what extent—social media algorithms and filter bubbles should be "blamed" for rising polarization and the spread of misinformation reinforces our point that new media technologies do not operate in a vacuum to influence American politics. Instead, the effects of new media technologies are entangled with those of legacy media, the economic realities of the media system, and the characteristics of media users, including not only their *ability* to process information, but also their *motivation*s for doing so.

Fitting Facts into Our Belief Systems

Building on this point, we wish to note that the selective exposure tendency described above is different from the idea of "motivated reasoning." In contrast to selective exposure, motivated reasoning occurs when we differentially weigh information in light of pre-existing beliefs and values (sometimes referred to as "priors"). Motivated reasoning is based on the assumption that information processing is not always geared toward accuracy but can instead be biased in favor of other desired outcomes (or "goals") (Kunda 1990), such as an impulse to protect value systems or belief systems that are critical to one's political identity.

As a result, people weigh new information more heavily when making choices or decisions that fit their priors (confirmation bias) and weigh new information less heavily if it contradicts their priors (disconfirmation bias). The outcome is "biased assimilation": essentially, audiences sometimes adjust their interpretation of new information so it fits existing belief systems (or "the pictures in our heads," as Lippmann would call them), rather than adjusting their viewpoints based on new information.

For example, if a political partisan cannot selectively expose herself to media and therefore *does* encounter disagreement, she will likely judge attitude-disconfirming information as "less convincing" than attitude-confirming evidence (Lord, Ross, and Lepper 1979). While this kind of biased processing can occur for many reasons, a desire to defend pre-existing political beliefs is among those reasons, especially for people who have formidable stores of political knowledge from which to generate counter-arguments (Taber and Lodge 2006). Motivated reasoning thus has important implications for any attempt to discourage the consumption and spread of fake news because it can make false beliefs particularly difficult to fix.

In fact, attempts to correct or fact-check misinformation and misperceptions have been shown to *backfire* among the most passionate and politically knowledgeable partisans, causing them to become more deeply entrenched in their false views (Nyhan and Reifler 2010). Furthermore, among partisans who are high in political knowledge and low in trust, motivated reasoning has been shown to predict greater support for factually disproven conspiracy theories (Miller, Saunders, and Farhart 2016).

Notably, in both of the above studies, the authors assessed possible differences among liberals and conservatives, and they found that their results were more pronounced for conservatives. However, in both cases, the authors argue that their findings may have less to do with innate psychological differences and more to do with contextual factors. For example, the fact that a Democratic president was in office at the time of data collection may have meant that popular anti-liberal conspiracy theories were simply more believable, or that "underdog" conservatives experienced stronger motivation to believe falsehoods than they otherwise would have under Republican leadership (Miller, Saunders, and Farhart 2016). Furthermore, the specific issues under discussion and the strength of their salience in a given political context may influence the "backfire" effect of corrective information (Nyhan and Reifler 2010). To this point, research on the complexity of thought among liberals and conservatives has shown that conservatives are not categorically more "dogmatic" or "simple-minded" than liberals, but that differences between these groups instead depend on the topic at hand, such that "liberals can be significantly more dogmatic if a liberal domain is made salient" (Conway et al. 2016).

Overall, the above discussion of selective exposure and motivated reasoning in a polarized political climate suggests that some of the most politically engaged citizens from both ends of the spectrum are unlikely to seek out information that disconfirms their pre-existing attitudes and beliefs, and, even if they do encounter disconfirming evidence, they may engage in motivated reasoning to discount it, thereby further entrenching their misperceptions. Flagging fake news (or fact-checking it) in an attempt to improve citizens' *ability* to identify and select truthful information is likely to be ineffective—or, worse, counterproductive—if citizens are not also sufficiently *motivated* to engage with information in less directional ways.

Moreover, our earlier discussion highlights the deep-seated nature of commercial and other pressures that exert constant pressures toward the production and circulation of many different forms of fake news for the foreseeable future. Together, these considerations suggest that in order for citizens to successfully navigate around fake news in the absence of sweeping changes to our media system, they will not only need improved abilities to process fake news, but they must also *be motivated* to exercise those competencies.

Politics: The Need for New Types of Citizen Competencies

We recognize that it is far easier to identify faults and limitations in already-proposed solutions than it is to carefully develop and articulate them in the first place. Nonetheless, it is possible to draw from the foregoing discussion a general sense of areas in which further study of possible remedies to the fake news problem may be more promising or at least offer opportunities for maneuvering around the considerable obstacles of long-standing patterns of media production and human cognition. The basic premises of such an approach are by no means new. Indeed, they draw on well-established lines of scholarship in communication and political theory. Though certainly more complicated and labor intensive, we believe that strategies which place more emphasis on motivations and competencies have great potential to address problems related to fake news.

The difficult and complex part of such an approach stems from the fact that the most reliable routes to stimulating careful information scrutiny in service of making the "right" judgment (as opposed to one that merely avoids offending one's priors) are social in nature. A wealth of research in psychology and communication underscores the sense in which fundamentally social dynamics—such as the overall climate of opinion, majority/minority positioning within reference groups, and, most influential, social expectations of being held publicly accountable for one's opinions—hold great potential for stimulating individuals to opt for information-seeking and processing strategies that privilege veracity and accuracy over the protection of prior beliefs (Scheufele 2014). Drawing from insights in these areas, we identify specific social dynamics that may have a reasonable potential for helping us deal with some of the more fundamental issues highlighted earlier.

The first of these is the simple "accountability effect" that emerges when individuals face an expectation that they will need to publicly discuss and/ or defend an opinion or judgment, as may be found in heterogeneous social or discussion environments. As developed in various experimental studies, the notion of "accountability effects" suggests that when individuals have an expectation that their views may be challenged by others, they are often more likely to increase cognitive effort devoted to understanding multiple sides of an issue and to carefully evaluate relevant information, as opposed to simply focusing on belief-consistent information (Xenos et al. 2011; Tetlock 1983). A similar set of dynamics is undoubtedly at work in communications research on the positive effects of heterogeneous discussion and social networks (Scheufele et al. 2004; Scheufeleet al. 2006). Though certainly no easy feat, the obvious implication here is that a more comprehensive approach to combatting fake news may need to involve increasing the odds that politically interested citizens find themselves in situations that promote civil discourse among those with divergent opinions, as well as helping individuals develop basic competencies for engaging in such conversations.

If such an approach seems difficult to scale in real-world conditions, similar principles point to two other social dynamics that may be more common or easily facilitated. Each of these draws on different sides of the same basic issue underlying the partisan polarization discussed earlier— namely, that principles of motivated reasoning often rely on in-group/out-group dynamics. The first of these is a proposal that has been identified in other discussions of the fake news problem, and it focuses on the cultivation of "co-partisans" who can help disseminate correctives to misperceptions propagated through various kinds of fake news (Lazer et al. 2017). For example, whereas a Democrat prone to motivated reasoning may easily brush aside a corrective coming from a mainstream source or an algorithm, similar information coming from a *fellow Democrat* would undoubtedly be more effective. The development of this proposal draws on research that points to the effectiveness of co-partisans in dispelling misperceptions (Berinsky 2017).

From another angle, although many social networks are rather homogeneous, research has identified the potential for cross-cutting social contacts to stimulate the kind of information-seeking and processing behaviors we believe are central to combatting fake news and misperceptions (Messing and Westwood 2012). With an approach based on this principle, rather than turning to co-partisans to correct misperceptions, the focus would be on facilitating cross-cutting information exchange and discussion among individuals with other things in common. By increasing diversity within social networks, we may be able to impact individuals' political attitudes and perceived importance of content circulated on social media (Messing and Westwood 2012). Taken together, these principles suggest a focus on social approaches to combatting political misperceptions that work with—rather than elide—some of the more deeply-rooted facets of contemporary issues surrounding fake news.

As a final note, we acknowledge that there will of course be pressures from the political fringe that tend to move discussion to the outer ends of the ideological normal curve, and, as a result, even if incentive is created to have cross-cutting conversations among centrists, there will be competing pressures from extremes to silence those centrists. This means two things for our suggestions above: (1) some of the strategies we've outlined may work better in different political contexts (e.g., a general election vs. a primary); and (2) we need additional research investigating the contextual factors that give rise to competing motivations, as well as the relative effects of competing motivations on information-seeking and information processing.

Conclusion

In line with the emphasis placed on root causes and fundamental underlying dynamics in our basic assessment of the issues surrounding "fake news," our brief discussion of possible ways forward has taken us to similarly fundamental issues of democratic theory. In particular, the approaches highlighted here resonate strongly with the notion—stressed by many in the literature on deliberative democracy—of an "enlarged mentality" that results from processes in which citizens directly engage with others as they process information and formulate opinions (Benhabib 1988; Arendt 1961).

As it happens, the ability and willingness of citizens to connect with non-like-minded others in meaningful debate is at the very core of combatting false or misleading information. As Kafka once wrote, "Altogether, I think we ought to read only books that bite and sting us. If the book we are reading doesn't shake us awake like a blow to the skull, why bother reading it in the first place? . . . [B]ooks that make us happy we could, in a pinch, also write ourselves."

Understanding the complex interplay of structural, behavioral, and social dynamics that drive debates will be crucial for maintaining enlightened debates (and disagreements) among citizens and political actors as one of the fundamental pillars of liberal democracies.

Lessons

- Fake news is not a new phenomenon, nor one that is bound only to social media.
- "Fake news" as a term captures an array of different phenomena (some new, some old). It is important to clearly distinguish which phenomenon is being discussed and, consequently, which solution is most appropriate.
- Approaches to addressing the "fake news problem" need to consider not only audience ability and technical solutions (such as automated fact-checking) but also audience *motivations*.
- Solutions to the spread of fake news should work to increase civic discourse among citizens with divergent opinions, as well as help individuals develop basic competencies for engaging in such conversations in a civil fashion.

References

Allcott, Hunt, and Matthew Gentzkow. 2017. "Social Media and Fake News in the 2016 Election." *Journal of Economic Perspectives* 31, no. 2: 211–235.

Amarasingam, Amarnath. 2011. *The Stewart/Colbert Effect: Essays on the Real Impacts of Fake News*. Jefferson: McFarland.

Arendt, Hannah. 1961. "Crisis in Culture." In *Between Past and Future: Six Exercises in Political Thought*, edited by Hannah Arendt, 220–221. New York: Meridian.

Bakshy, Eytan, Solomon Messing, and Lada A. Adamic. 2015. "Political Science. Exposure to Ideologically Diverse News and Opinion on Facebook." *Science* 348, no. 6239: 1130–1132.

Balmas, Meital. 2014. "When Fake News Becomes Real: Combined Exposure to Multiple News Sources and Political Attitudes of Inefficacy, Alienation, and Cynicism." *Communication Research* 41, no. 3: 430–454.

Barrow, Bill. 2017. "GOP Governors Launch 'News' Site Critics Call Propaganda." AP News, September 19. https://www.apnews.com/f97fbf53c0c84468ae046f861ecf3b64

Benhabib, Seyla. 1988. "Judgment and the Moral Foundations of Politics in Arendt's Thought." *Political Theory* 16, no. 1: 29–51.

Berinsky, Adam. 2017. "Rumors and Health Care Reform: Experiments in Political Misinformation." *British Journal of Political Science* 47, no. 2: 241–262.

Boxell, Levi, Matthew Gentzkow, and Jesse M. Shapiro. 2017. "Is the Internet Causing Political Polarization? Evidence from Demographics." (No. w23258). National Bureau of Economic Research, March. https://web.stanford.edu/~gentzkow/research/age-polar.pdf.

Bump, Philip. 2016. "Now You Can Fact-Check Trump's Tweets—in the Tweets Themselves." *Washington Post*, December 19. https://www.washingtonpost.com/news/the-fix/wp/2016/12/16/now-you-can-fact-check-trumps-tweets-in-the-tweets-themselves/?tid=sm_fb&utm_term=.4476c4e77abb.

Cacciatore, Michael A., Dietram A. Scheufele, and Shanto Iyengar. 2016. "The End of Framing as We Know It . . . and the Future of Media Effects." *Mass Communication and Society* 19, no. 1: 1–17.

Cacciatore, Michael A., Sara K. Yeo, Dietram A. Scheufele, Michael A. Xenos, Doo-Hun Choi, Dominique Brossard, Amy B. Becker, and Elizabeth A. Corley.. 2014. "Misperceptions in Polarized Politics: The Role of Knowledge, Religiosity, and Media." *PS, Political Science & Politics* 47, no. 3: 654–661.

Calfas, Jennifer. 2017. "Google Is Changing Its Search Algorithm to Combat Fake News." *Fortune*, April 25. http://fortune.com/2017/04/25/google-search-algorithm-fake-news/.

Campbell, W. Joseph. 2010. *Getting It Wrong: Ten of the Greatest Misreported Stories in American Journalism*. Berkeley: University of California Press.

Carlson, Matt. 2015. "When News Sites Go Native: Redefining the Advertising-Editorial Divide in Response to Native Advertising." *Journalism* 16, no. 7: 849–865.

CBS News. 2004. "60 Minutes Wednesday." [Television broadcast transcript.] September 8. http://wwwimage.cbsnews.com/htdocs/pdf/complete_report/1B.pdf.

Chrome Web Store. 2016. "Fake News Alert."

Conroy, Niall J., Victoria L. Rubin, and Yimin Chen. 2015. "Automatic Deception Detection: Methods for Finding Fake News." *Proceedings of the Association for Information Science and Technology* 52, no. 1: 1–4.

Conway, Lucian Gideon, Laura Janelle Gornick, Shannon C. Houck, Christopher Anderson, Jennifer Stockert, Diana Sessoms, and Kevin McCue. 2016. "Are Conservatives Really More Simple-Minded than Liberals? The Domain Specificity of Complex Thinking." *Political Psychology* 37, no. 6: 777–798.

Cooley, Charles Horton. (1987) 2004. "The Process of Social Change." In *Mass Communication and American Social Thought: Key Texts, 1919–1968*, edited by John Durham Peters and Peter Simonson, 21–25. Lanham, MD: Rowman and Littlefield.

Del Vicario, Michela, Alessandro Bessi, Fabiana Zollo, Fabio Petroni, Antonio Scala, Guido Caldarelli, H. Eugene Stanley, and Walter Quattrociocchi. 2016. "The Spreading of Misinformation Online." *Proceedings of the National Academy of Sciences of the United States of America* 113, no. 3: 554–559.

Dewey, J. 1927. "Search for the Great Social Community." In *The Public and Its Problems*, edited by John Dewey, 143–184. New York: Henry Holt.

Festinger, Leon. 1962. *A Theory of Cognitive Dissonance*. Mass Communication Series (Voice of America); 2. Stanford, CA: Stanford University Press.

Folkenflik, David. 2017. "Behind Fox News' Baseless Seth Rich Story: The Untold Tale." NPR, August 1. http://www.npr.org/2017/08/01/540783715/lawsuit-alleges-fox-news-and-trump-supporter-created-fake-news-story.

Galtung, Johan, and Mari Holmboe Ruge. 1965. "The Structure of Foreign News: The Presentation of the Congo, Cuba and Cyprus Crises in Four Norwegian Newspapers." *Journal of Peace Research* 2, no. 1: 64–90.

Garrett, R. Kelly, Brian E. Weeks, and Rachel L. Neo. 2016. "Driving a Wedge Between Evidence and Beliefs: How Online Ideological News Exposure Promotes Political Misperceptions." *Journal of Computer-Mediated Communication* 21, no. 5: 331–348.

Gary, Brett. 1996. "Communication Research, the Rockefeller Foundation, and Mobilization for the War on Words, 1938–1944." *Journal of Communication* 46, no. 3: 124–147.

Graves, Lucas, 2016. *Deciding What's True: Fact-Checking Journalism and the New Ecology of News*. New York: Columbia University Press.

Hassan, Naeemul, Bill Adair, James T. Hamilton, Chengkai Li, Mark Tremayne, Jun Yang, and Cong Yu, C. 2015. "The Quest to Automate Fact-Checking." In *Proceedings of the 2015 Computation+ Journalism Symposium*. http://ranger.uta.edu/~cli/pubs/2015/claimbuster-cj15-hassan.pdf

Hern, Alex. 2017. "Google Acts Against Fake News on Search Engine." *The Guardian*, April 25. https://www.theguardian.com/technology/2017/apr/25/google-launches-major-offensive-against-fake-news.

Herrman, John. 2016. "Inside Facebook's (Totally Insane, Unintentionally Gigantic, Hyperpartisan) Political-Media Machine." *New York Times Magazine*, August 24. https://www.nytimes.com/2016/08/28/magazine/inside-facebooks-totally-insane-unintentionally-gigantic-hyperpartisan-political-media-machine.html.

Holbert, R. Lance. 2005. "A Typology for the Study of Entertainment Television and Politics." *American Behavioral Scientist* 49, no. 3: 436–453.

Iyengar, Shanto, and Kyu S Hahn. 2009. "Red Media, Blue Media: Evidence of Ideological Selectivity in Media Use." *Journal of Communication* 59, no. 1: 19–39.

Jordan, Matthew. 2018. "A Century Ago, Progressives Were the Ones Shouting 'Fake News.'" *The Conversation*, February 1. https://theconversation.com/a-century-ago-progressives-were-the-ones-shouting-fake-news-90614.

Kull, Steven, Clay Ramsay, and Evan Lewis. 2003. "Misperceptions, the Media, and the Iraq War." *Political Science Quarterly* 118, no. 4: 569–598.

Kunda, Ziva. 1990. "The Case for Motivated Reasoning." *Psychological Bulletin* 108, no. 3: 480.

Kurtz, Howard. 2005. "Administration Paid Commentator." *Washington Post*, January 8. http://www.washingtonpost.com/wp-dyn/articles/A56330-2005Jan7.html.

Lasswell, Harold. (1927) 2004. "The Results of Propaganda." In *Mass Communication and American Social Thought: Key Texts, 1919–1968*, edited by John Durham Peters and Peter Simonson, 47–50. Lanham, MD: Rowman and Littlefield.

Lazer, David, Matthew Baum, Nir Grinberg, Lisa Friedland, Kenneth Joseph, Will Hobbs, and Carolina Mattsson. 2017. "Combating Fake News: An Agenda for Research and Action." Shorenstein Center, May. https://shorensteincenter.org/wp-content/uploads/2017/05/Combating-Fake-News-Agenda-for-Research-1.pdf.

Lippmann, Walter. 1922. *Public Opinion*. New York: Harcourt, Brace.

Lord, Charles G., Lee Ross, and Mark R. Lepper. 1979. "Biased Assimilation and Attitude Polarization: The Effects of Prior Theories on Subsequently Considered Evidence." *Journal of Personality and Social Psychology* 37, no. 11: 2098–2109.

Lynd, Robert S. (1940). 2004. "Democracy in Reverse." In *Mass Communication and American Social Thought: Key Texts, 1919–1968*, edited by John Durham Peters and Peter Simonson, 134–136. Lanham, MD: Rowman and Littlefield.

Memmott, Mark. 2004. "Scoops and Skepticism: How the Story Unfolded." *USA Today,* September 21. https://usatoday30.usatoday.com/news/politicselections/nation/president/2004-09-21-guard-scoops-skepticism_x.htm.

Messing, S., and S. J. Westwood. 2012. "How Social Media Introduces Biases in Selecting and Processing News Content." ResearchGate. https://www.researchgate.net/profile/Solomon_Messing/publication/265673993_How_Social_Media_Introduces_Biases_in_Selecting_and_Processing_News_Content/links/54d8e9620cf2970e4e7a399b/How-Social-Media-Introduces-Biases-in-Selecting-and-Processing-News-Conte.

Miller, Joanne M., Kyle L. Saunders, and Christina E. Farhart. 2016. "Conspiracy Endorsement as Motivated Reasoning: The Moderating Roles of Political Knowledge and Trust." *American Journal of Political Science* 60, no. 4: 824–844.

Molotch, Harvey, and Marilyn Lester. 1974. "News as Purposive Behavior: On the Strategic Use of Routine Events, Accidents, and Scandals." *American Sociological Review* 39, no. 1: 101–112.

Mosseri, Adam. 2016. "News Feed FYI: Addressing Hoaxes and Fake News." Facebook Newsroom, December 15. https://newsroom.fb.com/news/2016/12/news-feed-fyi-addressing-hoaxes-and-fake-news/.

Nyhan, Brendan, and Jason Reifler. 2010. "When Corrections Fail: The Persistence of Political Misperceptions." *Political Behavior* 32, no. 2: 303–330.

Oremus, William. 2016. "Trending Bad." Slate, August 30. http://www.slate.com/articles/technology/future_tense/2016/08/how_facebook_s_trending_news_feature_went_from_messy_to_disastrous.html

Oremus, William. 2017. "The Filter Bubble Revisited." Slate. April 5. https://slate.me/2oB6IkV

Pariser, Eli. 2011. *The Filter Bubble: How the New Personalized Web Is Changing What We Read and How We Think.* New York: Penguin.

Pew Research Center. 2016a. "Information Overload." http://www.pewinternet.org/2016/12/07/information-overload/.

Pew Research Center. 2016b. "Many Americans Believe Fake News Is Sowing Confusion." http://www.journalism.org/2016/12/15/many-americans-believe-fake-news-is-sowing-confusion/.

Pew Research Center. 2016c. "Partisanship and Political Animosity in 2016." http://www.people-press.org/2016/06/22/partisanship-and-political-animosity-in-2016/.

Pew Research Center. 2017a. "News Use Across Social Media Platforms 2017." http://www.journalism.org/2017/09/07/news-use-across-social-media-platforms-2017/.

Pew Research Center. 2017b. "Trump, Clinton Voters Divided in Their Main Source for Election." http://www.journalism.org/2017/01/18/trump-clinton-voters-divided-in-their-main-source-for-election-news/.

Prior, Markus. 2007. *Post-broadcast Democracy: How Media Choice Increases Inequality in Political Involvement and Polarizes Elections.* Cambridge Studies in Public Opinion and Political Psychology. New York: Cambridge University Press.

Ritchie, Hannah. 2016. "Read All About It: The Biggest Fake News Stories of 2016." CNBC, December 30. https://www.cnbc.com/2016/12/30/read-all-about-it-the-biggest-fake-news-stories-of-2016.html.

Rutenberg, Jim. 2016. "For News Outlets Squeezed from the Middle, It's Bend or Bust." *New York Times*, April 17. https://nyti.ms/2jMKOb5.

Sandvig, Christian. 2015. "The Facebook 'it's not our fault' Study." Social Media Collective Research Blog, May 07. https://socialmediacollective.org/2015/05/07/the-facebook-its-not-our-fault-study/.

Schaedel, Sydney. 2017. "Websites that Post Fake and Satirical Stories." Factcheck.org, July 6. http://www.factcheck.org/2017/07/websites-post-fake-satirical-stories/

Scheufele, Dietram A. 1999. "Framing as a Theory of Media Effects." *Journal of Communication* 49, no. 1: 103–122.

Scheufele, Dietram A. 2014. "Science Communication as Political Communication." *Proceedings of the National Academy of Sciences of the United States of America* 111: 13585–13592.

Scheufele, Dietram A., Bruce W. Hardy, Dominique Brossard, Israel S. Waismel-Manor, and Erik Nisbet. 2006. "Democracy Based on Difference: Examining the Links Between Structural Heterogeneity, Heterogeneity of Discussion Networks, and Democratic Citizenship." *Journal of Communication* 56, no. 4: 728–753.

Scheufele, Dietram A., Matthew C. Nisbet, Dominique Brossard, and Erik C. Nisbet. 2004. "Social Structure and Citizenship: Examining the Impacts of Social Setting, Network Heterogeneity, and Informational Variables on Political Participation." *Political Communication* 21, no. 3: 315–338.

Seitz-Wald, Alex, and Corky Siemaszko. 2017. "Seth Rich Case: Fox News Made Fake News to Protect Trump, Lawsuit Alleges." *NBC News*, August 1. https://www.nbcnews.com/news/us-news/seth-rich-case-fox-news-made-fake-news-protect-trump-n788541.

Shelbourne, Mallory. 2017. "Media Mistakes Intensify Debate over 'Fake News.'" *The Hill*, December 10. http://thehill.com/homenews/media/364193-debate-rages-over-media-mistakes.

Shell. 2014. "Cities Energized." *New York Times*. https://paidpost.nytimes.com/shell/cities-energized.html?_r=1.

Shoemaker, Pamela, and Stephen D. Reese. 1996. *Mediating the Message: Theories of Influences on Mass Media Content*. 2nd ed. White Plains, NY: Longman.

Silverman, Craig, Lauren Strapagiel, Hamza Shaban, Ellie Hall, and Jeremy Singer-Vine. 2016. "Hyperpartisan Facebook Pages Are Publishing False and Misleading Information at an Alarming Rate." BuzzFeed News, October 20. https://www.buzzfeed.com/craigsilverman/partisan-fb-pages-analysis?utm_term=.aoWP9JdvDD#.nkD7zLYeyy.

Sproule, J. Michael. 1987. "Propaganda Studies in American Social Science: The Rise and Fall of the Critical Paradigm." *Quarterly Journal of Speech* 73, no. 1: 60–78.

Stanford History Education Group. 2016. "Evaluating Information: The Cornerstone of Civic Online Reasoning." Stanford University. https://stacks.stanford.edu/file/druid:fv751yt5934/SHEG%20Evaluating%20Information%20Online.pdf.

Steinberg, Brian. 2014. "11 Top U.S. Magazines to Hawk NBC's 'Blacklist' on Fake Covers." *Variety*, August 18. http://variety.com/2014/tv/news/11-cost me top-u-s-magazines-to-hawk-nbcs-blacklist-on-fake-covers-1201285005/.

Sunstein, Cass R. 2007. *Republic.com 2.0*. Princeton, NJ: Princeton University Press.

Taber, Charles S., and Milton Lodge. 2006 "Motivated Skepticism in the Evaluation of Political Beliefs." *American Journal of Political Science* 50, no. 3: 755–769.

Tetlock, Philip E. 1983. "Accountability and Complexity of Thought." *Journal of Personality and Social Psychology* 45, no. 1: 74.

Tuchman, Gaye. 1978. *Making News: A Study in the Construction of Reality*. New York: Free Press.

Turow, Joseph. 1997. *Breaking up America: Advertisers and the New Media World*. Chicago: University of Chicago Press.

Vosoughi, Soroush, Deb Roy, and Sinan Aral. 2018. "The Spread of True and False News Online." *Science* 359, no. 6380: 1146–1151.

Xenos, Michael, Amy Becker, Ashley Anderson, Dominique Brossard, and Dietram Scheufele. 2011. "Stimulating Upstream Engagement: An Experimental Study of Nanotechnology Information Seeking." *Social Science Quarterly* 92, no. 5: 1191–1214.

Yeo, Sara K., Michael A. Xenos, Dominique Brossard, Dietram A. Scheufele, Elizabeth Suhay, and James N. Druckman. 2015. "Selecting Our Own Science: How Communication Contexts and Individual Traits Shape Information Seeking." *ANNALS of the American Academy of Political and Social Science* 658, no. 1: 172–191.

Zuckerberg, Mark. 2016, Facebook post, December 15. https://www.facebook.com/zuck/posts/10103338789106661.

PART II
PILLARS OF TRUTH IN JOURNALISM

Spotlight

Sophisticated Modernism and Truth

Edward Schiappa

Truth-deficient political discourse is nothing new and neither is questionable journalism that echoes false political discourse or sensationalizes stories with little regard to the facts. In the past, such journalism has been decried with labels such as yellow or tabloid journalism. We live now in a digitally enhanced media ecosystem that is saturated with political news coming at us from all directions, 24/7, which means that even if a small percentage of that news is false, the potential reach and influence is enormous. The persuasiveness of hyper-partisan news, conspiracy theories, and sensationalist journalism is aided and abetted by a variety of cognitive biases documented by psychologists, which refute Aristotle's belief that "that which is true and better is naturally always easier to prove and more likely to persuade" (*Rhetoric*, 1.1.12).

Propaganda, fake news, alternative facts—the silver lining behind the proliferation of terminology describing misleading or false news and political discourse is the evident desire to hang onto Truth. But how do we hang onto truth at a moment in history where we are caught between the Scylla of Naïve Modernism (which implausibly perpetuates a view of science that excludes all matters not capable of the scientific method as mere opinion), and the Charybdis of postmodernism (which in some forms equally implausibly sees all matters as mere opinion)? In both cases, the job of the journalist is severed from truth.

The answer is what I call Sophisticated Modernism. Such a view recognizes the fragility of truth—its dependence on human processes of persuasion and historical context—while not giving up on the concept altogether. Consider the concept of "the rhetorical construction of facts." The idea here is that facts are linguistic products and that "true" is an adjective we apply to claims that we believe have been proven. That process is a persuasive one, but that does not mean "merely" persuasive. For example, we regard the claim that "John F. Kennedy died in 1963" as true, even if it is possible to "deconstruct" aspects of the claim to demonstrate that its factual status depends on social agreement on such concepts as identity (JFK), life and death, and calendar systems. We give up the factual status of such a statement only at great cost.

The process of warranting a statement "true" is similar in most arenas of human interaction. Science, for example, only progresses when there is agreement on what counts as facts over time, and that process is one that relies on persuasion. There is no non-human algorithm that decides whether a claim is true, only other scientists can decide that. Hypothesis testing is done by humans.

It is also worth noting that an essential part of seeking truth involves *shared definitions*. Our ability to agree that "JFK died in 1963" depends on our agreement as to how to define the key terms—JFK, died, and 1963.

Now what does hypothesis testing and definition have to do with journalism and truth? To begin with, journalists construct facts through a process analogous to hypothesis testing: Evidence x Sources (+/– bias) = reliability of factual statements. A headline is, among other things, a claim about the world. It is then up to the journalist's story to persuade readers to accept that claim. The more and higher quality of evidence, then (we hope) the better the odds that a journalist can persuade the public that her/his claims are true.

Furthermore, even the simplest news article depends on shared understanding with the reader of key concepts. When a claim is put forward by a journalist, the language used must be one readers understand—there must be roughly shared definitions of key concepts.

Now what does all this have to do with journalism and social media? The age of social media complicates matters in two ways. First, the sheer volume of messages and conflicting sources means that the traditional epistemological role of journalists as information gatekeepers and hypothesis testers is challenged. Second, the cacophony of voices amplifies the problem of conflicting definitions. The idea that our word choice implies a particular point of view is certainly not new and is often described by George Lakoff and others as a matter of "framing" or "agenda setting." To call a situation a "crisis" is quite different than calling it merely a "problem," and there is a significant difference in describing a problematic statement a "lie" as opposed to an "exaggeration." Noting that "one person's patriot is another's terrorist" is not new, but social media amplifies the problem many times over, to the point that it often feels like we are not talking about the same things.

That journalists must make value judgments is also hardly new. There are constant personal, subjective decisions to be made about how to tell a news story. Narratives typically have three core elements—characters, plot, and lessons. Who is included or excluded in a story and how they are character-ized involves value judgments. Whether an event is described as an accident, a tragedy, a comedy, or pseudo-neutrally as "stuff happens" implies what, if any, sort of lesson we can draw and what sort of reaction is appropriate.

Indeed, virtually every adjective, noun, and verb choice carries with it characterizations that some readers/viewers will see as positive, others as negative. The late conservative literary critic Richard Weaver famously described language as "sermonic" and said we are all "preachers" of ways of understanding the world. Indeed, there is no way of escaping such a respon-sibility, for even the use of a passive voice in journalism that goes out of its way to assign responsibility advocates a way to view some part of the world, even if it is with a shrug of indifference. In the digital age, the number of "preachers" capable of reaching a large congregation is increased dramat-ically. Religious terminology seems apt, as social media seems full of true believers, heretics, reformers, those who would claim to speak infallibly, and those who would launch crusades or issue fatwas.

Not only is the question of *how* to tell a story value-laden, *whether* to tell a story is a value judgment that takes place under the banner of deciding which stories are "newsworthy." Journalists have no choice but to navigate between two poles that each sound objectionable in isolation—*either* every decision is made by what is usually a profit motive (what do people *want* to hear about) *or* journalists have to decide what consumers *should* and *need* to hear about. The first choice leads to pandering and sensationalism, while the second choice promotes a kind of paternalistic elitism that leads many people to distrust "the media" altogether. We need to recognize that there is no absolute solution this dilemma. It is one that every journalist and editor *constantly* must navigate, and hopefully does so with humility.

Judgments about newsworthiness cannot help but be informed by the constant presence of social media. Fail to report a story based on a judg-ment that it is not relevant to enough readers, and one may find social media correcting and counterbalancing that judgment by promoting someone else's account. In a sense, social media creates a hive mind that is always ready to challenge what we used to call mainstream media's judgments about what is newsworthy.

In a sense, the era of Sophisticated Modernism brings an end to the Myth of Objectivity in journalism. All journalism is now seen as "partial"— partial in the sense of being at least implicitly partisan, and partial in the sense of being an incomplete part of a larger picture. Though the excesses (and sometimes outright lies) of hyper-partisan journalism are worthy of censure, we may all end up better off without the Myth of Objectivity. At the same time, to claim an end to the Myth of Objectivity is not to embrace mere relativism or imply that any point of view is as valuable as the next. But it does mean that we need to stress other values of good communication— are journalists being *fair*? Are their accounts *trustworthy*? Whose *interests* are they serving? And yes, are they telling us the *truth*?

Collectively, the various challenges to journalism and truth in the 21st century challenge us all. Journalists must see themselves as persuaders who must earn readers' trust. Readers must be sophisticated consumers of news and news sources. Social media platforms must recognize that there is no such thing as a neutral algorithm and that they, too, function as preachers of how to understand the world. As we plunge forward into the digital age, we must all expand our notion of what is required in media literacy for the 21st century so that future generations can assess critically the messages with which they are inundated.

5

"The True" in Journalism

Juliet Floyd

Introduction

The business of journalists is Truth. As a philosopher addressing the topic of Truth in journalism, it is necessary to engage with the concept of Truth and its meaning. Truth is central to those who take on journalism as a career and should be central to those who consume journalistic products, which of course is nearly all of us. Moreover, philosophical reflection about Truth and its value are, inevitably, part and parcel of life with and in journalism: questions that turn, ultimately, on what kind of persons, as journalists or consumers, we are going to be, and what kind of society we want to inhabit and sustain.

The very first directive of the Society of Professional Journalists' (2014) code of ethics is to "Seek Truth and Report It," and in connection with this comes a clutch of ethical terms: journalists should be "accurate" and "fair," "honest" and "courageous" when "gathering," "reporting," and "interpreting" information; as well as "taking responsibility for the accuracy of their work," they should "verify information before releasing it."[1] Ultimately, people report the news, and it will be no better, with respect to Truth, than they are. If journalists as individuals fail to value integrity and courage in their peers, their professional norms will lose their grip.

There has been a lot of recent discussion of whether we live in a "post-Truth" era. We do not. But skepticism and doubt are increasingly lived experiences in everyday life, partly manufactured by "news," and partly by the lack of respect for the consequences of words—including words about Truth and "scientific expertise"—on the part not just of individuals but also academics and ideologues (McIntyre 2015, ch. 5).[2] Feeding such skepticism about our institutions of knowledge is the fact that our everyday environments are more and more densely populated with rapid dissemination of words and images in social settings marked by the "absent presence" of observers and "perpetual contact" with one another.[3] There are representations of injustice, shock, and norm-breaking behavior broadcasted, amplified, and delivered with ease. These realities come to us in a blooming, buzzing confusion, taking on an increasing variety of politicized forms in a globally connected world, forcing us to respond. Doubt's manufacture exposes the fragility of meaning.

The very human felt need to interpret these rapidly evolving symbolic forms is deep, and our discourse is inevitably epideictic, moralizing. The political niche orientation of much journalistic commentary is a kind of offloading of thought for many of us: too many issues, too little time to discuss face to face with neighbors and friends; too much effort to deal with objections, especially fringe ones. And then we realize that the offloading, the lack of face-to-face conversation about politics, the lack of nuance and tolerance of error, is damaging to all public discourse and to politics itself.

Disorientation and disappointment are facts in our lives, and so is the fear and anger over our imagined sense—real or not—that those with whom we believe we disagree are out-organizing us, and those we think are representing our voices, formally and informally, are letting us down. Institutions are being more and more asked for transparency because we live in a time when things are less and less transparent, and knowledge of inequalities and injustices grows. The public is increasingly dissatisfied by "the press" because it is getting more difficult to produce and consume the flood of information wisely, productively, and without mishap. Gwen Ifill's sage directive to her mentees, "never assume," is more important than ever, but more difficult than ever to implement. Complaints are legion that the norm of "objectivity" is mispracticed by journalists who feel a need to present "both sides" evenhandedly when there are not really sides, but prejudices (McIntyre 2015, 349).

Journalists and consumers of news, as well as politicians and powerful interests, are all trying to impose structure and meaning on the flood. There are newfangled toxicities in the media ecology we inhabit. Emotions of fear and anger are enemies of Truth, for they beget cynicism, and this gradually wears down the urge to care about Truth. The study of skepticism since ancient times trained its practitioners to face down differences of opinion rationally: unplugging periodically to protect oneself from the maelstrom is probably a good idea. But we live in a knowledge and information economy in which professing ignorance is not always possible, and journalists have a responsibility to convey what is True.

Emotions of outrage are relatively easy to produce, and, in any case, they are part of our moral nature. Fear, expressing our subjective sense of vulnerability, causes us to reach out and try to defend and control our environment at all costs (Nussbaum 2018). In fact, some of the worst of our emotional responses are really enemies within us. Just as cyberwar turns tools developed in defense against the defender, so fear, related to contempt and disgust, turns us against our own better ideals and against one another. Courage is not an accidental virtue for the journalist, who must increasingly rely on the streams emerging from social media, and at the same time surf their waves with judiciousness, allowing the truly democratic forces of passionate utterance their place at the table.[4]

The dialectic between Truth and doubt, fear and courage, ignorance and knowledge is not new terrain for philosophy. Simultaneous with the invention of the printing press in the fifteenth century and its flooding the public sphere with new media, there entered into Europe long-lost manuscripts of Greek philosophy in which ancient forms of skepticism as a way of life were contained. The philosophical interpretation of these techniques of argumentation and ways of thinking and coping with life provided a rich playing field for those living through the Wars of Religion in the 16th century, faced as they were with murderous debates about ultimate seats of authority and power (Popkin 2003). Throughout that time, just as today, people cared very much about truthfulness, getting things right, fitting what we say to the ways the world is. Philosophers such as Montaigne developed lasting and humane responses to the skeptical play of thought and emotion, this problem of fitting words to reality, showing its ethical depths. As he wisely wrote, "the thing I fear most is fear," for "he who fears he shall suffer, already suffers what he fears" (Montaigne 1948, ch. 18). Recall Franklin D. Roosevelt's line that "the only thing we have to fear is fear itself." The unruliness in our imaginations, emotions, and ideals matter to our very idea of Truth, for we all crave to order them. Yet some of the greatest dangers stem from false orders.

In what follows I want to spell out a view of Truth designed to take account of this for our era.

Relativism and Absolutism

One position is that there are many truths. Some hold that one's life experiences or demographic identity or tribe or culture determines what is true. This view is known as Relativism, and if correct it surely problematizes the view that there can be but one Truth which truth-seekers pursue together. If Truth is only partisan or culturally determined, there is no one way the world is.

The opposing position, what we may call Absolutism, is that what is True is true, and we do not have a choice in the matter. The world reaches beyond each one of us. Any other picture of Truth is not *Truth*, but only a confusion of Truth with interpretation or with power.

In this stark form, the two positions are obviously incompatible. Moreover, each is puzzling from the other's point of view. If there is but one realm of absolute, unqualified Truth that truth-seekers (journalists) pursue, then how are we to make sense of the fact that journalists make constant choices about which truths to enunciate and report on? How and in what ways are we to weigh a journalist's biases, modes of presenting facts, verifying the facts, and so on? If a journalist is to verify, then are there not facts to *be* verified? Moreover, as recent theorists of intersectionality have stressed, each and every one of us is a site of *multiple* identities, standpoints, cultures: Which are we to say determines what is said to be "true" (Allen 2016)?

The conundrum turns on a shared assumption: both the Relativist and the Absolutist share one overarching idea. Each makes irrelevant the delicate but profound capacity we have to *fit* our words and thoughts *to* the facts, suitably for an occasion or a narrative or identity or discussion, thoughtfully and helpfully, giving people what they need and want and care most about.

Interestingly, this making irrelevant the task of fitting—the pragmatic and procedural norms we devise for representing reality—is also a hallmark of skepticism. Each of these philosophical positions paints a picture of the detailed human labor of fitting and juggling our interests as something pointless, giving up on all of it a priori, ahead of time, as if it is a fundamentally poisoned well.

We see now that these classic conundrums about Truth are also a practical challenge for journalists. The challenge is to make sure that the labor of "fitting" words to reality by people is made to be, and is perceived to be, worthwhile and compelling, useful and valuable, and in service of Truth. This is no easy task.

There have been recent cultures in which this challenge is not met. In these situations, Truth is no longer held to be important, and in a very real sense, as Orwell described, the whole idea of Truth fades away, being bent to the interests of those in power. Lies, zipping through the airways, can manufacture credulity or belief, but also doubt and sheer exhaustion with the business of Truth, the business of struggling to fit words to situations. Truth may cease to *matter* (Diamond 1994). In our age of mass-produced information, which includes images, deep fakes, and pronouncements made through voice-activated technology, there is a continuing danger of this.

Authoritarians make public enemies of journalists whose views they do not like. In part this is done to frighten and discourage journalists from exposing what these politicians do not wish to be known. But in part it is to revel in concocting what appears to be something they can call "The True," flexing their muscles. It has happened before and will doubtless happen again. Being able to *tell* big lies with impunity, to *say* what is True becomes a public marker of "power." The recent apparently very gruesome death of Jamal Khashoggi forms in this way a theater of Truth and journalism itself, not simply an individual tragedy.

In discussions during the 1980s, the idea of the "postmodern" took on a political edge in academic circles in the United States (Kakutani 2018). The term "post-Truth" piggybacks on this in our time. Deconstructionists stressed the ways in which claims to Truth have often been ultimately a matter of communicating and enforcing norms and power structures. Their point is that Truth *itself* can be weaponized as an ideal, turned against itself—just as the ancient skeptics knew. They had a point here.

Deconstructionists shocked certain members of their audiences with reinterpretations of old Enlightenment norms: of Truth, freedom of speech, the human, gender, and so on. Far from serving as norms leading the way toward ideas of progress, these notions were portrayed as Trojan horses, smuggling in oppression by the back door, undermining and exhausting themselves. Pointing out that all truths must be communicated by way of signs or symbols of some kind, Deconstructionists argued that media are never intrinsically meaningful, but achieve meaning only in concrete situations, in the context of social arrangements and enunciations. Events of claiming-to-be-true enacted by people in particular historical moments and in the physical realm (biological and physical processes) become embraced—or dismissed—ultimately as the outcome of power struggles in society. "Truth" on this view is not a mysterious property of thoughts or claims or sentences. It merely belongs to the evolving cultural process as an epiphenomenon.

Less emphasized in recent histories of the 1980s and 1990s is the fact that during the same period many philosophers in the Anglo-American world were also seeking to demystify, domesticate, and trivialize Truth by scientifically reducing it to causal processes. Some philosophers of an "analytic" bent, focusing on the nature of reasoning and logic, came to insist that Truth is nothing but "disquotation," a simple operation. Logically speaking, if I assert that "*p* is true," I may as well just assert "*p*." So we have, formally speaking, that "'*p*' is true if and only if *p*," an impeccable logical truth, by the lights of famed logician Alfred Tarski. Some Anglo-American philosophers of the 1980s liked to think of themselves as pragmatic naturalists and "deflated" True, reducing it to a causal story about how we actually talk or an instrumental poetics.[5]

Richard Rorty was one of the most famous among them. Rorty argued that if, for example, we discuss the measuring practices of 17th-century archeologists, saying that they came out with "true claims" about the age of bones, we are doing nothing but "complimenting" them in our own tongue. The only techniques we have are *our* techniques. When philosopher Hilary Putnam countered that Truth is not a notion that reduces to techniques, he was criticized by Cora Diamond for evading the difficult challenge, raised by Rorty, of how we are to fashion our techniques of fitting words to reality, including the reality described by people who are far from us in culture, time, and situation (Diamond 1999). Putnam agreed. How we *represent* Truth matters (see Floyd 2017). Yet Rorty, like the Deconstructionists and the Deflationists, did not believe there was any issue of representation of reality at all.

On the views of the Deconstructionists, of Rorty, and the Anglo-American eliminativists, "truth" is relative but also absolute within the group. Crucially, their claim that what is true amounts to nothing more than the artful and evolutionarily adapted ability to bend the group in one direction rather than another, to play one game rather than another, is a claim about what Truth *is*. And if there is no more to Truth than the fact that psychologically, socially, historically, and biologically the group reaches the verdicts it does, then the experts on Truth will be psychologists, fashion experts, sociologists, evolutionary biologists, and engineers who specialize in devising methods of "nudging" our behavior this or that way. Those who break with their own group's claims, or thwart the generalizations, are rendered meaningless.

This all sounds very scientific, as if it explains Truth and counters the skepticism of the Deconstructionists. But, perhaps surprisingly, it does not. All these philosophers share the idea that claims are made with language, hence via conventions, which are imposed and ordained, rather than being simply True. If either the Deconstructionists or Rorty or the Anglo-American disquotationalists are right, then there *are* no objective facts backing up the truth of claims. There are only more or less interested parties at the table saying what they hold to be true, engaged in an evolving struggle.

These views harken back to the 17th century. Thomas Hobbes, preoccupied with the horrors of civil war, had his Leviathan, the supreme authority, decree the meanings of words. Hobbes's conventionalist theory of language and power is echoed in logician Lewis Carroll's *Alice in Wonderland* when Humpty Dumpty insists that words mean whatever it is that he wants them to. And the issue of language and power has been elaborated and refined sociologically and very perceptively by Pierre Bourdieu, who brought us to see the importance of how institutions designed to create social stratification and elites shape our own conceptions of personal refinement and accomplishment, the very language we use to discuss excellence and badness (Bourdieu 1984). The specific ways in which people do and do not make claims, speak, and present themselves and their points of view in the public sphere really do shape and reflect who dominates whom. And this is no less true of journalists than anyone else.

One would be naive to suppose that issues of power and prestige do not shape particular claims to be true. Truth is engaged with, both socially and historically. But is this itself the ultimate and only thing to say? Is there another way to try to overcome our conundrum?

"The True": Revisiting Frege

I believe there is. It is a form of pragmatism, but one in which we keep in view the idea of "The True," the facts, *the* way the world is, in view, facing head-on the struggle of fitting our words to reality. On this view, as Diamond puts it (2001; 2003) "The True" is *unfolded*: there to be revealed and concealed, uncovered. The root meaning of "True" is loyalty: what will not let us down, is genuine. And this is a very human matter, for better or for worse. Words in their dynamic flow are part of the reality around us, but algorithms can only do so much to craft and embed them in our world and lives meaningfully. Prior to the debate between the Relativist and the

Absolutist is the fundamental point that the notion of Truth is *irreducible*: it cannot be wholly analyzed away in terms of any more fundamental notion or value. It is also *normative*, reflecting our values and aspirations. This was long emphasized in the history of logic, in East and West, and I would like to bring it to our attention again, as it seems important for the practicing journalist, and often overlooked in recent discussions of whether we live in a post-Truth society.[6]

Let us begin with what philosopher Gottlob Frege called "The True," but now construed as an ultimate norm or value or horizon of judgment (Frege 1918). Insofar as we are judging what is true, we make claims about what is actually the case; what is a fact, what is true, and what is false. This is part of the basis of reasoning itself: we should be able to say what is True *if* such-and-such is True, and what is True *if* such-and-such is false. (If we judge that something is not the case, then we judge its negation to be True.)

The important contrast with this view is an idea that surrenders the norm of Truth altogether. If we are just engaged in what philosopher Harry Frankfurt called "bullshitting," shooting the breeze or entertaining, then of course "The True"—and reasoning itself—does not enter into what we are doing at all.[7] And those who insist on ridiculing, disrespecting, or purposefully flouting the ultimate norm or horizon are disrupters, skeptics, and others who want to undermine and eliminate "The True" (cf. Barney 2016 on trolling).

According to Frege's idea, we do not *create* "The True." Rather, we *acknowledge* it as a realm with normative content, reaching through all that we judge and say. We articulate, elucidate, and individuate what belongs to its purview, seeing what follows and does not follow from this or that particular truth, hypothesizing how things might be if they were different or not so, reasoning our way through. Just as it is the task of legal authorities to recognize or acknowledge or establish a person's dominion over a piece of land, so it is our task as judgers of truth to recognize or acknowledge what is so, to establish what belongs to the realm of "The True." We organize, justify, and correct our claims by way of this horizon. But "The True" is not relative to any particular legal system or culture. It is an ideal, not a fact. It belongs to no one in particular but also and equally to every judger that judges.

Of course, psychologically, economically, historically, and otherwise there are all sorts of ways in which we swerve from the task of acknowledging "The True." We may have good reasons or unconscious reasons for refusing to see or admit it. We make erroneous and false and partial and misleading claims—some of which are even true (cf. Soysal's chapter in this book). Life is a tissue of illusions and mistakes and misarticulations, and white lies and competing emotions, as journalists know and often observe. As professionals, they are even party to producing such things.

But for Frege, such human frailties show us exactly why we need to get to the right angle on the notion of "The True." In order to speak of falsity or error or bias or systematic illusion or any other such failure, we must already have in mind the goal of judging correctly. We should think of the horizon of "The True" as something to be deviated from. It is important, among many other things, for allowing us to say when someone is *not* pursuing this goal properly or well or at all.

The main point is that "The True" cannot be reduced to or confused with what it is that people actually judge or say to be the case in such-and-such a time or situation or place. "The True" cannot to be reduced to what is in fact *claimed* to be true. This point, Frege held, is a grammatical one. This seems to be widely appreciated by the public and by journalists. The facts are the facts, what is true is what is true, and if I judge that p is so, then either I am right or I am wrong—though of course in the same breath I may also be misleading or boring or misguided or any one of a number of other things. If I judge rightly, acknowledging what is true, this doesn't mean that things are so because I or my tribe or my group of friends say so. There are no alternative facts, according to Frege's norm of Truth. And this is a logical point. (There are of course alternative *interpretations* of the facts, to be sure.)

Frege's norm of Truth is a norm of journalism. Journalists must pursue "The True" even if this is sometimes a dangerous, expensive, unpleasant, uncomfortable, or unpopular thing to do. Consider the *Boston Globe's* Spotlight team: they needed great courage and encouragement to expose the Boston Catholic Church's flawed policies toward child molesters among their ranks, and that story opened up many, many others in its wake. Journalists' hope is that what they judge to be of significance will be so to their readership; they seek to uncover important truths, things that matter to us. It is their job to publicize and express what falls within the scope of the norm of "The True," illuminating the realm.

At the same time, journalists deal with "The True" in their own special way. Ideally, they contribute to the construction of meaningful public conversation. Obviously, they cannot pursue all truths, but should pursue the significant ones for their audience. They must sell their content. And they are there not only to inform their readers, but also to entertain, engage, uplift them, especially in times where social ways of conceiving and living our lives are being adapted and sometimes even lost. Therefore journalists must constantly exercise judgment as to which battles they will fight, which stories they will cover, and in what ways (piecemeal or all at once?). They must attend to how they help the public confront and respond and reconcile themselves to what they see as, and what is, reality, including social reality. The target or realm of "The True" is there, but there is no firm agreement about what lies at its center. Journalism is shot through with valuation and evaluation and struggle. This both journalists and their audience should admit. There is such a thing as making something *of* the reality you are delivered. And what you make of it is itself part of reality.

Articulations of "The True" always are, as Frege put it, *colored*. The tone of voice, the specific choice of words and their conversational implicatures ("nag" vs. "steed" was Frege's good example), the play of the eyes, gestures, clothing on television or video, the larger narrative conveyed or questioned, the social or political aims furthered: these are all fundamental aspects of human communication, what media theorists call its semiotics. And these always permeate our aim to acknowledge "The True." In fact, colorings are intrinsic to our sharing of claims about "The True." They are certainly intrinsic to our discussion of "The True" itself (discussions of Truth are often metaphorical and literary and philosophical, as Frege duly noted). Colorings are a crucial feature of the backdrop required for our pursuit of "The True," and each of us has our own sense of the realm.

In a world permeated by social media and citizen journalism colorings matter more than ever. Everyone who consumes and produces news is in the broad sense a "journalist." Every utterance and image is liable to rapid amplification, deep faking, mocking, and misquotation out of context. Words and images, as a part of the world all around us, really matter, but they are driven forward ever-more rapidly amongst us. It seems clear that our implementation of Frege's conception of "The True" is becoming ever more complex, ever more fragile and delicate. It requires more and more labor to build up contexts in which we may acknowledge "The True."

As we have seen, some such as Rorty, the Postmodernists, and the Deflationists have offered reasons to think that the norm of Truth is empty, covering up deeper interests of elites, "faking" us out, deceiving us, mystifying us. After all, there are always dogmatists and theologians and powermongers who misuse the ideal of Truth. As we have already seen, some argue that "The True" is nothing more than consensus, socially constructed. But then there is no such thing as "The True." For what is called "true" in one society or era is not called "true" in another one. Practitioners of journalism certainly know that what is held to be newsworthy at a given time is something that is temporary, partial, and artificial.

So why not give up on "The True"? Because journalists and their audiences must develop in themselves, and in their audience, the skills of humility, self-criticism, and care: the aim of fitting words to reality. This is what it takes to pursue the norm of "The True." Journalists concoct a narrative and manufacture something of social significance. They must keep in mind that there is a great difference between a story that matters, that conveys truths and experiences that may be unpleasant or controversial or lasting or up-lifting, and a story that does not. That is the point of Frege's lodestar, how-ever difficult—even impossible—it is to fully implement in reality.

Whether we speak in the broader or the narrower professional sense of "journalist," I think we should regard Truth as a kind of target at which we aim, as an archer aims: a norm in Frege's sense. We struggle to hit the golden center, the most "significant" and "important" truths, with arrows, our judgments. We compete with one another for the first best shot. We vie to establish what is counted inside the central, most important circle of facts, and what is taken to be more peripheral. We verify the shots that others take, crying foul when certain canons of play are broken. We some-times hit the dead center, and yet often only the periphery. We do not al-ways agree. Nevertheless, we play the game. This requires listening, taking in, caring, discussing reasonably.

That *is* the norm of "The True." We are subject to strong feelings about this norm, from an early age (out of the mouths of babes often come truths). We are astonished by what others judge to be true, uplifted by certain truths, amused by incompetent judgers who are far off-mark, frustrated by clichés, insistent on not making the same mistakes twice. We perform, as athletes do, positioning ourselves, seeking dominance, celebrity, influence, approval, and sympathy, pushing the game forward. We want to tell the truths that matter. We sometimes lie or trick ourselves. These are all truths about "The True" that must be acknowledged.

But such admissions do not overturn Frege's norm. They only indicate that we are human, that "The True" might not be wholly so, and that we must continually exercise and hone our skills with the ideal.

The Struggle for Truth

Just here, seemingly paradoxically, we see that a kind of pluralism and pragmatism about human judgment is necessary for Frege's non-Relativistic notion of "The True" to gain its foothold. As Wittgenstein wrote, it is what people *say* that is true or false, but this can only go on with the right kind of scaffolding in place: we need agreement, not in *opinions*—it is not a question of consensus—but agreement *in* our forms of life, our ways of living (2009, §240). In this case it means living with our various and multicolored struggles with and on behalf of "The True."

Journalists have a history of pursuing "The True": different styles, norms, procedures have been tried. Pamphleteering in the American Revolution was political and tactical; court reporting was filled with gossip; journalists went out into the world in the late 19th century as chroniclers of a world industrializing and forming a wider audience of readership with mass media; professional norms of "objective" reporting emerged in the 1950s in reaction to a period in the 1920s when journalists were hard-hitting, swashbuckling hounds. Some journalists have promoted psychoanalytic sensitivity to their own stances with their subjects, others the stance of advocacy. Bloggers seek attention over the relatively short term. Many posting on YouTube are simply sharing glimpses and small, but often tremendously useful, pieces of life. The *National Enquirer* entertains with outrageousness. And there is a style of *montage* on much social media.

How has the search for "The True" changed? Did an increase in female participation in journalism change things or not? Do TV shows and movies better help us develop a sense of popular culture, solidarity in the face of fear, than newspapers? Journalists need to know their own history with "The True," as a profession.

We should also combat certain naive ideas about big data and connectedness. When we have more and more data, and more and more "friends," it is not at all that the quantitative trumps the qualitative: exactly the reverse. When more and more people connect and can express themselves, things do not get nicer and more open. That old debate between the qualitative and the quantitative is not over. For we know less when we are faced with a sea of a billion tweets (what *is* it to "understand" a billion tweets?).

In real life, as opposed to statistically, managing the power of our "weak ties"—which are sometimes more effective and resilient and central to us than our "strong" ethnic, national, or family ties (Granovetter 1973)—requires sensitivity, discernment, and new forms of responsiveness in human life. Journalists can help communicate some of these new forms, as when the life experience of a troll is portrayed in detail, a coming to see that envy of others' sex lives was an illusion, or the errors of a journalistic organization are documented.

Increasingly the audience for journalism approaches the human community as a whole: a large market, unruly and various, often fearful and impatient, with varying degrees of literacy. People, including journalists, are strongly affected by moving images and the uses others are making of technology. Soon, with voice-activated technology, another billion users will be coming online. Journalists need to take all this into account. They face a new and difficult context in which to implement the norm of Truth.

Large-scale decisions are being made on the global scale. With the advent of social media and mobile technology, China has decided to control the forwarding of social media posts in an attempt to prevent street action. These methods may appear to some in the United States to work against freedom of expression, even though in China the specific content of what is posted is not the point, the number of forwards is.[8] And yet now Facebook is controlling the flow of information and sharing news posts as well, at the same time as it auctions off user information to advertising firms claiming to be able to psychologically profile users to a very fine degree of detail.

There will be legal developments, but they will remain ongoing: let no one suppose that there is a magic bullet we have found in controlling the flow and building up meaningful contexts. European laws mandate that YouTube videos posted be taken down within 24 hours if they are truly upsetting. But what about civilian videos made by desperate civilians in conflict zones as part of their documentation of their suffering? We must worry about the loss of evidence involved in this process, what the victims of terror have risked their lives to document. Alexa Koenig, executive director of the Human Rights Center at the University of California at Berkeley Law School, is busy crowdsourcing labor for Amnesty International, training her students to develop methods for verifying videos that might someday be accepted in international courts. She has urged the retention of this disturbing data.

Today the qualitative is, in a sense, becoming more important than the quantitative. For example, there are great differences among the conduct and practice of professional journalists. Even the life of a single journalist carries within it a great demand to manage varieties of coloring the truth. Journalists are writing op-ed pieces; some are tweeting, some are blogging, some are working with anonymous sources, or in dangerous areas, some pursue activist journalism, others report as accurately as they can on science or fashion or food. Each journalist must develop a sense of judgment about how to fit words to the context in which he or she writes, speaks, tweets, or posts. For there is not one right way. The Internet is not a context, but a co-evolving structure involving humans and machines. Thinking ahead carefully about what might happen to one's words in someone else's mouth is part of the game. In a sense, then, the life of a journalist is itself one with a variety of possible forms of life, forms of embedding words *in* life, words that matter.[9]

Journalists are undertaking something vast and important here as their responsibility includes providing aspirationally True characterizations about the world. Their work is liable to be increasingly contested by skeptics and cynics in the near term, not to mention those whose political and economic interests are harmed or supported by their reports. But Truth will be there still, a target or norm or judgment, given life by the pragmatism and pluralism about human judging that, I have just argued, our attitude toward "The True" requires. It will be supported by improving our understanding of the social science surrounding the uses of new technology: what it reveals about our tendency to make fallacies (confirmation bias, the reiteration effect, the backfire effect). But we also need to keep articulating philosophies of "The True" that dare to face its complexities and depth, as well as its meaning, in human forms of life. Philosophy will and should become more and more foundational, as a practice, in our world.

The great German playwright Lessing offered wise words about our pursuit of the ideal of Truth:

> Not the truth which some human being possesses, or believes he or she possesses, but the sincere effort made to get at the Truth: this constitutes a human being's worth. For it is not through the possession of Truth, but through its pursuit, that a human being's powers are enlarged, and it is in this alone that one's ever-growing perfection lies. Possession makes one passive, lazy, and proud—
>
> If God were to hold the whole of Truth in his right hand, and in his left only the steady and ever-active drive for Truth, albeit with the proviso

that I would constantly and eternally err, and said to me: "Choose!",
I would humbly take the left hand, and say: Father, give!—the pure Truth
is for You alone. (Lessing 1778, 97)[10]

In this essay I have argued against existing attempts to reduce or define
away "The True" in favor of something else. Truth is a struggle for and over
what really matters. A biased description of reality can still be True, an apparently objective one false. It is not surprising that sometimes journalists
cheat or plagiarize or advocate for their own political views, get important
matters of fact wrong, rush to deadline, allow themselves to be fed stories
by the powerful, are dogmatic or complacent or self-serving, or run off-
target: they are human, and they are in business.

But journalists are also a profession, and journalism a vocation. What is
important is that journalists share the sense that there is an ideal, a target.
They should care enough to call out colleagues and others who would urge
us further off track; they should persist in correcting or at least acknowledging the worst of their own biases to the extent that they can. They
should canvass eye witnesses and colleagues and experts in the thorough
ways they know. They should draw consequences from what they say, scru-
tinize alternative courses of action or articulation, listen to voices coming
from outside the journalist's world and respond. Not every debate belongs
in the center of the target. When journalists move debates into and out of
the center, they are engaged in a serious business.

Truth is a task, not a foundation. We should have confidence in the ideal
but be pragmatic and realistic in its pursuit. In the end, I believe that our
new communicative context has the potential to create new and better
forms of human understanding and philosophy, just as the context of the
17th century did. Journalists should take heart from the fact that Frege's
norm of "The True," pragmatically employed, is becoming even more important, and explicitly so, to journalistic-consuming publics. We may yet
see a renaissance of "The True."

Journalism's job is to establish and verify the most worthwhile, interesting, and important facts, as presented by others and themselves, communicating these in an interesting and compelling way that can be grasped by
the public. Its challenge is to test and bring about those harmonies of feeling
and interest among us that help us acknowledge "The True." By coloring the
game with "The True," by mediating experiences and expertise and voices,
getting us to focus on the truths that matter, journalists are assigned the

task of overcoming disharmonies when they occur. By taking on difficult assignments that are not impossible, they help us reconcile ourselves to reality, to fit our words to it, and—hopefully—pursue its betterment.[11]

Notes

1. https://www.spj.org/ethicscode.asp, accessed November 7, 2018.
2. McIntyre (2015) notes Lynch's point (2004, 35) that "postmodern" is itself an obscure term with fuzzy edges. Compare Lynch 2004, ch. 3 for a discussion of Relativism and the reply in Benson and Strangroom 2006.
3. On the ideas of "absent presence" as a feature of our "perpetual contact" with one another in an age that may be conceive of through the concept of *Apparatgeist*, see Katz and Aakhus 2004.
4. On the unruliness of passionate utterance and its importance in meaning what we say, see Cavell 2005.
5. Not all "pragmatists" followed this line, and there are important differences within this tradition (West 1989). The philosopher C. S. Peirce believed that in the long run, we could define Truth as the limit of ideal inquiry over time: with objective scientific pursuit, he believed that we will get closer and closer to the center of the target. W. V. Quine was neither an eliminativist nor a disquotationalist about truth, and explicitly disagreed with Peirce's attempted definition, or reduction, of truth (Quine 1960, ch. 1; cf. Quine 1992).
6. Edsall (2018) canvasses a variety of philosophers on whether postmodernism is expressed in the verbal behavior of the current US president. None of them entertain the view I defend here.
7. Frankfurt 2005. Frankfurt (2016) struggles with predicting what Trump will do while in office by emphasizing the difference between lying (knowingly saying false things) and bullshitting (saying things with no regard at all for the truth).
8. King, Pan, and Roberts 2014; Floyd and Katz 2016; cf. the interview with King at http://www.bu.edu/buniverse/view/?v=1ai53r0.
9. On the difference between "forms of life" and "culture" in the philosopher Wittgenstein, see Floyd 2018.
10. I have slightly modified the English translation.
11. Thanks are due to two anonymous referees and the editors for several crucial improvements to this essay, and to James E. Katz for inspiration and his deft and creative organization of the conference which led to this book (at http://www.bu.edu/com/academics/what-we-do/emerging-media/journalism-and-truth-in-social-media/, accessed March 25, 2019). Zeynep Soysal and Peppino Ortoleva gave me stimulating ideas, as did the audience at the conference Katz organized. The Andrew J. Mellon Foundation's Boston University Mellon Sawyer Award, 2016-2019 is to be thanked for giving us the resources for this venture.

References

Allen, Amy. 2016. "Feminist Perspectives on Power." In *The Stanford Encyclopedia of Philosophy*, edited by Edward N. Zalta. Stanford, CA: Metaphysics Research Lab, Center for the Study of Language and Information. https://plato.stanford.edu/archives/fall2016/entries/feminist.

Barney, Rachel. 2016. "[Aristotle], On Trolling." *Journal of the American Philosophical Association* 2, no. 2: 193–195. doi: 10.1017/apa.2016.9.

Benson, Ophelia, and Jeremy Strangroom. 2006. *Why Truth Matters*. London: Continuum.

Bourdieu, Pierre. 1984. *Distinction: A Social Critique of the Judgment of Taste*. Cambridge, MA: Harvard University Press.

Cavell, Stanley. 2005. "Passionate and Performative Utterance: Morals of an Encounter." In *Contending with Stanley Cavell*, edited by Stanley Cavell and Russell B. Goodman, 177–198. Oxford University Press.

Diamond, Cora. 1994. "Truth: Defenders, Debunkers, Despisers." In *Commitment in Reflection: Essays in Literature and Moral Philosophy*, edited by Leona Toker, 195–221. New York: Garland.

Diamond, Cora. 1999. "How Old Are These Bones? Putnam, Wittgenstein and Verification." *Aristotelian Society Supplementary Volume* 73, no. 1: 99–134.

Diamond, Cora. 2001. "Truth Before Tarski: After Sluga, After Ricketts, After Geach, After Goldfarb, Hylton, Floyd, and Van Heijenoort." In *From Frege to Wittgenstein: Perspectives on Early Analytic Philosophy*, edited by Erich H. Reck, 252–279. New York: Oxford University Press.

Diamond, Cora. 2003. "Unfolding Truth and Reading Wittgenstein." *SATS* 4, no. 1: 24–58.

Edsall, Thomas. 2018. "Is President Trump a Stealth Postmodernist or Just a Liar?" *New York Times*. January 25, 2018, Opinion Section.

Floyd, Juliet. 2017. "Positive Pragamtic Pluralism." *Harvard Review of Philosophy* 24: 107–115.

Floyd, Juliet. 2018. "*Lebensformen*: Living Logic." In *Language, Form(s) of Life, and Logic: Investigations After Wittgenstein*, edited by Christian Martin, 59–92. Berlin: deGruyter.

Floyd, Juliet, and James E. Katz. 2016. "Big Data and the Big 'Conversation,' Interview with Gary King." In *Philosophy of Emerging Media: Understanding, Appreciation, Application*, edited by Juliet Floyd and James E. Katz, 383–398. New York: Oxford University Press.

Frankfurt, Harry G. 2005. *On Bullshit*. Princeton, NJ: Princeton University Press.

Frankfurt, Harry G. 2016. "Donald Trump Is BS, Says Expert in BS." *Time*, May 12.

Frege, Gottlob. 1918. "Der Gedanke." *Beiträge zur Philosophie des Deutschen Idealismus*, 1: 58–77. English translation: "Thought." In *The Frege Reader*, edited by Michael Beaney, 325–425. Malden, MA; Oxford: Blackwell.

Granovetter, Mark S. 1973. "The Strength of Weak Ties." *American Journal of Sociology* 78, no. 6: 1360–1380.

Kakutani, Michiko. 2018. *The Death of Truth: Notes on Falsehood in the Age of Trump*. New York: Tim Duggen Books.

Katz, James E., and Mark A. Aakhus, eds. 2004. *Perpetual Contact: Mobile Communication, Private Talk, Public Performance*. Cambridge: Cambridge University Press.

King, Gary, Jennifer Pan, and Margaret E. Roberts. 2014. "Reverse-engineering Censorship in China: Randomized Experimentation and Participant Observation." *Science in Context* 345, no. 6199 (Aug.): 859–892.

Lessing, Gotthold Ephraim. 1778. *Eine Duplik*. Waisenhauses: Buchhandlung des Fürstl. English translation: "A Rejoinder." In *Lessing, Philosophical and Theological Writings*, translated and edited by H. Nisbet, 95–109. Cambridge Texts in the History of Philosophy. Cambridge: Cambridge University Press.

Lynch, Michael P. 2004. *True to Life: Why Truth Matters*. Cambridge, MA: MIT Press.

McIntyre, Lee C. 2015. *Respecting Truth: Willful Ignorance in the Internet Age*. Abingdon, Oxon: Routledge.

Montaigne, Michel. 1948. "Of Fear." In *The Complete Works of Montaigne: Essays, Travel Journal*, 52–53. Stanford, CA: Stanford University Press. Translated by Donald M. Frame, based on the 1588 Bordeaux (5th) edition in the Municipal Library of Bordeaux, photographic reproduction by Fortunat Strowski (Paris: Hachette, 1912).

Nussbaum, Martha. 2018. *The Monarchy of Fear: A Philosopher Looks at Our Political Crisis*. New York: Simon and Schuster.

Popkin, Richard. 2003. *The History of Scepticism from Savonarola to Bayle*. Revised and Expanded edition. Oxford: Oxford University Press.

Quine, W. V. 1960. *Word and Object*. Cambridge, MA: MIT Press. Reprint 2013 with a Preface by D. Føllesdal.

Quine, W. V. 1992. *Pursuit of Truth*. Rev. ed. Cambridge, MA: Harvard University Press.

Society of Professional Journalists. 2014. "SPJ Code of Ethics." https://www.spj.org/ethicscode.asp.

West, Cornel. 1989. *The American Evasion of Philosophy: A Genealogy of Pragmatism*. Madison: University of Wisconsin Press.

Wittgenstein, Ludwig. 2009. *Philosophical Investigations*. [*Philosophische untersuchungen*.] Rev. 4th ed. Translated by G. E. M. Anscombe, P. M. S. Hacker, and Joachim Schulte. Chichester, West Sussex, UK; Malden, MA: Wiley-Blackwell.

6

Truth in Journalism

Zeynep Soysal

Introduction

An important criticism of professional journalists is that they too often fail to deliver truths. Since the early 2000s, Gallup polls show a steady decline in the American public's trust in the mass media to report the news "fully, accurately and fairly"; the percentage of people who put either "a great deal" or "a fair amount" of trust in the media stayed below 50% since 2007 (Swift 2017; Gallup/Knight Foundation 2018). Some fear this trend could have dangerous consequences: lack of trust might lead the public to disengage from the traditional news media and turn to less reliable sources of information.

Generally, in such discussions, both critics and defenders of journalism assume that any departure from truth shows that something has gone wrong in the journalistic process. In this chapter, my primary goal will be to show that this is not quite right, and that it can lead to unjustified criticisms of journalism. More specifically, I will explain that

1. truth-telling is one of the most important requirements for achieving the goal of journalism, but it is not the only one;
2. some of the other requirements for achieving the goal of journalism make it more difficult for professional journalists to deliver truths and may even force professional journalists to depart from truth in certain ways.

I draw two practical conclusions from these claims. The first is that we should be more nuanced in criticizing journalists for not delivering truths: when journalists fail to deliver truths, this need not be because they are not properly pursuing the goal of journalism—because they are, for instance, dishonest, politically or financially motivated, or simply incompetent—it might also be because of the inevitable trade-offs they have to make in order to best pursue the goal of journalism. The second conclusion is that to regain the public's trust, journalists might try to be more transparent about when their job requires them to make trade-offs, what these trade-offs are, and why truth-telling, at least sometimes, may be compromised.

Preliminaries About Truth

The claim that journalists should not always be blamed for failing to deliver truths is not new. Some have argued for it by claiming that there is no such thing as "objective truth" to begin with (see for instance the discussion in Baggini 2003). This is not my view. Let me thus briefly explain what I will be assuming about truth in this chapter.

Truth is a property of sentences, propositions, or beliefs—in general, of things that "represent" the world. For example, a sentence is true or false depending on whether the world is the way the sentence describes it. In this chapter, I will assume *realism*, that is, the claim that the world exists independently of the way we think or speak about it, and that our thoughts and claims are about that world. So, the only constraint I put on a theory of truth is that it should be compatible with realism (for criticisms of anti-realist views of truth, see, for instance, Goldman 1999; Boghossian 2006; McIntyre 2018).

Of course, not every sentence is either true or false. For instance, some sentences are not even in the business of describing the world (among them are sentences that include so-called expressives such as "Hurray!" or "Ouch!"). And some sentences do not have a determinate meaning (for instance, by being vague or ambiguous), which means that they fail to describe the world to be one way rather than another. By and large, however, the sentences that journalists produce do have determinate truth values. Most sentences about worldly things, such as political events, social trends, the weather, the economy, crime, punishment, and so on, are either determinately true or determinately false, depending on whether the world is the way they describe it. So, on the view I will be assuming in this chapter, there are many truths for the journalist to tell—there is no fundamental problem with the notion of truth or objective truth. In what follows, my discussion will instead focus on is how hard it can be for journalists to *find out* and *tell* these truths to the public, as they are pursuing the goal of journalism.

The Goal of Journalism

First off, then: what is the goal of journalism? I mean this to be a question about the role that journalism as a social institution should ideally play in our society. I thus ask about the reason why individuals or societies need journalism as an institution in the first place.

To approach this question, consider the following commonsensical observations. We all need *information* to achieve our goals. For instance, if one of my goals is to vote for a candidate who will invest in a new airport for my city, then I need information about the candidates' stances toward this kind of investment; if one of my goals is to stay away from a particular hurricane, then I need information about the hurricane's trajectory. However, we cannot get all the information we need by ourselves—most of us usually do not have the time, resources, or expertise to do so. Therefore, we need to rely on others to provide us with most of the information we need. And this is where journalism comes in: in our society, journalism is one of the most important social institutions with the role to provide us with such kind of information. As stated by the American Press Institute, "the purpose of journalism is . . . to provide people with information they need to make the best possible decisions about their lives, their communities, and their governments" (Dean n.d.). The best possible decisions for individuals are also the ones most likely to help achieve their goals.

Now, when we say that we need information to achieve our goals, what we really mean is that we need *true* information. Suppose I am falsely told that the hurricane is not going to hit my city. If I act on this report, then I will most likely not achieve my goal of staying away from the hurricane. As a general rule, we need to know (or believe) truths to make the best possible decisions to achieve our goals.

We can thus already conclude that truth-telling is an important requirement for achieving the goal of journalism: if journalists are to achieve the goal of providing us with the information we need to make important decisions in our lives, they need to deliver truths (i.e., true information). What I explain next is that truth-telling is not the only requirement for achieving the goal of journalism. There are at least three other requirements we need to make explicit.

The first concerns the *kind* of (true) information journalists should deliver. As we just saw, we need information to make important decisions in our lives in order to achieve the various goals we have. And journalism's task is to provide us with precisely *this* kind of information, that is, information that is *useful* for making decisions to achieve our goals. For instance, journalists should not report the exact number of hairs on some politicians' head—that information would be useless for most people. Of course, given that they have limited resources, journalists cannot provide all the information each of us needs to achieve all of our personal goals. In a particular context, and given a particular audience, journalists should thus aim to provide information that is important and useful for a sufficient number of people in that audience to make their own important decisions, in that context. (Dale Jacquette [2007] similarly argues for a requirement to provide "maximally relevant" information.)

As with the number of hairs example, a lot of information is useless for most audiences, in most contexts. The "usefulness constraint" is thus a way to rule out information as not newsworthy. And it is, of course, also a way to rule in information as newsworthy. For example, in general, it is not enough for people to know what a particular politician said at a particular time. In order to make decisions, people also need to know whether what was said was true. Assume, for instance, that a sufficient number of people in some city have the goal to vote for a candidate who will invest in a new airport. Then it will not be enough for them to know that Candidate 2 said "Candidate 1 told me she would not invest in a new airport." They also need to know whether it is *true* that Candidate 1 previously spoke against investing in a new airport, and whether this really indicates that she will not support the investment if elected to office. Without this information, knowing what Candidate 2 said is not useful enough for these people to make a decision that will help achieve their goal—it is newsworthy but not informative enough. The "usefulness constraint" here thus provides a way to rule in further information as newsworthy, namely, information about whether what was said is true.

The second requirement I want to make explicit concerns the *way* in which the (true and useful) information should be delivered to the public. The goal of journalism is not simply to tell useful and important truths, it is also to tell them in a way that facilitates making use of these truths (see Goldman 2008, 113, for a similar point). After all, the information we need is out there somewhere, and most of it is recorded—in libraries, in witnesses' or experts' minds, and so forth. The whole point of journalism is to have an institution that *brings* the information to the general public, by making it easy for the public to *understand* and *believe* the information. If one does not understand or believe a piece of information, then one cannot use it in making decisions. If, for instance, I am told correctly that the hurricane will hit my city, but I either do not believe or do not understand this information, then I will once again most likely not achieve my goal of staying away from the hurricane. So, for information to be useful to the public, it needs to be delivered in a way that will make it easy for the public to understand and believe (i.e., possess) the information.

Finally, there is a third requirement of the goal of journalism I want to make explicit here. People often have many false beliefs, for instance because they get misinformation from unreliable sources. As explained above, false beliefs are often harmful to making the best decisions to achieve one's goals. So, given that journalism's overarching goal is to provide people with information they need to make the best decisions about their lives, sometimes, journalists might need to correct certain prevalent and important falsehoods believed by their audiences—where one might call a falsehood "important" for individuals if believing it will likely prevent them from achieving their central goals. Fact-checking journalism might be an example of a kind of journalism that is exclusively concerned with pursuing the goal of correcting prevalent and important falsehoods (see for instance Graves 2016).

Now, one might argue that correcting falsehoods should really count as part of the requirement to deliver *useful* truths, since sometimes information that is useful and important for people to know is that something is false. Nonetheless, I think it is worth setting the correction of important and prevalent falsehoods as a separate requirement of the goal of journalism, if only because, as Bill Kovach and Tom Rosenstiel note, this requirement might be gaining importance as people have more and more access to information from everywhere in the world and from many sources, inter alia, through social media and the Internet:

In the networked world, audiences may have heard differing assertions about an event before they encounter a formal journalistic account. Thus the role of the new journalist, more than the old, is to work with audiences to sort through these different accounts, to know which of the facts they may have encountered they should believe and which to discount. (Kovach and Rosenstiel 2014, 27)

To summarize, we have teased out the following four requirements for achieving the goal of journalism. Journalists should aim to

(i)   give *true* information;

(ii) give information that is *useful* for people in making important decisions about their lives, communities, and governments;

(iii) give information in such a way that the public *can use* this information in making decisions;

(iv) correct prevalent and important falsehoods believed by the public.

Note that this is not meant as an exhaustive list of all the requirements of the goal of journalism. Just as an example, one might argue that part of the goal of journalism is also to satisfy people's curiosity or "intrinsic desire" for knowledge, and information that is given to satisfy one's curiosity or desire to know need not be useful (see for instance Kovach and Rosenstiel 2014, 21–22 and Goldman 1999, 3–7). In any case, surely (i)–(iv) are at least some of the most important requirements of the goal of journalism. What I want to explain next is that it can be very difficult to satisfy all four at the same time, and, in particular, that the truth-telling requirement, (i), can come into conflict with the other three.

Some Tensions Within the Goal of Journalism

Truth and Usefulness

It is not always easy to know truths, and *useful* truths can often be particularly difficult to know. Consider once again the claim that, in general, a report of what some person of public interest said is less useful to the public than a report of both what that person said and whether what was said is true (see also for instance Keller 2013 and Cunningham 2003 for criticisms of the media based on this point). Now consider the difference between the justification journalists usually have for the claim that some person of public interest said something (during a public announcement, say), versus the justification they need to have to know whether what was said is true. There are almost always recordings, transcripts, and witnesses that can confirm that a person of public interest made a particular statement. But to know whether what was said is true often requires a lot more investigation.

So, putting forward the more useful truth comes at a greater risk of putting forward a falsehood, because the useful truth is less epistemically justified. In other words, trying to reach the goal of providing useful truths, (ii), makes reaching the goal of providing truths, (i), more difficult.

Let us consider another example. In a recent article, Andrea Wenzel et al. investigated the roots of mistrust in the media in Philadelphia (Wenzel et al. 2018). One complaint they reported hearing often is that journalists fail to provide enough "constructive coverage." The idea is that the news should not merely report, say, that a crime occurred, but also help the public answer the question of what could be done to reduce crime. As some respondents to their surveys stated:

> [Y]ou need to talk about more positive things and not if it's going to be a shooting in the community. Have a series on like, how we can stop shooting? They just like to show stuff and don't show no solutions.
>
> Let's be strategic in how we . . . report issues. Not just . . . whatever the problem is and sensationalize it and cause fear, but you know, let's provide the facts so then who is going to be looking at a solution, and what is that? What are potential solutions to this as well? (Wenzel et al. 2018, §5)

These complaints exemplify that people need useful information to achieve their goals. The goal of reducing crime is surely important for a sufficient number of people in this community, and, in order to achieve this goal, they need more information than just the information that a crime was committed. But, of course, it is much more difficult to know what would help reduce crime. Once again, then, it is hard for journalists to reliably report truths that are *also* useful because it is harder to have justification for useful truths—it is more likely that what one says will be false.

As we saw in the introduction, many people nowadays complain that journalists do not deliver truths. Some people think that this is because journalists are intentionally deceptive to their audiences—which might (unfortunately) sometimes be the case. But there is also another explanation for why journalists might sometimes fail to deliver truths, which is that journalists need to give more information than they are perfectly well-justified in asserting. As we just saw, journalists need to provide useful truths, but useful truths are often more difficult to know, and thus providing them comes at a greater risk of providing falsehoods. So, what could journalists do to both achieve their goal of providing more useful information and gain back the trust of the public that thinks journalists are not well-justified in asserting many of their claims?

One idea might be to use more evidential expressions in news reporting, that is, expressions like "this is partly speculative," or "the reliability of these sources has not been confirmed," or "evidence points in this direction, but . . ." and so forth. In other words, journalists could try to make it clear to their audience *that* some of their claims are epistemically more tentative, and preferably also explain *how* they are less epistemically justified, and *why*. For the "why?": journalists could be explicit in conveying that part of their role as journalists leads them to make more tentative claims because part of their goal is to provide useful truths to their audiences. For the "how?": journalists could explicitly say how strong their evidence is for making these claims, for instance, by explaining their evidence. These kinds of practices are not very common in journalism nowadays. In particular, it is uncommon for journalists to flag how confident they are in making various claims.

Journalism handbooks and guidelines often recommend that journalists should practice "transparency." Journalists are told, for instance, to disclose their sources, the updates or additions to their reports, their personal or organizational links to sources (Silverman 2014, §2 and §5), and to provide information about the reports' author(s) (Goo 2017). There are a number of obvious reasons why this kind of practice of transparency is important, in particular, for accountability. But proponents of transparency also propose it as a way of solving the kind of problem I am interested in here, namely, the problem of how to regain the public's trust. For instance, Kovach and Rosenstiel note that the "Spirit of Transparency" provides ways for journalists to "be as open and honest with audiences as they can be about what they know and what they don't" (Kovach and Rosenstiel 2014, 114). These recommendations of transparency sound similar to my proposal. But mine differs in important ways, and it has some important advantages for the issue at hand. Including information about sources or updates to a news report does not guarantee the reader will fully understand that some of the claims made in the news article are thereby more tentative, let alone that they will understand which claims are more tentative. It can be difficult, for instance, to know what exactly to infer from a disclosure line at the end of an article such as "My wife works with the company . . ." (Silverman 2014, §5). Or, take the recommendation that journalists should disclose their sources: usually, knowing the source of some information will not enable readers to infer how secure that information is because the readers often will not know how reliable these sources are. The kind of transparency I advocate here is thus a bit different: I suggest that journalists should explicitly flag that some of their claims are more tentative, and why they are more tentative, by adding a statement about how well their evidence supports those particular claims. So, for instance, instead of (or in addition to) listing the sources she used, a journalist might want to say something like "Source X said Y. But there is some reason to think that X might be unreliable, because Z." Or, for instance, when journalists are reporting the findings of a scientific study, they might want to say what can (and what cannot) be inferred from such a single study.

Whenever one asserts a claim, one should already have figured out to what extent one's evidence supports that claim. This is a general principle that epistemically responsible agents should follow. Responsible journalists, then, should already know to what extent the evidence they have supports the claims they assert. What I propose here is that journalists should just make this more explicit for their readers. I suggest that this might help journalists regain the trust of the public that thinks journalists are not well-justified in asserting their claims. Note that the complaint that journalists are intentionally deceptive might also be partly the result of the difficulty of providing useful truths: journalists end up saying some things that are false, people notice this, and assume journalists are lying. Thus, my proposal here with respect to the complaint that journalists are not well-justified in asserting their claims might also help against the complaint that journalists are intentionally deceptive. Beside the potential benefit for regaining the public's trust, being explicit in this way might also help journalists come closer to reliably giving people information they need to achieve their various goals. Indeed, if the public is told explicitly why and how some of the claims journalists make are more tentative, they could make more careful use of the journalist's reports. Moreover, if they expect the journalist to flag the claims that are more tentative, they might be more trusting of the claims that are not flagged. More generally, there would be less risk of the public being led astray by basing their decisions on epistemically less well-justified claims.

Truth and Usability

Let us now turn to component (iii) of the goal of journalism, namely, that journalists should convey useful and true information in a way that the public *can make use* of when making important decisions. What I explain here is that pursuing (iii) sometimes requires deviating from the truth in some ways and hence comes into conflict with the goal of providing truths, (i).

Here is one way in which conflict arises. A lot of the information we need to make important decisions is too complicated for us to understand. For this reason, being told the truth is often less useful to us than being told something that is close enough to the truth and easier to grasp. For instance, if a journalist is to report certain medical information, she will often need to simplify, and hence distort, that information. Simplified medical information, though it may be strictly speaking false, will be more useful for people to achieve their goals than true but incomprehensible information. Similar considerations apply to science journalism more generally, or even to historical journalism, where one often needs to use simplifications to convey information in a way that can be understood and thus possessed. This issue relates to traditional discussions in philosophy on the usefulness of idealization or simplification (for a recent discussion, see for instance, Appiah 2017). In particular, some philosophers think that most of scientific inquiry involves "useful untruths," and so, on this view, any kind of journalistic reporting of science would have to involve such useful untruths.

Here is a second way in which conflict between truth and usability arises. Many ways of conveying true information are tedious and boring. This means that the public will not even read certain kinds of news reports, which will go against the goal of getting people to possess information they need to make important decisions. Here is, for instance, how Kovach and Rosenstiel state what comes close to our goal (ii):

> Perhaps it is best understood this way: Journalism is storytelling with a purpose. That purpose is to provide people with information they need to understand the world. . . . Part of journalism's responsibility is not just providing information but also providing it in such a way that people will be inclined to listen. (Kovach and Rosenstiel 2014, 214f.)

On their view, storytelling is sometimes the best way to get people to possess the information they need to make important decisions. Storytelling is very common: journalists pick a particular person's story to report on a phenomenon that affects many. But storytelling like this can, and often does, come apart from truth-telling: it either involves telling (or at least implying) a certain narrative that is not entirely true (and thereby conflicts with (i)), or it involves omitting certain important truths (and thereby also conflicts with (ii)).

Achieving the goal of getting people to read, understand, and possess information so they can make use of this information may thus require departures from the truth, either via the simplification of information or the use of narratives or fictions. It follows that trying to achieve the goal of getting people to possess useful information, (iii), sometimes comes into conflict with the goal of truth-telling, (i).

Once again, then, the question arises: how can journalists both achieve their goal as journalists and regain the trust of the public that thinks they are failing to deliver truths? This is a difficult question, which requires more in-depth examination than I can provide in the space of this chapter. One suggestion is that the kind of transparency that I was suggesting above in "Truth and Usefulness" might be of use here as well: journalists might try to be explicit about what is omitted from a particular narrative or story and when simplification is used, and why. But how exactly to avoid conveying false beliefs in one's audience when one uses "useful untruths" or fictions is a very important question for future exploration, for both journalists and theorists alike.

Correcting Falsehoods

Finally, let us turn to component (iv) of the goal of journalism, namely, the requirement of correcting prevalent and important falsehoods believed by the public. What I explain here is that this requirement can also come into conflict with the other requirements of the goal of journalism. Moreover, these conflicts might be more prominent now that a lot of information is conveyed through social media platforms and online resources.

It is a well-known and much-discussed fact that, given their limited air-time, journalists have to choose very carefully which piece of important, useful information they report to their audiences. Discussions have often focused on the question of which statements journalists should report— it is surely important for most people to know what some famous politician or expert said about an issue, but is it really good to report a statement even when what was said was blatantly false, or misguided, and especially without commenting on the fact that it was false or misguided? (For recent discussions, see for instance McIntyre 2018 or Van Norden 2018.)

An important point that is often neglected in these discussions is that even if journalists actually report on the content of what was said (and thus come closer to achieving goal (ii), as discussed in "Truth and Usefulness"), and even if they correct important falsehoods (and thus achieve goal (iv)), they might nonetheless end up producing more false beliefs in their audiences, thereby coming into conflict with requirement (iii). Studies suggest that merely giving voice to some falsehood, even while reporting it to be false, can have the adverse effect of having people believe the falsehood (see for instance the discussion in Levy 2017). Neil Levy argues on this basis that consuming "fake news" even in a report that exposes it as fake can get people to believe the fake news (2017). This would mean that the problem of selecting what to correct and what to authenticate given the goal of creating true beliefs in one's audience is very far from trivial. Moreover, the correct choice might depend on results from psychology about how exactly people process information. Given that, nowadays, so many people have the ability to reach a public—through social media and online platforms—and thus also to convey falsehoods, journalists have to pick very carefully which statements to report and which falsehoods to correct, to avoid potentially exacerbating the effect of the widespread false information.

Conclusion

Journalism is a crucial social institution; we all need it to make the best possible decisions about our lives, our communities, and our governments. Its proper functioning depends not only on journalists doing their jobs but also on the public being receptive to the information journalists provide. It is thus very important to maintain or restore trust in journalism—this trust should not be given up without good reasons. My goal in this chapter was to show that, sometimes, departure from truth in journalism might not mean that journalists are not properly pursuing their goals as journalists, and hence that we should be more nuanced in criticizing journalists for failing to deliver truths. More specifically, I explained that part of the goal of journalism is to provide *true* information that is *useful* to the public and that is *usable* by the public, and that journalists sometimes also need to correct important and prevalent falsehoods believed by their audiences. Sometimes, providing useful information comes at the risk of providing false information, because it can be harder to have justification for useful truths. Sometimes, providing usable information requires providing "not-quite true" information because in order to get people to possess useful information and be able to make use of it journalists need to simplify, idealize, or use narratives, which can distort the truth. And sometimes, correcting important and prevalent falsehoods believed by the public might backfire and convey more false beliefs in their audience. Thus, when journalists fail to deliver truths or correct falsehoods, this may well be because of the inevitable trade-offs they have to make to best achieve the goal of journalism, and this need not imply that they are malicious or incompetent. We should thus be more attentive to the goal of journalism, and aware of how difficult it can be to achieve it, before we blame journalists for failing to deliver truths.

That being said, I also suggested that journalists could try to be explicit about the kinds of trade-offs they have to make, how exactly they make them, and why truth, at least sometimes, may be compromised. I suggested that this kind of transparency might help journalists achieve the goal of providing true, useful, and usable information to the public, while maintaining the trust of the public: they would be making the public aware of when truth may be compromised.

Finally, and more generally, I think that getting clear about the goal of journalism and the various tensions that arise within it—both as journalists and as consumers of news—is an important step toward better journalism and toward better consumption of journalism.

References

Appiah, Kwame Anthony. 2017. *As If: Idealization and Ideals.* Cambridge, MA: Harvard University Press.

Baggini, Julian. 2003. "The Philosophy of Journalism." *Open Democracy*, May 15. https://www.opendemocracy.net/media-journalismwar/article_1218.jsp.

Boghossian, Paul. 2006. *Fear of Knowledge: Against Relativism and Constructivism.* New York: Oxford University Press.

Cunningham, Brent. 2003. "Rethinking Objectivity." *Columbia Journalism Review*, July/August. http://archives.cjr.org/feature/rethinking_objectivity.php.

Dean, Walter. n.d. "Journalism Essentials." https://www.americanpressinstitute.org/journalism-essentials/what-is-journalism/purpose-journalism/. Accessed July 4, 2018.

Goldman, Alvin I. 1999. *Knowledge in a Social World.* New York: Oxford University Press.

Goldman, Alvin I. 2008. "The Social Epistemology of Blogging." In *Information Technology and Moral Philosophy*, edited by Jeroen van den Hoven and John Weckert, 111–122. New York: Cambridge University Press.

Goo, Sara. 2017. "Guideline for Bylines on NPR.org." *NPR Ethics Handbook*, March 1. http://ethics.npr.org/category/g-transparency/.

Graves, Lucas. 2016. *Deciding What's True: The Rise of Political Fact-Checking in American Journalism*. New York: Columbia University Press.

Keller, Bill. 2013. "Is Glenn Greenwald the Future of News?" *New York Times*, October 27. http://www.nytimes.com/2013/10/28/opinion/a-conversation-in-lieu-of-a-column.html.

Jacquette, Dale. 2007. *Journalistic Ethics: Moral Responsibility in the Media*. Upper Saddle River, NJ: Pearson/Prentice Hall.

Gallup/Knight Foundation. 2018. "American Views: Trust, Media and Democracy." https://kf-site-production.s3.amazonaws.com/publications/pdfs/000/000/242/original/KnightFoundation_AmericansViews_Client_Report_010917_Final_Updated.pdf.

Kovach, Bill, and Tom Rosenstiel. 2014. *The Elements of Journalism: What Newspeople Should Know and the Public Should Expect*. Revised and updated 3rd ed. New York: Three Rivers Press.

Levy, Neil. 2017. "The Bad News About Fake News." *Social Epistemology Review and Reply Collective* 6, no. 8: 20–36.

McIntyre, Lee. 2018. *Post-Truth*. Cambridge, MA: MIT Press.

Silverman, Craig. 2014. "The Best Ways for Publishers to Build Credibility Through Transparency." *American Press Institute*, September 24. https://www.americanpressinstitute.org/publications/reports/strategy-studies/transparency-credibility/.

Swift, Art. 2017. "Democrat's Confidence in Mass Media Rises Sharply From 2016." *Gallup News*, September 21. http://news.gallup.com/poll/219824/democrats-confidence-mass-media-rises-sharply-2016.aspx.

Van Norden, Bryan W. 2018. "The Ignorant Do Not Have a Right to an Audience." *New York Times*, June 25. https://www.nytimes.com/2018/06/25/opinion/free-speech-just-access.html.

Wenzel, Andrea, Anthony Nadler, Melissa Valle, and Marc Lamont Hill. 2018. "Listening Is Not Enough: Mistrust and Local News in Urban and Suburban Philly." *Columbia Journalism Review, TOW Reports*, March 26. https://www.cjr.org/tow_center_reports/mistrust-and-local-news-urban-and-suburban-philly.php.

PART III
CRAFT OF JOURNALISM AND TRUTH

7

Canards, Fausses Nouvelles, Paranoid Style

Classic Authors for an Emerging Phenomenon

Peppino Ortoleva

Why a Historical Approach to Fake News

In the past few years, fake news has become an urgent issue, and even the subject of a form of moral panic. The expression itself is often presented as novel. It may seem strange that I propose to read the topic through the lenses of classic authors, writing between the 1840s and the 1960s. In fact, the best "reading" of the present is not that which considers it as an isolated moment in time, devoid, like a *geometrical* point, of any length. Rather we should consider it as a *meeting* point where a variety of processes converge, some of which have their roots in events and trends dating decades, even centuries ago.

It has been already noted in this volume and elsewhere that fake news is not a totally new development; on the contrary, forms of fabricated information have existed in previous periods in history. In this chapter, I weave together some disparate historical threads that may all shed light on the phenomenon as we see it now. They may shed light also on another aspect. The invention of information has not been equally present in all periods; on the contrary, it has emerged in some historical moments while it has been less visible, or submerged, in others. We may speak of a cyclical disappearing and reappearing. The classic authors I will consider will help us understand the dynamics of this cycle.

A brief introduction to my authors: I will first consider the French novelist Honoré de Balzac and one of his friends, and a famous writer himself, Gérard de Nerval. Balzac, whose incomes were for a great part the fruit of his contributing stories and novels to the leading daily papers, was very curious and competent about the journalistic profession and the newspaper industry, which was growing very rapidly at the time. "I have the whole of a society in my head," he said of himself, and also spoke of his work as daguerreotyping a system of social relations (Ortoleva 2018). Some of the main characters of *La comédie humaine*, the gigantic work in which he endeavored to describe and to invent at the same time the French social, economic, and cultural life of the 1830s and 1840s, are in fact newspapermen. The novel *Lost Illusions*, first published in installments between 1837 and 1843, is centered on the life and career of a young journalist. In this novel, generally considered one of Balzac's masterpieces, some attention is reserved for the phenomenon then known as *canards*: this word included both the insertion of consciously invented or inflated news in the pages of regular newspapers and the creation of improvised sheets containing fabricated information, which were diffused in the streets by newsboys.

Exactly about this subject his friend Gérard de Nerval wrote a pamphlet, *Histoire véridique du canard*, published in 1844. The title itself is an oxymoron: "a truthful history of untrue news" may be a faithful enough translation. Like Balzac, Nerval dates the origins of the phenomenon to the very beginnings of modern journalism, and he shows that it was purposely used by newspaper publishers and editors. These classic authors invite us to view fabricated information as a sort of shadow that has always followed the newspaper industry: not a marginal phenomenon, the work of amateurs or lunatic fringes, but a part of the profession itself.

A third classic author who will guide us into the nature and evolution of fake news is a great historian: Marc Bloch. A specialist in the Middle Ages, in some moments of his life Bloch tried his tools, his "craft" as he famously defined it, on the historical events that he was experiencing, before being executed by the German army in 1944 as a fighter for the Resistance, and a Jew. His century-old essay (1921), had a telling title: *Reflections of a Historian on the False News of the War*. Bloch was particularly curious about the psychological and cultural dynamics of false rumors: where fake news came from, what pushed people to circulate, and to "believe," them. One of the most interesting aspects of the essay is the connection that Bloch established between the bottom-up formation of this "news" category and the loss of credibility of the official (and censored) press.

Finally, we will turn to an American historian: Richard Hofstadter, active between the early 1940s and the late 1960s, who remains famous not only for great syntheses of US history, like *The American Political Tradition*, but also for keen insights into the mentality of his time. *The Paranoid Style in*

American Politics, in its original form a speech given at Oxford in 1963, is one of the most famous of these contributions. It focuses on the obsession on conspiracies, which creates, so to speak, a level of "truth" more coherent than real life may possibly be. It may be surprising that some of the phenomena he described more than 50 years ago are similar to those we are familiar with today. So, for instance, the "news" that described the fluoridation of water as part of a communist campaign to pollute the physical and mental health of American children may remind us of some of the recent wave of false information: against vaccination or "manipulated" food.

Fake news as a professional inclination of the journalists, fake news as part of a psycho-social crisis, fake news as the product of a paranoid world-view: the four authors lead us through three different paths, all of which show us where the contemporary phenomenon of false information comes from and help explains what is happening now.

Balzac, Nerval, and Journalists as Falsifiers

In a famous passage in *Lost Illusions* Honoré de Balzac wrote: "*Canards . . .* is our word for a scrap of fiction told for true, put in to enliven the column of morning news when it is flat. We owe the discovery to Benjamin Franklin, the inventor of the lightning rod and the republic" (Balzac 1951, 361). And he added: "In journalism everything that is probable is true."

However rapid in his writing, Balzac was careful in his choice of words. He did not use the word "invention," as we might think when speaking of fabricated news, but "discovery." In his view, a single *canard* might be the fruit of invention, but *canards* as an idea, and as a technique, were, so to speak, there to be found. They were a part of the journalistic profession's environment. In any case, the mention of Franklin, who by the way was also the initiator of *Poor Richard's Almanack* (with its own share of dubious news) was meaningful: the inventor of the republic. In Balzac's opinion, there was a connection between fake news and democracy: in his (conservative) view, a *régime* of freedom is always open to abuses of freedom.

As already said, the word *canard* could be applied both to the publication of manipulated news in the column of regular newspapers and to the printing of leaflets, which were sold in the streets with their sensational—and fabricated—titles. (A last echo of that phenomenon is in the name of a famous French weekly, *Le canard enchaîné*, whose editorial line is in between satire and scandal). Nerval defined the phenomenon, in his *Histoire véridique du canard,* as "canards are news that are sometimes true, always overstated, often fake" (Nerval 2007, 3).

What Balzac and his associates were most curious about was what moved journalists and their publishers to overstate and/or fabricate news. According to them, there were two typical reasons for the flourishing of *canards.* One was the lack of "real" news during holiday periods; it was boredom that gave the impulse to great hoaxes, like the story of a big sea snake threatening Paris. After all, one of their publishers was Emile Girardin, whose role in the ascent of journalism as entertainment, based on advertising revenues, was unequaled in the European press. The *canards* Balzac and Nerval wrote about thrived in a newspaper world in which the attention of readers had already become a merchandise in itself. But fake news was also created, according to our authors, when the government wanted to distract public attention from some serious problems. Or to deform what was really happening.

But why was the metropolitan audience of the 1840s willing to accept information that would later disappear or prove false? Or to buy sheets which from their very face showed their dubious origins? Balzac also published in 1842 a semi-serious treatise, *Monographie de la presse parisienne,* which portended to define the rules governing the journalistic world. There he gave some surprising and funny examples of pseudo-facts that were published as news *exactly because* they were impossible to believe. In other words, accepting or buying news is not always the same as believing. In many cases the value of these "news" is not based on their being recognized as facts. In order to understand why this may happen we should turn to another French classical thinker, Alexis de Tocqueville, writing more or less in the same years: "A newspaper is an adviser that does not require to be sought, but that comes of its own accord and talks to you briefly every day of the common weal, without distracting you from your private affairs. Newspapers therefore become more necessary in proportion as men become more equal and individualism more to be feared." These lines were published in the second volume of *Democracy in America* in 1840, as an afterthought to the devastating critique of the American (and French) press the same author had expressed five years earlier, in the first volume. In Tocqueville's view, news had a social role that went beyond the more or less reliable representation of facts: it was an indispensable instrument of social cohesion in a more and more individualistic society. In this role, legends and rumors, and also *unbelievable* news, may be more effective than "real" news. Particularly in moments in which the need to give a meaning to an abstract and anonymous world is more intense. Paris in the 1830s and 1840s, one of the earliest metropolises of the industrial age, was going through such a moment.

In this situation, the attitude of readers might incline toward what Jan Harold Brunvand (1981), in a famous book on urban legends, has called "half-believing": that is, accepting information "as if" it were true without seriously evaluating evidence in favor or against. In this situation, it was possible for some journalists, as Nerval noticed, to become famous *exactly because* they were the inventors of spectacular *canards*. This is the case of Joseph Méry, a semi-legendary figure, journalist, poet and fiction writer, credited with having personally fabricated the famous sea snake story, the prehistoric monster threatening Paris, which regularly re-emerged in the press and in the leaflets, and other spectacular hoaxes. How could people appreciate a journalist for deceiving them? Evidently because the entertainment he provided was perceived as a value in itself, independent of truth, or rightly because of the ingeniousness of the falsification. "An angel heart, a poet mind, a satanic spirit": so the novelist Alexandre Dumas defined Méry, who by the way also was a friend and collaborator of Nerval (Dumas 1851, 293): the world of fiction, that of fake news, and that of the critical study of *canards* was in many ways the same, as Filip Kekus (2012) has recently demonstrated.

But when the professionals of information start fabricating news, the amusing stories of a Joseph Méry are just one of the possibilities. In another novel by Balzac, *Bureaucracy,* we find a powerful clerk, the secretary-general of a minister, who "sang to the journalists his fake news and swallowed theirs." It is worth noting that, in this case, the terms used are *fausses nouvelles,* literally "fake news," not *canards*. In Balzac's description, invented information is a currency exchanged between journalists and politicians, or high-ranking bureaucrats. Just one step away are those who serve politicians or other powers not just by distracting the public opinion but also by consciously misleading it: like the Russian journalists who in the very early 20th century created the *Protocols of the Elders of Zion*, one of the most powerful weapons of anti-Semitic propaganda, later to be reprinted in installments in Henry Ford's *Dearborn Independent,* in the 1920s.

So, let's go back to the final considerations of Nerval's *Histoire véridique*: "what is strange is that *canards*, these children of the coupling of paradox and fantasy, always turn out to become true" (Nerval 2007, 11). Fake news may originate as false, but they may also actuate themselves, in time. A danger we should never overlook.

Fake News Between Orality and the Press

In *Reflections of a Historian on the False News of the War*, Marc Bloch declared an opinion on professionally fabricated fake news that at least partially coincided with that expressed by Balzac and Nerval: "often, false news in the press is simply a fabrication, crafted by the hand of a worker in a predetermined plan—to affect opinion or to obey an order—or simply to embellish a story" (Bloch 2013, 4). But his focus was more on the circulation of fake news in particular moments, in situations of social alarm: a phenomenon that could not be attributed to the conscious work of single professionals but was the fruit of more complex, and collective, movements.

A mass war like World War I was a typical culture broth for fake news. But what Bloch said may be applied also to different situations of crisis, including economic recessions. In fact, in many countries the 1929 Depression was another moment in which fake news and conspiracy stories were widely circulated. We should consider this if we want to understand the possible relations between the recent explosion of fake news and the long economic crisis that has started in 2008 and is still with us.

"One easily believes what one needs to believe" (Bloch 2013, 8). This is one of the crucial elements of Bloch's analysis. Demand for information does not necessarily mean a search for something real on which to base our behavior. It may also mean a search for something that confirms what we already think (including prejudices) or for something that meets our hopes or for signs of the times, as in oracles or prophecies. It is possible to extract from Bloch's essay some general statements: what we might call some basic laws of *fausses nouvelles*.

According to the first of these laws, the diffidence against official truths, which is always latent, grows proportionally to the real or perceived power of censorship. "The opinion prevailed in the trenches that anything could be true except what was allowed in print" (Bloch 2013, 10). This diffidence fostered, at the same time, the need for reliable news, and the impossibility to get them from the sources that are generally considered reliable. So, the usual authority of "the press" was diametrically reverted. Authoritative sources losing their credibility, their place was taken by unofficial "news": this could circulate in oral form or also through the proliferation of various unofficial media, including leaflets and handwritten posters. And nobody could correct or even contradict them: trying to establish an authoritative "truth" was the best way not to be believed. It is important to add, anyway, that, in the Great War, and in many later occasions, the opinion that "prevailed in the trenches" was all but unfounded. We should never forget that hesitancy toward official truth is, in itself, often justified. And that along with fake news much information may circulate that may be inflated but basically true.

Second law: "an item of false news always arises from preexisting collective representations" (Bloch 2013, 10). These narrations can be produced by more or less consciously assembling fragments of pre-existing stories or by reproducing them with different names and locations. Fake news does not come out of nowhere. Much of fake news' credibility comes from its being embedded in social memory. Even when purposely fabricated, it is often inspired by the personal memory of the fabricators and the social memory that surrounds them. This is an indication for the study of fake news that has been rarely pursued: to analyze their roots and precedents, to disassemble it in order to find older nuclei and practices of adaptation to present contexts.

The third law is the most important for understanding the fake news phenomenon. In a situation of crisis and alarm (not necessarily a war), people tend to look for signs everywhere: signs that may help them to make sense of what's happening and to have an idea of their destiny. To read a piece of information looking for signs is intrinsically different from reading something looking for facts. In the latter case what is relevant is the sequence of events that are narrated, a sequence that may be verified or falsified, and deemed more or less credible. In the former, what is relevant is the possible meaning, independently from the concrete truthfulness. A familiar example: a person who reads in a perfectly rational way a newspaper to know what has happened the previous day, may totally change his/her way of reading when moving to the horoscope column. In this case what counts is not what concretely happens or even what will plausibly happen, but the possible direction one's life may take. The horoscope does not give us facts, but inspiration or just some food for our fantasy.

If fake news is read as news, we can define it as a more or less well-fabricated manipulation of reality, which we may detect by instruments of verification. If it is read in terms of signs, what makes it relevant is not its information value, but its ability to fulfill a need. The critique of fake news as false descriptions of facts simply does not apply to those who read them as oracles. In Bloch's opinion, looking for signs also often means to over-interpret reality. "Who had not taken the most innocent lights for suspicious signals or even (I can vouch for this story) the alternating shadows cast on a church steeple by the erratic flight of a couple of owls?" (Bloch 2013, 9). Fake news may also be the fruits of bona fide over-reading of real facts, and one of their most uncanny aspects is their tendency to cumulate details: which may contradict each other, but may also, on the contrary, support a disturbingly coherent representation of the world.

Fake News and Collective Fear

Richard Hofstadter's essay on the paranoid style in American politics focused on how fake news may originate from a collective state of mind, the fear of treacherous enemies and of conspiracies. A state of mind, we may add, that in some historic moments is limited to what is generally defined as a "fringe," but in others may extend to larger areas of the public opinion. One of the examples of Hofstadter's paranoid style was the campaign against water fluoridation. To prevent dental disease, addition of fluoride to the water supply had become an official policy of the US Public Health Service in 1951. Immediately, the extremist McCarthyites targeted this health policy as the product of a communist conspiracy to poison and even to "brainwash" American children, surely a foolish contention. But Hofstadter hastened to state that although the paranoid style was particularly evident in the far right it was "not necessarily right-wing" (Hofstadter 1964, 77) that gave rise to this style (as was also earlier said by two Frankfurt school scholars, Leo Löwenthal and Norbert Guterman, in *Prophets of Deceit*, about the radio agitators they studied in the late 1940s.)

A "paranoid style": both words in this expression are carefully chosen. "Style has more to do with the way in which ideas are believed than with the truth or falsity of their content" (Hofstadter 1964, 77). The paranoid style is not really interested in information, rather in what Hoftadter calls "ideas."

The word is intentionally vague: we might speak of a *Weltanshauung*, a world vision in classical German terms. It is a "way to believe," or a way to choose what one "needs to believe" according to Bloch's interpretation, and it is not verifiable or falsifiable as such. In the "style" that Hofstadter defined the feeling of persecution is central and, indeed, systematized in a grandiose theory of conspiracy. For a paranoia to exist, an enemy has to be identified, and its presence has to be perceived as pervasive. It must be nowhere and everywhere. The enemy, who has a central role in the world vision of paranoid politics, is also the protagonist of all kinds of possible narrations. Evoking the enemy makes even the most incredible stories credible. The enemy is a sort of metaphysical figure, which generates all sorts of possible "news" and transcends it. "Unlike the rest of us, the enemy is not caught in the toils of the vast mechanism of history, himself a victim of his past, his desires, his limitations. He is a free, active, demonic agent" (Hofstadter 1964, 85).

There are more elements in Hofstadter's interpretation that deserve our attention. The first: the enemy is everywhere, but the paranoid style tends to see him more as an agent from inside than an aggressor from outside. He is a *traitor*. He disguises as one of us, he can be one (or more) of our friends, he acts like a virus. Typically, Sen. McCarthy and his acolytes were far more concerned about American "communist agents" than about Russian military power. All conspiracy theories tend to focus on invisible powers that act inside our society to subvert it or to manipulate our minds. The case of the anti-fluoridation paranoia is an example: the invisible enemy wants concretely to "penetrate" us, acting like a slow poison. We find an analogous attitude, 50 years later, in the many stories about supposedly poisonous food, or GMOs (genetically modified organisms). Or in the campaigns against "Big Pharma": paranoid fake news invites us to mistrust everybody, even those who are supposedly the most trustworthy. Precisely because they should be trustworthy.

A second intuition we may get from Hofstadter's analysis: the paranoid mentality pushes its adoptees to imitate the enemy, to behave exactly like those it fears. Hannah Arendt once noted, in *The Origins of Totalitarianism* (1951), that while the *Protocols of the Elders of Zion* were clearly a mystification, the Nazis themselves tried to make them come true. They ended up adopting exactly the representation of power and conspiracies that the *Protocols* attributed to their arch-enemies, the Jews. People influenced by the "paranoid style" create secret societies to contest invisible demons and imitate the organizational tactics they attribute to those they fight. And they create fake news to contrast the lies that the enemy is spreading, by definition, constantly.

In this mentality, fake news is a method, a legitimate method, Hofstadter added, because the enemy "controls the press; he has unlimited funds; he has a new secret for influencing the minds (brainwashing)." In fact, paranoiacs are in great need of information and at the same time want the information they gather to always confirm their prejudices. "The paranoid mind is far more coherent than the real world" (Hofstadter 1964, 86). All the news, the opinions, the documents they collect tend to form a unitary system, more "credible" than reality itself, if one considers coherence a criterion of credibility.

This accounts also for another tendency Hofstadter noted: "Respectable paranoid literature . . . carefully and all but obsessively accumulates 'evidence.' . . . What distinguishes the paranoid style is not . . . the absence of facts but rather the curious leap in imagination that is always made at some critical point in the recital of events" (Hofstadter 1964, 85–86). In any case, Hofstadter added ironically, sometimes the love of facts is such that they are led to manufacture them.

A third important intuition in Hofstadter's considerations is what he called "the ecumenicism of hatred." This is why for centuries, from the Know-Nothings in the 1850s up until today, accusations against Catholics could be coupled with ones against Jews, or more recently those against Opus Dei can be coupled with those against Freemasons. The paranoid world vision seems based on the fall of all non-contradiction principles. The world of fake news is in fact surrealistic more than simply unreal.

Some Observations

With this short synthesis I have tried to demonstrate that an emerging phenomenon of fake news may be better understood as the meeting point of different threads, each going back to a moment of historical emergency: the birth of the modern metropolis and of modern information in 19th-century Paris; the great military, but also psycho-social, crisis that opened the 20th century; the cultural crisis that accompanied the ascent of the United States to global power. The "newer" a tendency is, the more we need the past to understand it and to see the different strata that compose it. Fake news may be the product of professionals or may be spread by the most informal of vehicles. It may be made credible by a generalized mistrust in official sources and/or generated by professional journalists. It may be credible even though spectacularly unreal, and exactly because of that. It fascinates people who are looking for signs of the times, more than for simple and verifiable facts.

True and False

All our authors show us that it is impossible to fight fake news by simply demonstrating that it is simply *not true*. As Balzac and Nerval emphasize, its strength does not lie in its being believed in the classic sense of the word; in some cases, it lies in entertainment value that goes beyond any credibility. As Hofstadter shows, it may be perceived as more coherent, therefore more credible, than reality itself, and any attempt to demonstrate its falsity may, in a paranoid mentality, revert into an evidence of their truth. From this point of view the most meaningful lesson is the one we find in Bloch: we may prove that *news* is false not that *oracles* are. If those "news" items are not assumed as facts, rather as signs, their value is not in a concrete and verifiable (or deniable) truth, rather in their possible meaning. "The lord whose oracle is at Delphi neither speaks nor conceals, but gives signs" we read in a fragment attributed to Heraclitus.

The Politics of Fake News

Both Bloch and Hofstadter attract our attention on the oppositional character of fake news. It is generated *against* official truths, which censorship makes unreliable, or which by definition are deemed false by a paranoid mentality. It is accepted as reliable by those who mistrust the powers that be: an area of public opinion that always exists as a fringe but may become much larger in moments of crisis. In any case, both these authors lead us to see fabricated information as anti-political more than properly political.

This is where the most ancient of our authors, Balzac and Nerval, send us a note of caution. Ministers and parties may also be involved in the fabrication and circulation of fake news: they may be useful in the art of government in order to distract attention and (we may add) to sow confusion. They are part, as "real" news is, of the continuous exchange between the political professionals and the newspaper professionals. In some moments in history (we should add) what was generated in fringe politics became part of mainstream politics: Nazism is the most evident case but by no means the only one.

The Communication of Fake News

What all our authors tell us about the media which propagate fake news may be particularly relevant today.

In Bloch the expression *fausses nouvelles* clearly refers to something that circulates orally more than in written form, but the choice of not using the word *rumeurs*, the French correspondent of the English "rumors" is careful. What he describes does not have the vague form of legends or of the continuous flow of word of mouth, it takes precisely that of reported facts. It works, we may say, in an area in-between traditional orality and the printed media.

On the other hand, Balzac and Nerval concentrated on printed fake news, which could be part of a newspaper but also used in a peculiar medium—the leaflets sold in the streets by newsboys. The sociologist Tamotsu Shibutani (1966) famously defined rumors as "improvised news"; we might define *canards* that circulated in the streets of Paris as "precarious news," printed like books and newspapers but bound to disappear in a few hours, a few days at most, like oral communication does. Again, in-between orality and the printed media.

Today, social media, blogs, tweets, and many forms of web information are written (or audio/visual) information that circulates with the speed, and the precariousness, of orality. This may explain much of their power and their irresponsibility: a new phenomenon with very old roots.

Some Concrete Lessons for Practitioners and/or Consumers of News

- Fake news is an old phenomenon, which tends to be more evident in moments of social crises, like wars or serious economic recessions.

Understanding the deep reasons of disorientation that push areas of public opinion to accept and circulate fake news is at least as important as fighting it.

- Fake news is often accepted not as "true" but as signs of oracular value. To understand fake news, and fight its consequences, simply demonstrating that it is untrue may be useless. It is better to address the deep needs they answer.
- Fake news tends to reproduce old stories in new forms and contexts. To understand the process, salient fake news content should be disassembled to force their (often ancient) nucleus to emerge and to analyze how it has been adapted to present realities.
- Much fake news, particularly of the "paranoid" kind, is almost impossible to belie, because any attempt to demonstrate its falsity creates a vicious circle. It is taken as evidence that some power (the government, the established press, Big Pharma, and so on) do not want them to circulate: a demonstration of their reliability.

References

Arendt, Hannah. 1951. *The Origins of Totalitarianism*. New York: Harcourt, Brace.

de Balzac, Honoré. 1951. *Lost Illusions*. London: John Lehmann.

de Balzac, Honoré. 2010. *Bureaucracy*. Project Gutenberg edition.

de Balzac, Honoré. 2002. *Les Journalistes. Monographie de la presse parisienne*. Paris: Editions du Boucher.

Bloch, Marc. 1953. *The Historian's Craft*. New York: Alfred Knopf.

Bloch, Marc. 2013. "Reflections of a Historian on the False News of the War." *Michigan War Studies Review* 51: 1–11.

Brunvand, Jan Harold. 1981. *The Vanishing Hitchiker*. New York: W. W. Norton.

Dumas, Alexandre. 1851. *Impressions de voyage: Midi de la France*, tome 2. Paris: Michel Lévy frères.

Hofstadter, Richard. 1964. "The Paranoid Style in American Politics." *Harper's*, November.

Kekus, Filip. 2012. "Du canard romantique: enjeux de la mystification pour la génération de 1830." *Romantisme* 2: 39–51.

Löwenthal, Leo, and Norbert Guterman. 1949. *Prophets of Deceit*. Studies in Prejudice Series. Vol. 5. New York: Harper and Brothers, American Jewish Committee.

Nerval, Gérard de. 2007. *Histoire véridique du canard—et autres textes*. Lyon: Moments de Presse.

Ortoleva, Peppino. 2018. "In the Time of Balzac. The Daguerreotype and the Discovery/Invention of Society." In *Photography and Other Media in the Nineteenth*

Century, edited by Nicoletta Leonardi and Simone Natale, 149–161. University Park: Pennsylvania State University Press.

Shibutani, Tamotsu. 1966. *Improvised News. A Sociological Study of Rumors. An Advanced Study in Sociology*. Indianapolis: Bobbs-Merrill.

Tocqueville, Alexis de. 2006. *Democracy in America*. Vol. 2. Project Gutenberg edition.

8

Scoop

The Challenge of Foreign Correspondence

John Maxwell Hamilton and Heidi Tworek

In 1938, Evelyn Waugh published *Scoop*, a satirical novel about foreign correspondents. *Scoop's* protagonist, William Boot, who had been writing a nature column "Lush Places," is mistaken for another journalist with the same name and sent to report on a crisis in the fictional East African state of Ishmaelia. The inept Boot somehow scores a scoop, but there's plenty of falsification and misrepresentations along the way.

Scoop might be a satirical novel—so beloved among journalists that Tina Brown named her online news site *The Daily Beast* after Boot's newspaper—but Waugh based it on real life. As he almost always did when writing a new novel, Waugh first published a book of reportage. In this case, *Waugh in Abyssinia* (Waugh 2007), published in 1936, detailed Waugh's experience covering the Second Italo-Abyssinian War for the *Daily Mail*. The book chronicled Waugh's travails, such as sending a scoop by telegraph in Latin just to be sure his colleagues would not scoop him, only to learn later the editor of the desk in London spoke no Latin and thought it was just another Waugh prank. In another incident, one of Waugh's more colorful and inventive colleagues reported that 2,000 people perished when the Italians marched into the town of Adowa. In fact, six died (Deedes 2003, 76).

Scoop was not the first or last time someone would associate foreign correspondents and foreign reporting with ineptitude, exaggeration, or misrepresentation. How could you blame Ethiopians for doubting Western ways, Waugh wrote, when the best example they saw was "journalists, press photographers, and concession-hunters" (Waugh 2007)? For postmodern French theorist Jean Baudrillard (1995), the (very real) first Iraq War "did not take place." It was a foreign war made for domestic TV consumption through CNN.

Technology, whether the telegraph in Waugh's day, TV for Baudrillard, or the Internet today, has always played a role in how foreign correspondents work. Each new iteration heralded as an advance also has had disadvantages. The current wave of technological innovation has taken journalists to a summit that they have long wanted to scale. They know more than they ever did about their readers through "likes" and precise data on the uptake of their stories. They seem to have achieved the long-desired "annihilation" of time and space, as James Gordon Bennett and others put it in the 19th century (Hamilton 2009, 55). A reporter virtually anywhere in the world can file instantly and receive near-instantaneous responses from readers. But the quality of the information reported is not necessarily better—and often worse.

Claims about the impact of social media and new technology often devolve into either-or assertions about the state of journalism. Either social media have altered journalism completely or changed little about journalism's ultimate task to uncover facts. Either social media will make professional journalists superfluous because we will have citizen journalists or social media will make journalists more important than ever because they have the professional capability to sift for reliable material. Either our current new technologies are unprecedented in disrupting media or these technologies repeat patterns from the past. These simplistic narratives make less sense than understanding our current moment as a recalibration of three trade-offs in foreign correspondence: independence, speed, and sources. We will examine these trade-offs by looking at modern American and European foreign correspondents, who have long grappled with truth and trust in news.

One of those who fretted over these problems was the German Hans von Huyn. Writing in exile in London in 1939, because he had refused to work for the Nazis, Huyn still had faith in foreign correspondents and their work. Huyn had been a reporter in Warsaw in the 1920s and believed that of all beats, the foreign correspondent "occupies an especial position." Although dismayed by how the Nazis distorted his own country's news, Huyn held on to a core belief: up to now, he averred, no one had succeeded "in arresting the march of truth" (Huyn 1939, 142–143).

Huyn thought that foreign correspondents needed to work particularly independently because no one at the home office could as knowledgably assess a far-flung land with many stories from which to select. For Huyn, as for many others, the "truth value" of foreign correspondents lay in their ability to set their own program and decide how to ensure accuracy, balance, and completeness. The trade-offs we discuss in this chapter have put pressure on foreign correspondents to recalibrate how they achieve those goals.

The Antecedents

Anyone who doubts that fabricated foreign news has a long history need only pick up a copy of George Bronson Rea's *Facts and Fakes About Cuba*. It recounts the shoddy coverage of the Spanish-American War by a responsible correspondent sent there for the *New York Herald*. Indeed, throughout the history of modern journalism, which we date to the middle of the 19th century (Hamilton and Tworek 2017), foreign newsgathering has been more susceptible to distortion and error than any other kind.

To start, correspondents have an enormous brief. They often cover not only a country but also a region. They are frequently shifted to even more distant, less familiar places when major stories break. Their range of subjects is similarly broad—politics, economics, culture, and so forth. At home, any one of these subjects would be a beat for a number of specialists. This broad range makes foreign correspondents more liable to make errors of interpretation and fact, for example because they have little time or ability to find credible sources for all their beats or because in many instances they have to depend heavily on handlers whom they may not know well.

Related to the problems of enormous topical and geographical coverage are the limitations of working in a foreign language. Few correspondents can master all they need. They rely on interpreters whose skills vary or, more recently, unreliable translation apps. At the very least, nuance is lost in translation.

While editors value language proficiency, as well as background in the history and culture of a foreign place, they worry about correspondents being too expert—"going native"—which puts them in touch with the region but out of touch with the home audience. An extreme case of this was the quirky Colonel Robert McCormick of the *Chicago Tribune*. In 1927 he asked a gathering of his correspondents in Paris who among them spoke no foreign languages. One raised his hand: Larry Rue. McCormick made Rue his roving correspondent. "I don't want my fine young boys ruined by these damn foreigners," McCormick said (Smith 1997, 300).

None of the correspondents who covered the Italian invasion of Ethiopia in 1935—the setting for *Scoop*—spoke the local language. They relied on government press releases, interpreters with poor English-language skills, and paid informers who made themselves valuable by passing along sensational news (Hamilton, in Waugh 2007, xxi). Correspondents working under such limitations can play it safe and use the same notes as the colleagues with whom they are dossing down—to use a phrase Waugh liked.

Although they were limited by language and often overwhelmed by a broad mandate, foreign correspondents also had more freedom and less supervision because they were farther from home. Until well after the mid-19th century, the foreign editor at the *New York Times* had little power over his reporters compared with other desks. The general rule was to run what a correspondent sent in or kill the story—but to do little editing. One correspondent for the *New York Times* during the Spanish-American War was none other than the great hoaxer William Mannix. He made up stories while sitting in his Havana hotel room, at one point faking quotes from a rebel general that drew from dialogue in *The Pirates of Penzance* (Hamilton 2009, 97).

The famed English-born correspondent Henry Stanley ("Dr. Livingston, I presume.") had no compunction about faking, right down to his name, which at birth was Henry Rowlands. He falsely claimed he was adopted by a New Orleans merchant named Stanley. Stanley wrote a stirring story in 1868 about linking up with guerillas in Crete, apparently without going there (McLynn 1990, 77–78).

At the height of his career in the 1960s and 1970s, the famous Polish journalist Ryszard Kapuściński technically covered 50 countries as the foreign correspondent for the Polish Press Agency. He wrote travel books that were translated into dozens of languages; he was even considered for a Nobel Prize in Literature. Since his death in 2007, however, a biography (Domosławski 2012) has suggested that Kapuściński often mixed reporting and fiction by inventing scenes to give his journalism greater aesthetic value, providing inaccurate details, and claiming to have witnessed events that he did not. The revelations were highly controversial in Poland where Kapuściński is celebrated for his vivid portrayal of fact. The biographer argued not that Kapuściński was a fraud; rather, he wrote, the biography was meant "to start a debate over the relationship between truth and fiction" (Harding 2010). Others argued that the whole debate missed the point: one journalist defended Kapuściński by saying that "there is no sharp frontier between literature and journalism" (Ascherson 2010).

Imaginative news reporting has lived on to our own time. *USA Today* correspondent Jack Kelley was celebrated for an uncanny ability, year after year, all over the world, to be in the right place at the right time—until it was learned he was a serial faker. In late 2018, internationally award-winning and apparent young superstar *Spiegel* journalist Claas Relotius was exposed for fabricating quotes, stories, or people in at least one-quarter of his stories about topics like the US-Mexico border or a Yemeni prisoner in Guantanamo. Boris Johnson, former London mayor and British foreign minister since 2016, was a foreign correspondent in Brussels for the *Telegraph* in the late 1980s and early 1990s. He got the job after being fired from the *Times* for making up a quotation. Johnson spent his time in Brussels fabricating and exaggerating stories about the European Union. Johnson's papers were complicit, providing headlines for his stories like "Snails are fish, says EU."

One foreign correspondent, Martin Fletcher, worked in Brussels at the same time as Johnson. After the Brexit referendum in 2016, Fletcher called Johnson "a mendacious pundit, one who achieved prominence by writing entertaining but dangerous nonsense." Other British newspapers took their cues from Johnson and also filed exaggerated stories bashing Brussels. During the referendum campaign in mid-2016, national newspapers continued the trend "by peddling lies and phoney [*sic*] patriotism," (Fletcher 2016). Technology may have changed by 2016, but fabrication and exaggeration remained the name of the game for many British papers.

"Snails are fish, says EU" is amusing. But foreign correspondents like Johnson have long exerted real political power. Consider, for example, the Sisson Documents, named for an American propagandist in Russia who was the object of a disinformation campaign in 1918. Sisson acquired the forged reports from anti-Bolshevik elements in Petrograd and then oversaw their distribution around the world. These forged papers aimed to delegitimize the Soviet government by purporting that Lenin and his comrades were German agents. Like the best fake news, the papers contained an element of suspected truth, namely that the Germans had given financial support to the Bolsheviks. It left out the nuance that virtually every Russian political party had taken foreign money and that the Bolsheviks were seeking to spark a revolution in Germany. The documents were endorsed by leading American news organizations. Their release by the Wilson administration coincided with and helped validate the United States' decision to join the Allies in launching an invasion of Russia. The Sisson Documents also gave oxygen to the administration's communist witch hunt immediately after the war (Kennan 1956).

Several decades later, the outbreak of World War II relied upon an elaborate scheme to falsify news. To provide a pretext for invading Poland, Gestapo director Reinhard Heydrich ordered SS troops to disguise themselves as Poles and attack the German radio tower at Gleiwitz. This attack on August 31, 1939, became known as the Gleiwitz Incident. The organizer of the Gleiwitz Incident, Alfred Naujoks, revealed at the Nuremberg trials after the war that Heydrich had justified the false-flag attack by saying that "actual proof of these attacks of the Poles is needed for the foreign press, as well as for German propaganda purposes" (Naujocks 1945). Heydrich viewed foreign correspondents as highly useful instruments of diplomacy.

Journalists had begun to emerge as important diplomatic figures at the end of the 19th century with the rise of the mass-circulation newspaper. Foreign correspondents of prominent newspapers like the *Times* and *Frankfurter Zeitung* were "politically more influential than the ambassadors of their countries" (Huyn 1939, 144). Foreign correspondents contributed to increasing tensions between Britain and Germany before World War I; many German foreign correspondents portrayed the UK as a hostile nation, building suspicion among German politicians of British actions (Geppert 2007; Bösch and Geppert 2008).

During the interwar period, European governments sought to cultivate and control foreign correspondents. In Germany, for example, the Press Department determined whether foreign papers were allowed interviews with German ministers. As the Press Department did not control domestic journalists' access to ministers, it focused on foreign correspondents. As part of a broader move toward modern opinion management through scheduled interactions with journalists, the Press Department organized press teas, weekly press conferences, and interviews with various ministers and high officials. More generally, embassies of Western governments also cultivated closer relations with foreign correspondents from their countries, often seeing them as extensions of their foreign policy (Tworek 2019, ch. 5).

Since then, the relationship between governments and foreign correspondents has continued to develop and intertwine in new ways. During the second Iraq War, foreign correspondents embedded with the military, which resulted in a potentially distorted picture of reality on the battlefield and directed attention away from the larger strategic issues. These close relationships between governments, embassies, armies, and foreign correspondents have always introduced the possibility of distortion in exchange for access. Trade-offs, then, have always existed. The question is how social media have changed the dynamics.

Three Trade-Offs

Number One: Managed News Versus Independence

Until the computer keypad and the satellite phone replaced the portable typewriter and cables, foreign correspondents were highly independent of the home office. "Rarely does the telegraph editor find it necessary to give orders to these representatives," a 1907 American primer on the news business said of foreign correspondents. "They forward the news they think worth forwarding without waiting to ask questions, and most stories they write can be turned over to the printers just as they are received" (Given 1907, 224–225).

Correspondents had such great freedom to set their own agenda that it was not unheard of for reporters from the same newspaper to assign themselves to the same story. Three *New York Times* reporters filed a similar report on Pierre Laval, the head of the Vichy government, who was about to be tried at the end of World War II. The problem, said one of the three, Drew Middleton, was "communications, pure and simple" (Hamilton 2009, 451).

This same lack of communication made it difficult to check reporters. If a reporter were unethical or sloppy, he or she had much more latitude than today to fabricate and make mistakes. Supervision is now much easier. Shortly after the revelations of Pulitzer Prize finalist Jack Kelley's transgressions in 2004, *USA Today* editors matched story datelines with expense accounts and contacted correspondents to double-check on precisely what sources they used.

Today, editors can be in touch daily, or hourly if they wish, with their correspondents. And having these abilities, editors use them. They can do what they once did with domestic stories, by thinking of packages in which several reporters in different places file reports that can be arranged into a complex story or stories. This leads to deeper, more nuanced reporting.

But the loss of independence has costs. One way to think about this is what political scientists call indexing.

In times of national security crises, the news is indexed to the views of officials. When the consensus is strong, as during the 2003 invasion of Iraq, which was predicated on the existence of weapons of mass destruction, few dissenting voices emerge in the news. "When other officials inside circles of power . . . fail to speak out against prevailing government claims . . . there is no engine to drive critical news coverage" (Bennett, Lawrence, and Livingston 2007, 10). Only when the consensus breaks does this change. Modern technology may give editors greater access to the foreign press, which sometimes offers alternative perspectives, but this does not change the imperative to look for reference points at home in times of crisis—or even in times of peace.

Indeed, a similar, albeit quotidian, problem exists in peace time with the close control exerted by editors at home. Foreign correspondents have never been wholly divorced from home country policy considerations. Often the top stories from abroad were less about political or economic issues than "Americans in trouble." But correspondents had more time to look for stories that might not be on the agenda of policymakers, either because those policymakers did not want them covered or did not know about them. Vincent Sheean, one of the United States' most prescient correspondents in the mid-20th century, correctly observed that "international journalism was more alert than international statesmanship" to the impending world war (Sheean 1946, 94).

For a more modern example, we have the *Washington Post*'s Jonathan Randal, who covered the first Iraq War. His editors "convinced themselves they had a better overall grasp of events than their men on the spot and wrote the overall lead story from Washington." Among other things, they overstated the accuracy of so-called smart bombs. "I unashamedly pine for the old cable office or the telex in the Third World that shut down at nightfall in the 1950s and 1960s," Randal recalled decades later. The freed time "allowed me time to meet and read about the people I was covering" (Randal 2000, 17, 19). Despite control from the center, Randal had far more latitude than correspondents today.

This indexing to domestic concerns is also abetted by readership statistics and social media shares. These measurements have confirmed what researchers and editors long suspected: most readers do not consume or care much about foreign news, unless it involves their compatriots.

Italy-based correspondents for the major American newspapers had nearly as many top-billed stories on the Amanda Knox trials as on the election and activities of popes. Italian and British papers (the murdered girl in the trial being British) paid her plight similarly large amounts of attention.

Number Two: Speed Versus Superficiality

The seeming annihilation of time and space by new technologies is a mixed blessing. Journalists are like dogs that try to bite their tales, succeed, and, still holding tightly, wonder what they have achieved. Even in the 19th century, William Howard Russell of the *Times* of London was unsure. He called the laying of the transatlantic cable "the greatest work of civilized man" but complained that "the electric telegraph quite annihilates one's speculative and inductive facilities" (Russell 2005, 105).

The need for visual images limited television news to places where cameras could go. But lightweight cameras and the need for smaller production crews in the field—not to mention the iPhone and drones—allow journalists to get pictures almost anywhere there is news and send them instantly. (It also helps that another technology—airplane flight—is cheaper and faster than ever.)

Still, the constant ability to file stories constantly becomes determinant. Because journalists have the technology and compete against people who use it, they must too. The resulting imperative for continual news reporting and knee-jerk reaction stories leaves less time for newsgathering, as CBS correspondent Marvin Kalb has pointed out based on his experience as a television reporter in Moscow in the late 1950s and early 1960s. In those days, he had to send his film home via airplane. The standard practice was to find someone at the airport willing to convey the raw footage to New York, where they would be met by someone from the network. In an allusion to 19th-century technology for moving news, they called these travelers "pigeons." While the film traveled to New York, Kalb had two or three days to think about the story, for which he could provide the voice-over via phone later. Modern correspondents, he says, don't have that kind of time and therefore are less authoritative. With live stories, they often say "I think" (Kalb 1993, 75–78). In other words, they have not had time to find out for sure.

A foretaste of this is one of the first cases of life radio coverage, the sinking of the *Graf Spee* in 1939 in Montevideo harbor: "We don't want to tell you what we think is going on. We want to tell you what we can see, and we can't see a great deal, due to the excessive action and movement" (Snyder and Morris 1951, 401).

Real-time reporting via the Internet, satellite telephone, and Twitter generates high audience engagement. We all love to know *right now* what is happening. In the hands of a seasoned, careful reporter, such accounts can be accurate in a technical sense of limited errors of fact. But another kind of falsehood often creeps in, to wit, lack of context and depth, which deprive accounts from conveying truth. This kind of reporting in turn deprives new audiences of the means to assess the significance of an event.

It is the instant news mentality that led a colleague of William Boot in *Scoop* to observe, "News is what a chap who doesn't care much about anything wants to read."

Although the need for speed limits "truth," foreign correspondents are also much more subject to speedy criticism—and correction, some of it salubrious. To be sure, social media users can be vicious if a correspondent holds a political position that they do not like or happens to be female or non-white. But swift corrections of fact and alternative interpretations by readers, commenters, and experts can create a more accurate record.

Number Three: Abundance of Sources Versus Reliability

The third trade-off is about sources. The advent of social media means that we have many new sources of foreign news; many of those sources can also be accessed from the newspaper's main office or by readers anywhere with an Internet connection. Before the Internet and social media, foreign correspondents could sometimes get away with rewriting stories from the major newspapers in a country, as the home desk didn't have access even to that basic information. Now, foreign correspondents both have more sources and more pressure to write something that cannot be found for free elsewhere.

The question is whether social media have provided enough new sources of information to compensate for the decreased number of professional foreign correspondents. Much of the debate in foreign news is over the loss of correspondents. In the American context, the number of traditional correspondents is way down. No more corps of correspondents for the *Baltimore Sun, Boston Globe, Newsday,* or the *Philadelphia Inquirer.* Television correspondents no longer span the globe the way they did when CBS styled itself the elite Tiffany Network.

But even this trend is subject to debate in key ways. First, the decline in the number of foreign correspondents and the quality of international news began long before the Internet and social media. In Britain, international news stories declined from 20% of stories in 1979 to only 11% in 2010. The stories also lost prominence, falling from 33% to 15% of the first 10 pages of newspapers (Moore 2010). Second, alternative sources of foreign news reporting have emerged. Bloomberg News, with hundreds of editors and reporters abroad, is one example. Its news is very high quality, though limited to a business audience that can pay the steep monthly fee for a connection. Further to this point, content analysis of the *New York Times* suggests that its foreign reporting is growing in important ways, not only by volume but also by paying more attention to smaller, less economically powerful counties (Sobel, Kim, and Riffe 2017).

Beyond establishment media, however, new forms of foreign reporting are alive and well. Two other types of journalists have become much more prominent and provide new types of sources: independent journalists (or freelancers) and citizen journalists. In the past, independent reporters still had to work through editors. Now they are their own editors. They also make very little, or no, money and rarely stay in the business, reducing institutional memory. These factors increase the probability of making mistakes or being duped by malicious sources.

The contemporary news environment is increasingly filled with unaccredited journalists supplying news for free over platforms ranging from Twitter to the Huffington Post. People operate independently, without editorial supervision. Some individuals even act like foreign correspondents from their own homes, providing astonishing and unexpected expertise. Eliot Higgins, an unemployed Briton, became the leading expert on munitions in the Syrian civil war (Keefe 2013). Citizen journalists like Higgins are unpaid, but their skills and information provide crucial fodder for commercial media companies. They also create the potential for misinformation if media are not careful.

The development of the citizen journalist is part of a shift from "readers" and "viewers" to "the people formerly known as the audience" (Rosen 2006). These people can decide when to engage with media, how, and whether to respond and co-create stories. All of these developments are powered by new technology.

Alongside providing more sources for foreign correspondents and more feedback on stories, however, there is also less, or no, quality control. This creates space for made-up and tendentious news. Some of this news might emerge from honest mistakes made by citizens with little training; some might be deliberate attempts to mislead that fall in the category of reporting that can be legitimately called "fake news." The Russians, for example, have figured out how to send us made-up news about ourselves, as well as what is happening abroad. The Russian-funded Internet Research Agency provided faked videos from Syria that were picked up by the *Washington Post*, among others (Romm and Molla 2017).

Authentic-seeming fakes may become more problematic in the future. It is ever easier to doctor photos and videos. But it is also possible to detect a fake. Individuals can use the Internet to check facts and impressions, and traditional media have already enlarged their routine news "beats" to verify misstatements, identify disinformation campaigns, and generally do more to keep people honest. A historical analog is the way journalists met the rise of government propaganda during World War I with an increased attention in the news pages on such projects, albeit, investigating mainly those produced by the enemy.

The key to balancing the explosion of sources with reliability is verification. Foreign correspondents can remain invaluable if they bring the skills to deduce whether a report, photo, or tweet is "true" or not. They often have access to government, economic, and social elites that citizen and independent journalists generally do not. These sources must be checked, of course, since they are often the origin of misinformation. But that is nothing new for good reporters. Besides, they have back-up from newsrooms with technical capabilities to detect fakes and editorial capacity to check whether tweeters are real people and not bots.

In many ways, the problems of verification are more economic than technological. Changes in the media landscape over the past few decades have increased the pressure to publish constantly and chase breaking stories as well as reduced the number of journalists and editors who can check sources.

The current technological disruptions through social media are not unprecedented, however. They build on a longer pattern of challenges to the printed press that began with radio and television. These disruptions were offset because those media initially provided a limited amount of news and because the number of newspapers continued to decline, reducing print competition. Newspaper penetration halved from 1950 to 2000. As Picard has pointed out (2008, 113), declines in newspaper penetration began with radio and TV, but the Internet accelerated the decline across all news media. Foreign news is the most vulnerable to these changes: most people care much less about foreign news than national or celebrity news. Foreign news is also expensive, making it an easy target for cost-cutters.

One possible way forward will be news sites that focus on particular topics and build trust with their users. US-based News Deeply, for example, was created in 2012 to produce topic-focused detailed reporting on a few issues of pressing concern. One of the site's co-founders, Lara Setrakian, sees the site as one solution to the "broken system" of journalism that provides insufficient explanations, expects journalists to be experts in all topics, and fails to build trust with users (Setrakian 2017). One of News Deeply's verticals—or in-depth areas of coverage—focuses on the Syrian civil war (www.newsdeeply.com/syria). The site provides more information on that civil war than anyone could have received on, say, the Yugoslav wars in the early 1990s.

Conclusion

The state of foreign reporting today is paradoxical. New technology makes some aspects of foreign reporting faster and easier; it has also raised old problems of trust and of financing foreign news that we first saw in the 19th century. As we argue, foreign news has always been the most elusive because the high costs limit the number of reporters sent in search of news, because readers are less well equipped to judge stories from places they have never been, and because correspondents have so much to cover.

This has been a recipe for fake news, even at the zenith of journalism's prosperity and credibility. But it will become more of a problem as traditional media grows less robust. The new economics of news has reduced the number of foreign correspondents employed by legacy news organizations and created more freelancers with less support and training. For instance,

James Foley, a novice freelancer, was captured in Syria in 2012. One of the companies Foley worked for, the online outlet GlobalPost, tried to get Foley released, but failed. He was beheaded by ISIS in 2014. Jason Rezaian, on the other hand, was the Tehran bureau chief for the *Washington Post* when he was arrested and imprisoned in Iran in 2014 on espionage charges. Pressure from the *Post* and US government ensured Rezaian's release in 2016.

Technology has an impact. New technologies lower barriers to entry for citizens to document events and for news to spread virally. News delivery can be many-to-many through social networks. By providing new source material from citizens and new perspectives, social media can help more traditional foreign correspondents cover foreign affairs. At the same time, it can impede quality coverage (consider the need to file all the time). Also, it will be increasingly hard to verify sources from afar as we rapidly develop technologies to manipulate audio and visual materials. Even as more amateurs can become involved, the expert knowledge needed to discern reality from fiction may be more prized than ever.

But there are strong underlying reasons why foreign news is difficult to report that go far beyond technology. New technologies don't solve some of the fundamental problems associated with foreign correspondents, such as cost and lack of interest from the general public. In those respects, new technology sometimes takes us back to the future. It is easier than ever to be like the 19th-century author Theodor Fontane. Fontane ostensibly worked as a foreign correspondent in London (and had previously lived in London), but in fact he wrote all his articles sitting in Prussia. He gathered his news by mining newspaper reports from London papers. Fontane's actions were so typical that by the 1850s the phenomenon had a generic name: "fake foreign correspondent's letter" (*unechte Korrespondenzen*) (McGillen 2017). While it may be tempting to dismiss this as trivial, the Sisson Documents and the Nazi false-flag operation show they often were consequential. The errant reporting on weapons of mass destruction in Iraq has roots deep in history.

This is not to say that everything is the same today as it was. While the tendencies toward fake news are long existing, the ability to produce them is greater than it was. Just as the telegraph energized bad reporting as well as good from abroad, the Internet and other modern communication technologies have made it possible to avoid editors and go straight to people with the most tendentious reports, who in turn can tweet it to their friends. Our understanding of the psychological weak points in people's ability to process information is also much greater. Still, it is worth noting that we have a lot to learn ourselves about how influential fake news has been. As much as journalists and media scholars are right to deplore fake news—since their enterprise is about truth—we have no clear understanding how much it makes a difference.

For that reason, we maintain, the best way to see new developments in media economics and technology is as a return to how the three trade-offs of independence, speed, and sourcing functioned in the 19th century, when foreign news was full of hoaxes and bogus reporting as well as outstanding correspondents on the ground. We even have an old-new name for this enduring phenomenon: "fake news." Understanding this historical discontinuity *and* continuity is vital if we want to move past trite assertions of novelty in the age of social media.

Recommendations

Our history of foreign correspondents suggests three main lessons for the present and future.

First, foreign correspondents can develop procedures to verify material. Foreign correspondence will never be free of fakery and mistakes. What matters is trying to reduce the possibility of such problems as far as possible. Foreign correspondents will need to be particularly alert to the development of so-called deep fakes, meaning fake audio and video. Fake visuals have existed pretty much since the dawn of photography. One German news agency, Transocean, created fake photos during World War I. Stalin had his smallpox scars airbrushed out. Fashion magazines have photoshopped models for decades. Each time, we have found ways to detect fakery. New technologies have empowered faking but also given us tools for combating it. There is no reason why the future should be different as long as we prepare for it.

Second, news organizations will need to devote increasing resources to help foreign correspondents verify their materials. Verification will not be impossible. But the right procedures will be key. One small organizational change to promote vigilance is the creation of a regular schedule for revisiting and updating verification guidelines. Setting a regular time to update guidelines creates an in-built mechanism to keep organizations up-to-date on the latest technological developments and pushes editors to think about how their newsrooms might adapt (Tworek 2018).

Third, foreign correspondents thrive with freedom. Journalists in the field may not always know best, but the tradition has been to put the best correspondents in the field. This is because the task is so demanding and because they can be trusted. The benefits of giving correspondents freedom is that they can find out not only what we don't know but also what we didn't think to ask. News media need to be watchful that over-management tends to produce stories that are more predictable. Scholars can help bring greater clarity to this problem by comparing reporting from an earlier time with today to determine the extent to which this sort of indexing of stories to Washington is occurring.

References

Ascherson, Neal. 2010. "Ryszard Kapuściński Was a Great Story-Teller, Not a Liar." *The Guardian*, March 3, sec. Books. http://www.theguardian.com/books/booksblog/2010/mar/03/ryszard-kapuscinski-story-liar.

Baudrillard, Jean. 1995. *The Gulf War Did Not Take Place*. Bloomington: Indiana University Press.

Bennett, W. Lance, Regina G. Lawrence, and Steven Livingston. 2007. *When the Press Fails: Political Power and the News Media from Iraq to Katrina*. Chicago: University of Chicago Press.

Bösch, Frank, and Dominik Geppert, eds. 2008. *Journalists as Political Actors: Transfers and Interactions Between Britain and Germany Since the Late 19th Century*. Augsburg: Wissner.

Deedes, W. F. 2003. *At War with Waugh: The Real Story of* Scoop. London: Macmillan.

Domosławski, Artur. 2012. *Ryszard Kapuściński: A Life*. Brooklyn, NY: Verso.

Fletcher, Martin. 2016. "Boris Johnson Peddled Absurd EU Myths—and Our Disgraceful Press Followed His Lead." *The New Statesman*, July 1. https://www.newstatesman.com/politics/uk/2016/07/boris-johnson-peddled-absurd-eu-myths-and-our-disgraceful-press-followed-his.

Geppert, Dominik. 2007. *Pressekriege: Öffentlichkeit und Diplomatie in den deutsch-britischen Beziehungen (1896–1912)*. Munich: Oldenbourg.

Given, John L. 1907. *Making a Newspaper*. New York: Henry Holt.

Hamilton, John Maxwell. 2009. *Journalism's Roving Eye: A History of American Foreign Reporting*. Baton Rouge: Louisiana State University Press.

Hamilton, John Maxwell, and Heidi J. S. Tworek. 2017. "The Natural History of the News: An Epigenetic Study." *Journalism: Theory, Criticism, Practice* 18, no. 4: 391–407. https://doi.org/10.1177/14648849/15625630.

Harding, Luke. 2010. "Poland's Ace Reporter Ryszard Kapuściński Accused of Fiction-Writing." *The Guardian*, March 2, sec. Books. http://www.theguardian.com/world/2010/mar/02/ryszard-kapuscinski-accused-fiction-biography.

Huyn, Hans von. 1939. *Tragedy of Errors. The Chronicle of a European*. Translated by Countess Nora. Wydenbruck: Hutchinson.

Kalb, Marvin. 1993. "In the Days of Carrier-Pigeon Journalism." *Media Studies Journal* 7: 73–79.

Keefe, Patrick Radden. 2013. "Rocket Man: How an Unemployed Blogger Confirmed That Syria Had Used Nuclear Weapons." *The New Yorker*, November 25. http://www.newyorker.com/magazine/2013/11/25/rocket-man-2.

Kennan, George F. 1956. "The Sisson Documents." *Journal of Modern History* 28, no. 2: 130–154.

McGillen, Petra S. 2017. "Techniques of 19th-Century Fake News Reporter Teach Us Why We Fall for It Today." *The Conversation*, April 6. http://theconversation.com/techniques-of-19th-century-fake-news-reporter-teach-us-why-we-fall-for-it-today-75583.

McLynn, Frank. 1990. *Stanley*. Chelsea, MI: Scarborough House.

Moore, Martin. 2010. "Shrinking World: The Decline of International Reporting in the British Press." Media Standards Trust, London. http://mediastandardstrust.org/wp-content/uploads/downloads/2010/10/Shrinking-World-The-decline-of-international-reporting.pdf.

Naujocks, Alfred. 1945. Nuremberg Trial Proceedings, vol. 4, 24th Day, December 20, 1945, Morning Session, 242. http://avalon.law.yale.edu/imt/12-20-45.asp

Picard, Robert G. 2008. "News Consumption and the Business of Journalism." In *New Models for News*, 112–119. Baton Rouge, LA: Manship School of Mass Communications. http://uiswcmsweb.prod.lsu.edu/manship/ReillyCenter/PublicationsandResources/papers/item25318.pdf.

Randal, Jonathan. 2000. "The Decline, But Not Yet Total Fall, of Foreign News in the U.S. Media." 2000–2002. Working Paper Series. The Shorenstein Center on the Press, Politics and Public Policy, Cambridge, MA. https://shorensteincenter.org/wp-content/uploads/2012/03/2000_02_randal.pdf?x78124.

Romm, Tony, and Rani Molla. 2017. "Russia-Related Twitter Account Citations per Day in U.S. News Stories." Recode. November 3. http://apps.voxmedia.com/at/recode-russia-related-twitter-account-citations-per-day-in-u-s-news-stories.

Rosen, Jay. 2006. "The People Formerly Known as the Audience." *Pressthink* (blog), June 27. http://archive.pressthink.org/2006/06/27/ppl_frmr.html.

Russell, William H. 2005. *The Altantic Telegraph*. Stroud: Nonsuch.

Setrakian, Lara. 2017. "3 Ways to Fix a Broken News System." TEDNYC presented at the TED, New York City, January. https://www.ted.com/talks/lara_setrakian_3_ways_to_fix_a_broken_news_industry?

Sheean, Vincent. 1946. *This House Against This House*. New York: Random House.

Smith, Richard Norton. 1997. *The Colonel: The Life and Legend of Robert R. McCormick, 1880–1955*. Boston: Houghton Mifflin.

Snyder, Louis L., and Richard B. Morris. 1951. *They Saw It Happen: Eyewitness Reports of Great Events*. Harrisburg, PA: Stackpole.

Sobel, Meghan, Seoyeon Kim, and Daniel Riffe. 2017. "The International News Hole: Still Shrinking and Linking: 25 Years of *New York Times* Foreign News Coverage," *International Communication Research Journal* 52, no. 2: 3–27.

Tworek, Heidi J. S. 2018. "Responsible Reporting in an Age of Irresponsible Information." Policy Brief 9. Alliance for Securing Democracy, German Marshall Fund of the United States, Washington, DC. http://securingdemocracy.gmfus.org/publications/responsible-reporting-age-irresponsible-information

Tworek, Heidi J. S. 2019. *News from Germany: The Competition to Control World Communications, 1900–1945*. Cambridge, MA: Harvard University Press.
Waugh, Evelyn. 1964. *Scoop: A Novel*. London: Chapman and Hall.
Waugh, Evelyn. 2007. *Waugh in Abyssinia*. Edited with an introduction by John Maxwell Hamilton. Baton Rouge: Louisiana State University Press.

9

Searching for Truth in Fragmented Spaces

Chat Apps and Verification in News Production

Colin Agur and Valerie Belair-Gagnon

Introduction

During the 2014 Umbrella Movement protests in Hong Kong, as tens of thousands of young activists gathered in the city streets, an image circulated on social media showing what appeared to be an armored personnel carrier entering one of the tunnels connecting Hong Kong island to the Kowloon Peninsula. Using WhatsApp and Facebook Messenger—the two most popular means of digital communication for the Umbrella Movement—protesters shared and re-shared the image thousands of times. For many, the meaning was clear: the Hong Kong government, backed by allies in Beijing, had had enough and was mounting a response reminiscent of the crackdown on the Tiananmen Square protests in 1989. But while many people simply re-posted the image, a journalist we spoke to chose to verify it. That person found that the image, while real (in the sense that it had not been digitally altered), was from several years earlier and there was no evidence of imminent military action against the protesters. The diffusion of the image had taken place quickly, often in closed chat groups among friends and factions of the larger movement and had prompted a great deal of excitement and worry. But the truth moved much more slowly, frustrating local authorities who wanted to keep tempers from flaring, as well as moderate protesters who worried that the image might empower more radical factions within the movement and weaken the united front they were struggling to maintain.

This informational challenge was a recurring feature of the Umbrella Movement, in which mobile chat apps—with closed groups and private messages—served as the primary means of digital communication. Since their emergence in the early 2010s, mobile chat applications (e.g., WhatsApp, WeChat, and LINE) have gained massive user bases and given enterprising reporters a new challenge: verify truth in a set of fragmented conversations. Chat apps are media, with a role somewhere between public and private communication. Some allow for conversations among a small number of users (e.g., Facebook Messenger or Telegram), while others enable interactions involving large sets of participants (e.g., WhatsApp and WeChat). Increasingly, encryption has become a common feature of chat apps (with some notable exceptions, such as WeChat), distinguishing them from other social media and giving users greater confidence that their conversations will be safe from surveillance.

In a few short years, chat apps have become popular around the world, with different apps dominating different regions and countries. According to Statista (2018), three giants—WhatsApp, Facebook Messenger, and WeChat—each have more than one billion active users, while QQ Mobile's user base is just shy of 800 million. Several other chat apps—including Skype, Viber, Snapchat, LINE, and Telegram—can claim 200 million or more active users. For reasons of language, user culture, and surveillance, different countries have embraced different chat apps. Often, it is homegrown chat apps that enjoy the most loyal followings, such as WeChat (China), LINE (Japan), and KakaoTalk (Korea). But there are exceptions: though developed in the United States, WhatsApp enjoys widespread usage worldwide, but less so in its country of origin. The significance of chat apps goes beyond user numbers. These apps have taken on new roles as carriers of social life, from daily conversations among friends to family logistics, to study groups for high school and university courses, to discussions among lawmakers concerning legislation. As they have become increasingly central in social life, chat apps have naturally attracted the interest of journalists who see them as tools for news production, distribution, and interaction with audiences.

Chat apps have emerged as major venues for storytelling—in private and public, and in the murky in-between—and journalists have followed stories to the spaces where they are told and retold by users. Given the possibilities of chat apps for newsgathering and sourcing, journalists have also sought to develop robust verification methods that can home in on truths quickly, especially for fast-moving stories of great public interest. For news organizations and individual reporters looking to check facts, chat apps present a set of new opportunities and challenges. Just as they have learned to use pre-existing social media (e.g., Facebook and Twitter) to verify statements, translations, and the integrity of evidence, such as photos and video clips, news organizations and reporters must learn to make use of a new and evolving set of features on chat apps.

One of the distinguishing features of chat apps is their encouragement of private conversations rather than public, searchable posts. This means that discourse on chat apps tends to be fragmented into private and unsearchable group discussions. This fragmentation fosters an intimacy and frankness among participants that, for journalists privy to these conversations who are able to gain access to these conversations, can deepen reporting and enhance storytelling opportunities (e.g., gaining access to student activists' rolling press conferences in WhatsApp groups). But the closed nature of many conversations means that notions of truth are highly contextual; not only divergent facts but also entirely different worldviews can exist simultaneously in separate conversations on the same chat app and in different groups on these apps.

Chat apps are a distinct communicative form and require a distinct approach for journalists reporting on discussions in these spaces. Several features make chat apps distinct from other kinds of social media: the group-oriented structure fosters a fragmented, kaleidoscopic discourse that is home to many different informational priorities, contextual facts, and differentiated senses of reality. For example, in a political protest, different groups might be more or less inclined to believe police estimates of crowd sizes or might differ in their understanding of controversies (for example, if violence erupts between police and protesters, who should bear responsibility). Even photographic evidence is subject to group-level biases, as multiple camera angles could allow for a variety of interpretations (including those that distort the nature of the incident), and of course, photographs can be cropped or altered to give false impressions.

At the same time, there are questions—about building trust within a set of digital structures and interactions—that also apply in other contexts. If online users have met each other in real life or have some kind of social context in which they know each other, they are better able to situate their conversations and decide how to act. In other words, on chat apps and in other fragmented digital spaces, truth-searching involves a process by which reporters and other social media users understand the sociotechnical structure of social media in different contexts. Truth, we argue in this chapter, thus resides in and is shaped by a socio-technical context.

For those who wish for a shared set of facts, chat apps pose troubling questions: when chat apps emphasize group-level discussions that direct conversations away from open, searchable platforms, how can journalists verify claims in fast-moving stories? When group-level "facts" emerge, what authority can journalists claim when reporting truths on contentious topics? And can widely held truths endure as a rapidly growing form of communication encourages further fragmentation of conversations, interpretations, and notions of truth?

In response to these questions, this empirical and inductive chapter identifies several implications for journalism and the search for truth in an age of social media. It begins by highlighting some salient contributions to the relevant literature on chat apps in journalism, then uses a study of chat apps as tools of verification by major news organizations covering political unrest in Hong Kong, then moves to a conceptual discussion of the challenges of journalistic verification in fragmented political spaces. We conclude with a discussion of near-term truth-finding and truth-telling in digital journalism, in which chat apps seem likely to play a significant role.

Mobile Chat Apps: New Trends in Journalism

Any communication technology that allows for greater speed and collaboration will prompt new thinking among journalists and editors about how to integrate that technology into news production. For chat apps, one overarching question is whether they can—or should—blur the notion of "stages" in news production. For example, many practitioners and scholars might think of verification and editing as activities that take place relatively late in the process of producing a news piece. Similar to other social media, with chat apps, reporting teams can create closed groups to share images, videos, quotes, and other material—including user-generated content—that might need to be verified. In response to the growth of social media, the larger news organizations have developed forensic verification teams whose purpose is to locate the origins and veracity of content (e.g., Storyful or the BBC's User-Generated Content hub). These forensic teams have also proven useful with content provided via chat apps by reporters in the field. As these teams review materials from closed or semi-open chat app groups, they provide real-time checks on content and claims. Similarly, editing can take place with reporters still at the sites of newsworthy events, as a real-time and collaborative process rather than as a stage.

This change, while helpful in certain respects, has led to new challenges and complications for journalists seeking truth. Especially when covering fast-moving events, journalists' and news organizations' use of "traditional" social media (e.g., Twitter and Facebook) in verification complicates truth-gathering and truth-telling. Scholars of journalism have found that news organizations, in their efforts to establish and disseminate facts, have made use of the communicative features of social media, bringing audiences closer to—and in some cases, inside—the news production process (see Belair-Gagnon 2015). In this way, workplaces become the intersection of technological infrastructures and human behavior, news gathering, and dissemination of constructed truths. Integration of audiences into news production has created a digital relationship between journalists and audiences, requiring a shared trust of the digital channel and of each other, which goes beyond the face-to-face interactions that journalists have traditionally valued in their work. Recently, mobile technology has taken on a growing importance in reporters' uses of social media, leading notably to complex cross-platform news production and to new sets of practices in verification (e.g., crowdsourcing).

In some respects, chat apps offer a familiar set of crowdsourcing opportunities possible on Twitter or Facebook. For example, by soliciting updates and details from individuals present at a fast-moving event, reporters can view events from multiple vantage points, keep an eye on stories before deciding to go to a particular place, and integrate user-generated content into stories. Chat apps also offer novel possibilities for news organizations, including a mixture of open and closed conversations, as well as interactions on a wide range of scale (from one-to-one to hundreds of participants). As an example, WhatsApp is a combination of mass and interpersonal communication channels. Every day, millions of people use it to communicate with other individuals, much like one-to-one email or text messages. At the same time, WhatsApp functions at different scales, with group sizes from a handful of participants to hundreds of people. Thus a single app is a free and more secure replacement for text messaging and a means for sharing messages and content with an audience of hundreds.

Chat apps have attracted journalistic attention for their use in recent instances of political unrest. With protesters using Viber, Voxer, and others to coordinate protests, journalists have sought to understand and deploy these same apps in their reporting. And in contexts of surveillance, encrypted chat apps such as Signal, Telegram, and WhatsApp allow for secure communication channels with sources. In this context, scholars have emphasized the importance of trust in news organizations' and journalists' relationships with audiences (McBride and Rosenstiel 2013). And in online interactions, trust is crucial in how audiences decide which reporting is reliable and with which journalist or news organization the public may want to interact (see Belair-Gagnon et al. 2017).

Building on this work, this chapter extends old questions about truth-gathering and truth-telling to a new type of media. Chat apps have new features and new complexity, and thus provide a renewed set of contexts for debates about truth. This is a twofold process: chat apps are part of a wider fragmentation of informational structures, including legacy media, websites, and social media. Also, chat apps offer a new and distinctive kind of fragmentation and result in challenges for truths in journalism. To understand this topic, we next explore journalistic trust-building on chat apps in moments of political unrest. By doing so, we can glimpse how journalists and news organizations are developing processes and principles for truth-seeking in fragmented online spaces such as chat apps.

Our Study of Journalistic Uses of Chat Apps During Political Unrest

Large-scale protests can reveal the strengths of individual reporters and entire news organizations, but they also pose challenges for reporters seeking to cover events quickly and accurately. Reporters must make sense of vast quantities of social media content, the heightened pace at which claims and counterclaims arrive in news feeds, and the wide gulf that often forms between opposing sides. Standing in the middle, reporters are often overwhelmed by the speed and volume of information flows, and aware that a great deal of mis- and disinformation is circulating.

In such contexts, reporters have made especially active use of chat apps to verify claims in their coverage of political unrest. This section involves a study of reporting by foreign correspondents during major political unrest, focusing on Hong Kong and China in 2014 and 2016. Given its institutional importance as a major Asia hub for many large news organizations, Hong Kong is an essential context for studying journalistic chat app usage in truth-seeking. In Hong Kong and mainland China, chat apps have become part of everyday communication as WhatsApp (in Hong Kong) and WeChat (in China) are ubiquitous in social life and in news production. Reporters routinely use these apps and others (especially Telegram and Signal, for sensitive inquiries) to gather news, contact sources, and verify information, resulting in renewed challenges for journalists seeking truth in various dialogic and digital spaces.

To study chat apps in journalism, from June 2015 to March 2016, we conducted 34 in-depth semi-structured interviews with foreign correspondents at major international news organizations in Hong Kong and China.[1] This approach had several advantages. First, journalists encountered challenges posed by fragmentation when covering fast-moving events such as political unrest. In Hong Kong and China, the journalists we interviewed sought to be at the forefront of news—knowing, for example, when key announcements were made, when important participants were arrested, or when significant events took place in a large-scale, multi-site protest movement. At the same time, they wanted to verify the claims and evidence (especially photos and videos) they saw on Facebook and WhatsApp groups. Journalists were also keenly aware of another challenge: surveillance. In addition to revealing the scale of the challenge for reporters, our study also had a second advantage: it showed how a range of journalists (from stringers to solo foreign correspondents to reporters working in teams for large news organizations) integrated chat apps into all stages of their reporting. As part of a socio-technical system, journalists use chat apps in newsgathering, sourcing, verification and, in some cases, as digital extensions of the newsroom. Below, we highlight journalists' views on truth in the fragmented spaces that have developed on chat apps. These views are contextualized in terms of how journalists try to adhere to a set of professional values while navigating a polarized set of political voices.

The evidence we gathered reveals divergence in how reporters used chat apps based on their organizational and structural capabilities as reporters, thus offering a variety of options how they do their truth-seeking. News organizations have used chat apps as an extension of their newsrooms, with editors, reporters, and forensic verification teams in constant dialogue on closed groups, cut off from competitor news organizations. Solo reporters, especially those who have flown in to cover a story on short notice and are less connected with local sources, joined chat app groups populated by other reporters similarly trying to sift through large amounts of information (often in an unfamiliar language) or sort out which sources are trustworthy and which claims are facts. Although they were rivals in the sense that they represent different news organizations, these solo reporters often found that they could improve their coverage thanks to the knowledge and contacts available via these groups. In these divergent ways—as mobile and digital extensions of newsrooms and as sites for crowdsourcing and trading favors among journalists—chat apps have emerged as distinct forms of news spaces.

Verifying Claims and Content in Fragmented Spaces

As protests evolve over days and weeks, factions and small groups can deepen, resulting in a more divided set of communicative spaces. In the Umbrella Movement, for instance, the initial moment of unity proved difficult to sustain, as competing subgroups—each with an agenda, leaders, preferred modes of communication and, often, a geographical base within the encampment—focused on digital narrowcasting messages to core supporters. The fragmenting of discourse into closed digital spaces creates new problems for journalists: how to catalogue and verify claims of fact, and how to build trust with potential sources.

Verification on Chat Apps

For journalists following fast-moving events using chat apps, searching for updates involves their networks of sources and the communication methods favored by those individuals. Increasingly, this means that journalists join small online group discussions, where members (using real or assumed names) claim to have witnessed events or have information that could update or change a story. Journalists can join groups in a variety of ways. Frequently, encounters in real life (at public meetings or social gatherings) might lead to an online connection between a reporter and a source, as well as an invitation to join a private group. Sometimes reporters might be invited by a group that seeks news coverage of its activities. Other times, because journalists often develop ties to local communities or to organizations with topical specialties, the journalist might learn of a chat app group and ask a member if she can join. In each of the instances described above, reporters identified their occupation and employer before asking questions of other group members or using content from private groups in reporting.

An online first journalist summed up a frequent problem: "It's hard to verify those claims, but . . . I think that when I've opened some of those chat rooms, you see a bunch of random people talking, and since it's random people that don't know each other, and they're all anonymous." While the online form of these fragmented spaces may be new, verification has a long history in news production, and news organizations have sought to apply some old tried-and-tested measures in these new contexts. One digital journalist who follows newsroom policy found that having a "rigid system" is an essential trait for anyone trying to assess claims on chat apps:

> Our [news organization's] nature now is just to not assume that something is true face value, and in the case that you are unsure, and I want to tweet something I would just say, "This has not been verified but this is something that is been circulating around Hong Kong media. I do not vouch for it is accuracy, but this is what people are saying." From a professional point of view, I cannot tweet things that we [the news organization] have not deemed to be true so I am pretty safe on that front.

In the verification process, journalists also question group members who make claims about events. This means introducing themselves as reporters, identifying the claim(s) they wish to verify, giving the individual an opportunity to provide evidence. This might include a video, photo, or audio recording, or a detailed eyewitness account with contextual information that establishes the credibility of the claims. One journalist explained the process by which the reporter relied on formal sources (i.e., the police) to verify claims on chat apps:

> I would say, "Hey, I am a reporter, can I verify with you that a police officer used pepper spray? Can you describe for me how they used the pepper spray, and how many times did they use it, on how many people they used it?" I ask multiple people just to verify a single claim that pepper spray had been used at one of the major points of confrontation during the later days of the Occupy protest. I did that as part of my verification, and then I would of course call the police to ask them to verify if pepper spray was used there, and if they would give me any details. The police very often do not have the information immediately available, so I did have to rely on eyewitness accounts, on secondary sources, meaning these protesters.

Thus the verification process involves a mixture of traditional reporting (calling the police to ask what level of force officers had used in a particular situation) and the application of old methods in different contexts (asking multiple members of chat app groups individually about their experiences in that same situation). In this instance, the reporter's efforts established that there had been pepper spray, but it was unclear whether it was by police or agent provocateurs or counter-protesters. Accordingly, when writing the piece, the reporter signposted to the audience what had and had not been verified: "I would write that protesters said they had been pepper sprayed, but not that the police pepper sprayed protesters to distinguish between what I saw and what protesters said." As political organizers have made active use of chat apps, reporters and news organizations have learned not only the benefits of reporting in these spaces but also the risks. While it may be tempting to run some of the claims and user-generated content that emerge from group discussions on chat apps, unverified material and claims can discredit stories and the people who report them. Thus, news organizations have established editorial policies on what to include and what thresholds must be met in terms of verification. For example, a foreign correspondent told us: "If we verify the date, we would still say 'unverified' just to be transparent with the readers. Sometimes we'll do that, and then obviously we will replace it with verified information as soon as we get that."

In this sense, verification emerges not just as an internal process but as a set of internal newsroom policies and signals to the reader. News organizations can include verified and unverified content and make clear to the reader what has gone through a robust set of checks and what may be the latest developments but has yet to be as thoroughly examined by institutional processes and individual fact-checkers.

When covering political unrest and other fast-moving stories, reporters and news organizations have developed editorial policy and processes and sought to communicate them to readers (e.g., signposting), as well as relied on a network of trusted or formal sources to demonstrate the rigor of verification for content sourced from chat apps. In doing so, reporters have highlighted their role as arbiters of trusted facts in the socio-technical system of chat apps and in their reporting.

Trust and the Role of Journalists in Verification

Chat apps can empower the voices and claims of participants and undermine the authority of journalists as providers of fresh, factual updates.

In their efforts to retain professional authority, journalists must make decisions about what types of facts to convey and how to be transparent about the verification process, such as by relying on formal sources and personal observation on the ground:

> During Occupy, most facts that we put in there are what people say. Like, an official said that the protest was unlawful, and they would trust someone with whatever charges they were going to make. These claims are easily verifiable, like going straight to the source, which is the government. If the police make claims, and you can call the police spokespeople, and then ask for a comment from them, straight from the source, that I consider is confidently verified. Then the other kind of fact that I put in that story is observation of things that happen on the ground.

By making decisions about what facts to privilege and how to present the verification process to audiences, journalists reinforce their role as monitors of facts. Journalists also reinforce their authority through sourcing by using traditional practices. As with other communication technology, journalists make themselves visible on chat apps as individuals who want fresh, useful, and truthful content, and who can be trusted to protect sources from surveillance and from those who would threaten those sources.

Journalistic communication on chat apps with users also may mean developing long-term relationships with trusted, often senior, members of a group. These relationships give journalists reference points when trying to understand the validity and meaning of user generated content, said one journalist: "there are certain accounts that you follow. I mean, as a journalist you can make that judgment whether an account is reliable or not if somebody is posting." Similarly, reporters also use sources on chat apps not just to follow up within an online discussion but also to decide which facts to verify via other traditional methods: "I would definitely take a look at the [activist's Twitter] feed. If there was something crazy happening, we would either send somebody there on a scene or again, and verify through actual things you can see rather than just a photo," said a journalist.

For reporters covering the Umbrella Movement, this often meant calling one of a few visible student leaders who made themselves available to media. The volume of content (text, videos, and photos) on WhatsApp led journalists to pause, make note of certain claims, and get in contact with

Joshua Wong (a prominent figure in the movement) or another protest leader:

> Let's say somebody tweeted, or wrote on WhatsApp, or there was a news article that said, "they're planning to lead all of the students out of the camps tonight," either we would word it really carefully, like "so-and-so suggested that this is happening" or we would really always try to verify directly, by asking Joshua, "Hey are you really planning on retreating tonight?"

But it is not always so easy to sort truth from misinformation on chat apps. As a foreign correspondent lamented, "it is quite hard to find the original uploader on a lot of these chat programs, WeChat obviously being the biggest one. I think you really need to have somebody who is entrenched in WeChat and uses it regularly." Similarly, another journalist pointed to the difficulty of developing and maintaining meaningful contacts in fragmented spaces.

In these interactions, both in person and on chat apps, trust is essential for journalists establishing their authority. By developing relationships the old-fashioned way—in face-to-face encounters, often on the source's home turf—journalists establish that they are serious about the story, its details, and the people who can provide those details. As sourcing relationships continue in digital spaces, journalists can leverage trust to gain other contacts and access to closed groups.

While journalists and news organizations have learned ways to search for truth and maintain their professional authority on chat apps, a more fundamental challenge is presenting itself. With the one-too-many model of broadcast and print media struggling to compete with the more personalized and dynamic social media, and with group-based discussions so popular on chat apps, journalists may find that truth-telling becomes more difficult.

Truth as a Socio-Technical System

The Umbrella Movement involved a fragmented set of conversations in closed chat app groups, as well as reporters each trying to find a distinct way of covering the protests. The result was a differentiated set of approaches (teams of varying sizes, and a variety of practices in newsgathering, sourcing, and verification). Yet some journalists—especially stringers, solo foreign correspondents, and those who lacked language skills or local knowledge—used chat apps to collaborate, verify claims and content, and piece together fragments of a larger conversation. For example, a reporter described the potential chat apps offer for cooperative reporting between journalists and across news organizations by claiming that a chat app "makes the information [during unrest] much more transparent to a journalist."

Yet, journalists who were based in Hong Kong and had language skills and local knowledge had less of an incentive to share their findings with other journalists, especially those who had just flown in to cover the story. And reporters who worked for large, well-resourced news organizations tended not to contribute to these collaborative projects, either by choice or because of policies that prescribed certain practices for chat apps. Yet to get a sense of the competition and to see the larger picture of reporting, reporters kept an eye on what took place in these groups: "The journalists group we kind of ignored, to be honest. We are not going to rely on competitors. But it would give us a gauge. It would give us an idea of what they are talking about."

While the closed nature of many chat app discussions enables many group-level "facts" and evidence, journalists try to keep their eyes on a larger picture. This means maintaining a broad set of contacts, with competing viewpoints and differing agendas, in groups that might not communicate with one another. This also means developing a set of robust processes to check claims across different contexts, use trusted sources as reference points in contentious or fast-moving discussions, and strike a balance between patience and speed in publishing the latest development. And last, this means conveying to the reader the processes used to find and verify information from chat apps. While fragmented spaces present a new set of challenges for broadly held truths, but as reporting from the Umbrella Movement shows, journalists and news organizations have developed a set of approaches to piece together large-scale truths from small, isolated discussions on chat apps: from developing internal editorial policy about trust to relying on official sources on these apps. Yet, these approaches vary from the solo reporter to the legacy newsroom with a large foreign bureau abroad. These apps nevertheless may offer reporting speed and scale and opportunity for the solo journalist.

Discussion: Truth-Finding and Trust-Building in Digital Journalism

In sum, while journalists use chat apps for news production by seeking truthful information, they interact in these diverse fragmented spaces at different speeds and scales, thus allowing for gaps and different levels in knowledge production of newsworthy events. Journalistic uses of chat apps highlight organizational and political power struggles also present in dialogic forms of communication. In other words, the journalists' uses of the apps are the outcomes of interactions between humans and the apps they use. As a first example, evidence shows that the encryption of a handful of chat apps and journalistic uses of these apps may be the result of journalists' need to have trustworthy and confidential conversations with sources in contexts of political censorship and surveillance. As a second example, and in contrast to the first example, the user-profile section available on some chat apps acts as an identity-shaping mechanism that signals who claims to be a journalist or who may not in the system of truth-seeking. Thus, chat apps create opportunities for reporters to signal professional intent in building trust and relationships with apps users. A related point is that profile names and pictures allowed reporters to access protesters within WhatsApp private groups. And, as a third example, coordination efforts among foreign correspondents seeking truth on chat apps during unrest highlight a need for these journalists, who have a similar set of professional experiences compared with local reporters, to report news on the fly as news organizations report on nimble budgets and crisis events unfold in different and sparse locations. These apps thus represent a complex socio-technical system that reflects tensions in professional news making and truth-seeking in the knowledge economy.

Some of the same developments as described above will continue to pose challenges for journalists seeking truth in fragmented spaces as a socio-technical environment. Chat apps will become more multifaceted (e.g., Facebook taking on characteristics of Snapchat and other chat apps). These changes in the structure of these apps will require technical skills and communicative nuance from reporters. Chat apps will also continue to emphasize group-based conversations (meaning that more and more useful content will exist in closed spaces, as opposed to open discussions on microblogging sites such as Twitter). A particular challenge for journalists and news organizations will be the ephemeral nature of much content, due in some cases to design, as in Snapchat. And due to the popularity and convenience of chat apps, they will be the preferred sites for protest organizers and for dissemination of protest-related content. More and more critical discussions (protest planning and coordination) will take place on chat apps, meaning that these spaces will be of greater significance to reporters.

While the functionalities of chat apps are important, the medium does not make or break the truth. Rather, the functionalities of a medium, combined with its user culture, provide users with a set of communicative norms that aid or hinder efforts at truth-gathering and truth-telling. As with other social media, journalists and other chat apps users navigate the socio-technical system of chat apps when seeking truth. In these different contexts, truth becomes a process by which journalists and chat apps users make sense of facts that emerge in different settings and attempt to establish a shared sense of an emerging reality.

Lessons for Journalists and News Audiences

- For journalists in large organizations, a pressing challenge is to understand and deploy a set of (often complex and large-scale) processes to seek truth on chat apps.
- For journalists at small news organizations (or those with limited resources), mastering chat apps will involve learning a wide set of technical, social, and evaluative skills.
- For news audiences, finding broad truths will require self-awareness about filter bubbles and a desire to actively seek out a range of informed perspectives on political issues.

Note

1. We began by seeking interviews from reporters who had written the 2014 Umbrella Movement protests in Hong Kong; we then reached out to other journalists in foreign correspondents' communities, based on interviewees' recommendations and further discoveries of journalists who had covered protests in Hong Kong and China. Our interviews lasted an average of 60 minutes and focused on how reporters used chat apps to verify facts. Our subject pool included a range of journalists: 15 women, 19 men, from print newspapers and their digital editions, print magazines and their

digital editions, digital-first sites, wire services, and broadcast (television and radio). We coded the interviews by reading all of their contents and tagged segments of interest related to verification and truth in reporting using chat apps.

References

Belair-Gagnon, Valerie. 2015. *Social Media at BBC News: The Re-Making of Crisis Reporting*. New York: Routledge.

Belair-Gagnon, Valerie, Colin Agur, and Nicholas Frisch. 2017. "Mobile Sourcing: A Case Study of Journalistic Norms and Usage of Chat Apps." *Mobile Media and Communication* 6, no. 1: 53–70.

McBride, Kelly, and Tom Rosenstiel. 2013. *The New Ethics of Journalism*. Thousand Oaks, CA: CQ Press.

Statista. 2018. "Most Popular Global Mobile Messenger Apps as of April 2018, Based on Number of Monthly Active Users." https://www.statista.com/statistics/258749/most-popular-global-mobile-messenger-apps/.

10

The Use and Verification of Online Sources in the News Production Process

Sophie Lecheler, Sanne Kruikemeier, and Yael de Haan

Introduction

The abundance of information offered online is not exclusive to journalists, but open for the general public to consume, share, reuse, and even recreate news. Also, the world around us has become more complex with global political issues and conflicts in myriad policy realms. Information and misinformation can be spread rapidly. In this social media era, the task of journalists is now more than ever to inform the public with information that is both relevant and reliable. True, the online environment has facilitated the production process with journalists using online tools and quickly being able to find and select online information (Lecheler and Kruikemeier 2016; Lewis 2015; Jordaan 2013; Paulussen and Harder 2014). Yet, the online environment has put journalists to a difficult task as how to verify their sources and select information. Others have examined how the rise of the Internet changed the fundamentals of journalistic news production (see e.g., Hermida et al. 2014; Usher 2014). Still, we know surprisingly little about the selection *and* verification of information in the digital environment, especially given that not only journalists but also algorithms prioritize, filter, and classify information (Diakopoulos 2014).

Hence we will be evaluating how journalists today select online sources for their stories, how they interpret the validity of different online tools and sources, and how they evaluate the possibilities of verifying these when producing quality news. Consequently, this chapter examines the available research on *how* and *which* online sources journalists use today, and *how* journalists can verify information online.[1] We also discuss how the use of online sources affects the prevalence of balanced and objective reporting in mediated discourses. First, we will review research examining the use of sources (*selection*) and the credibility of online information (*verification*; Lecheler and Kruikemeier 2016). We argue that digitalization has not changed all that much. Indeed, scholars have found that journalistic routines as to which sources are selected remain relatively stable. What has changed, however, are verification techniques. Therefore, we see that there are newly developed online source verification strategies developing within the profession that allow journalists to find new paths toward reliable information selection.

The chapter's second section presents a short case study on how journalists in the Netherlands select and verify sources online. In a country with a highly professional journalism culture, a high level of pluralism, and a strong tradition of public service broadcasting (Hallin and Mancini 2004), online affordances have altered the way journalists produce the news. Based on empirical research of Dutch scholars, an elite survey ($N = 201$), and our online observational study of journalists' research activities, we answer the question of how Dutch journalists use and verify sources online.

Source Selection: Same Old Routines?

The study of source selection is integral to journalism research, as it describes the fundamental relationship between journalists and those persons, channels, and events that provide information during the news production process. In this sense, source selection has been of interest not only to those who study journalism as a professional routine but also to scholars within political research and political communication who are interested in how journalists select the elite and citizen voices that are ultimately heard in public discourse. In a digitalized society, one of the most important initial arguments along these lines was that selecting sources online will have a democratizing effect on journalistic production, allowing "normal" citizens easier access to the news through social and participatory media, and thereby shifting the power balance away from elites. Along the same lines, scholars have asked whether the emergence of online opportunities of sourcing has perhaps led to a displacement of proven-and-tested "offline" sourcing techniques (Sellers and Schaffner 2007), such as press conferences, press agencies, interviews, publications, or stakeouts.

However, as it is often the case when studying change, first results are not as groundbreaking as expected. Speaking generally, current work takes the point that online sources have not actually replaced offline sources. Instead they are more of an addition to journalistic sourcing routines. This generalization (or normalization) comes with the limitation that most existing studies focus on "traditional" journalistic setups, such as newsrooms and press corps, thereby perhaps not taking into account changing contexts of journalistic news production. For example, the increase of public-relations generated stories coming from outside the newsroom is influencing the newsgathering, selection, and verification of journalists (Lewis et al. 2008). Also, online practices such as the aggregation and curation of online news (Bakker 2014) and automated journalism, where stories are automated based on algorithmic writing (Van Dalen 2012; Van der Kaa and Krahmer 2014), have challenged journalistic sourcing routines. However, the above argument (of a power change in journalism due to online sourcing) has not yet been demonstrated; rather, elite news sources continue to dominate reporting.

Most journalists use online sources in their research process or information gathering and see it as vital (Jordaan 2013; Paulussen and Harder 2014). Hence, digitalization is a pivotal construct to consider when studying professional motivations and role conceptions. Yet while websites are important online sources for journalists (Lariscy et al. 2009), they continue to choose elite sources when gathering online information—precisely the same way as they would "offline." This trend is further evidenced in research that examined how social media were used as newsgathering tools in the UK news coverage of the Iranian elections in 2009. The study authors found that "although the mythology of the Internet as an equal place where all voices are equal, and have equal access to the public discourse, a kind of idealized 'public sphere' continues, the practices of journalists and the traditions of coverage continue to ensure that traditional voices and sources are heard above the crowd" (Knight 2012, 61). Thus, established routines of selecting formal elite sources still prevails as journalists adhere to traditional practices of selection, where they can easily verify their sources and information or that they feel might be most reliable, also because that is what they are used to. Machill and Beiler (2009) showed that online research tools complement traditional research strategies, but that journalists mostly prefer to use the telephone to do their research. Interestingly, Van Leuven et al. (2014) did not find that the more traditional ways of using sources changed or decreased, even after the use of online sources became important. It seems that online sources still function as a substitute for offline sources. However, they do function as *inspiration* for later news stories

(Tylor 2015). Thus, while there is definitely substantial use of online sources in news production, researchers seem to suggest that this new practice has not actually increased democratization in the news. Reliance on traditional styles of verification, as well as trust in established elites, is still very much prevalent in the news.

The question remains as to which factors determine whether an online source becomes part of a news story. We address this question along several lines. First, there is reason to believe that journalists will use online sources more when they report about news focusing on soft or human interest news (Moon and Hadley 2014). This perhaps indicates that journalists do not consider online sources as reliable or high in quality as traditional methods of information search. Second, it seems that the media outlet at stake makes a difference. Journalists working for online media seem to use online sources more often (Gulyas 2013). Journalists working for an online news outlet might feel more pressure to publish news at a much earlier stage, as news websites are constantly updated, especially when live-blogging news events (Thurman and Walters 2013). Finding, collecting, and using information from traditional sources is often slower, while information from online news sources, such as social media, can be obtained at any time. Further, journalists working for broadcast media are more likely to collect information from online sources compared to newspaper journalists (Gulyas 2013). Along the lines of the above, research has also indicated that journalists working for tabloid newspapers use social media more frequently as a news source compared with broadsheet journalists (Broersma and Graham 2013, but see Paulussen and Harder 2014). Broersma and Graham (2013, 460) note that "tabloids are bulk consumers of tweets," and "that both the working conditions and the journalistic norms in tabloid newsrooms might promote this practice." Seemingly, media that use less in-depth news reporting are more likely to use online sources. Hence, online and social media sources have become a part of daily journalistic routine, which is intrinsically related to the norms and values within the media organization.

When reviewing the literature on source selection, there are also differences according to methodological approaches within available studies. In interview and survey studies, journalists often state that social media are very important for their work due to the open nature of these sources and quick accessibility. Social media are often used to monitor events or to find spoken sources (Brandtzaeg et al. 2016). In those studies, it seems that journalists feel a need to learn additional skills to handle such new sourcing strategies (Braentzaeg et al. 2016 Jordaan 2013; O'Sullivan and Heinonen 2008). However, content analyses show that the actual use of, for instance social media as "direct" sources in news production is limited—they thus function as "inspiration" but are rarely visible in reporting. Even though there seems to be a lot of hype around their importance in journalism, scholars note that content coming from social media is not always detectable in the news (Knight 2012; Machill and Beiler 2009). Furthmore, research also indicates that social media are mainly used in the initial information-gathering stage for retrieving background information on elite source such as politicians, or social media are used to add opinions from ordinary citizens ("vox pop") to add "flavor" to a story (Broersma and Graham 2012; 2013).

Taking these studies into consideration, it seems that online information, for example, from social media, is important for journalists as they offer them new and useful ways of accessing information. However, more recent studies, focusing on specific cases, indicate that social media content is used when "other" information is unavailable. One illustrative example is research concerning the Arab Spring. Information coming from foreign journalists was limited during that period, and consequently, social media content was used intensively (e.g., AlMaskati 2012; Hermida et al. 2014).

Thus, given previous work that focused on online sourcing techniques and especially the use of social media, we cannot argue that the Internet has completely changed journalists' sourcing routines and source selection. As mentioned, journalists use online and social media content from the public ("vox pop") in the initial information-gathering stage or to enrich a news story. However, news stories remain dominated by elite sources, which indicates established power balances are largely intact.

Verification of Online Sources: Unknown Challenges?

Moving on from the mere selection of sources, we come to a more fundamental question: If online sources are selected, how can journalists reliably show that their informational value is there? This becomes particularly relevant in the contemporary era, where an increasing chorus of critical voices is directed toward the media and journalists (Egelhofer and Lecheler 2017). It is also relevant when we evaluate journalism as a profession that suffers from a time-pressured environment; an overload of information is available online, and information is offered by media outlets at a fast pace. In short, journalists are confronted with difficulties in verifying sources online (Hermida 2013). Journalists are not only challenged with a wealth of online information, but also the search and subsequent selection of information has shifted in the online environment. It seems that search engines now take a prominent role.

What is particularly striking is a change in the *architecture* of searching for information when researching a story. Before the Internet's rise, many journalists started their research by contacting people in their personal networks. Another way was to follow press agencies (Reich 2011). In the Internet era, journalists rely more and more on search engines to find relevant and reliable information. In the past, journalists often had exclusive access to sources (e.g., through use of press cards). Now, journalists and citizens are able to search for the same information online, often starting with a search engine such as Google (Carlson 2007; Tylor 2015).

Thus, it is common practice for journalists to use search engines in the initial research phase. What is crucial is that journalists consider search engines to be an accurate and professional strategy to find and select credible sources (Lecheler and Kruikemeier 2016). However, whereas journalists select sources based on journalistic principles such as relevancy and trustworthiness (thereby often reinforcing elite bias), search engines rely on the "rules" of algorithms (Gillespie 2014). Journalists might thus implicitly "fall prey" to the architecture of algorithms: research shows that journalism students favor sources offered on the first page of the search engine results, and those on the top of (personalized) result lists (Tylor 2015). Fink-Shamit and Bar-Ilan found in 2008 that Internet users invariably assess website quality in a particular way. This could indicate that journalists not only assess the quality by examining the rank of the source but also the title of the sources, the description given on the search engine, and whether the key words appear in the results. These relevant factors may affect which sources are selected when found through search engines. Consequently, the output of the research increasingly relies on the logic of computer algorithms, which in turn is based on the users' past research activities, as well as other invisible factors (Gillespie 2014). The open question is what the impact of that choice is on the trustworthiness of journalists' daily research activities. Note that we do not know how "positive" or "negative" this reliance on search engines vis-à-vis more traditional forms of information searches is. The idea of an algorithm inherently implies bias, but journalistic bias was already present and strong way before the Internet age. So, we must be concerned with whether algorithmic or search engine–led research is more or less balanced than that of human selection. This too is an open question.

In light of the above changes, it is even more important to emphasize a need for novel forms of online verification techniques. No matter how a journalist arrived at a specific source, how are they to know where a tweet came from, or whether a picture has been retouched? In a recent study, we suggest a categorization of online verification strategies, based on a number of ideas previously suggested by other authors (De Haan, Kruikemeier, and Lecheler 2017). We find that, online, journalists employ either (1) explicit, (2) hybrid circular, or (3) hybrid background verification techniques. *Explicit strategies* refer are the use of different computerized tools to verify information online (Schifferes et al. 2014; Silverman 2014). There are tools focusing on verifying images and the location of a specific event (Silverman 2014). While new tools are always becoming available, journalists are often unfamiliar with them or lack the skills to use them. Some even doubt whether these tools can verify the authenticity of the source, despite claims they can do so (Brandtzaeg et al. 2016; Schifferes et al. 2014).

While explicit verification strategies make use of specific verification tools, hybrid strategies combine searching, selection, and verification activities. When using a variety of sources to check and double-check the online information we refer to a form of hybrid verification called *circular verification strategies*. Shapiro and colleagues describe the process as journalists "interweaving between verification and original information gathering" (2013, 667). Social media sources are verified using other more elite online sources, or information found in media sources is traced to the original online source. The third, *background verification strategies*, describes another hybrid form of verification through a process where a journalist checks the origin or background of a specific source or platform. Social media profiles can be verified by checking the person's profile, number of followers, and friends. Verifying the origin of a website, by looking at the contact page or searching for background information, helps the journalists judge the relevancy and trustworthiness of a site. Even search engines can be checked by analyzing who the contributors are and the history of the content they have placed. In sum, we consider verification techniques the most fundamental part of studying online sourcing. Verification includes information and search strategies used to arrive at a source, as well as the explicit or implicit steps taken afterward to verify those sources. We assert that search engines now guide journalists' information search, who have in turn developed novel ways of understanding how reliable online sources are. This understanding is that there should be at least three types of verification strategies when checking sources online.

Case Study: Dutch Journalists and Digital Sources

To obtain in-depth insight into the use and verification of digital sources, we present evidence from a short case study in the Netherlands. The Netherlands presents an interesting case as it has a high Internet penetration rate; almost every citizen in the Netherlands has Internet access, which normalizes Internet use. Additionally, previous work has shown that many Dutch journalists use digital content when gathering news; around 75% of journalists spend more than two hours per day on the Internet (Hermans et al. 2011).

To begin our case study, we describe how Dutch journalists use digital sources and the extent to which they verify information obtained from these digital sources. To do this, we look at (1) previous work from colleagues in the Netherlands, and we give some ideas from our (2) empirical work by describing the outcomes of a questionnaire distributed among journalists in the Netherlands ($N = 201$), and the outcomes of a smaller observational study examining how journalism students verify online information. The questionnaire was distributed online in the Netherlands in November and December of 2016. The average age of a Dutch journalist in the survey was nearly 49 years old; 42% were female; 17% work as a journalist in an organization as a staff member (paid employment); 60% work as a freelance journalist; 6% does both (staff journalist and freelance); and 18% have another position. In our observational study, we asked journalism students ($N = 48$) to prepare a journalistic product (i.e., finding information online in preparation of writing the actual news article). These journalism students already completed, on average, four years of journalism school, and 43% were already working as a journalist. We tracked the online behavior of journalism students by recording their screens while they were searching for information their journalistic product. Afterward, we coded the recorded data (for full study details, see De Haan et al. 2017).

Results

The Use of Digital Sources

Previous work shows that the Internet plays a major role in the daily routines of journalists in the Netherlands, either searching for information or the channels they use (e.g., the websites they visit). Survey research, conducted in 2010 by Hermans, Vergeer, and Pleijter in the Netherlands found that most journalists feel that the Internet is a useful tool for their journalistic work. The study reported that 78.5% of journalists use the Internet to search for new ideas, 89.9% for new information sources, and 86.9% for finding new experts. In addition, the Internet is used to find information about events that happen faraway, for instance abroad (Hermans et al. 2011).

The Platforms Used for Digital Sources

Journalists' use of the Internet, especially social media, is also reflected in the platforms used, as Broersma and Graham (2012), for instance, discovered that tweets from politicians are often reported in Dutch newspapers. Our research confirms these observations. Our survey shows that Dutch journalists frequently use various digital channels to find information. The use of organizations' websites is popular among journalists and is therefore regularly used.[2] With regard to social media channels, we find some interesting results. First, Dutch journalists regularly use information from Wikipedia. It is also not a surprise that information from Twitter and Facebook is used in the research process. But, other social media, such as YouTube and Instagram, are used less frequently (see figure 10.1). Lastly, we found that journalists often use search engines, such as Google.

Digital Sources Used When Searching for Information

In line with those findings, Kemman and colleagues (2013) show that Dutch journalists mainly use standard digital channels when searching for information online, particularly general search engines. More advanced channels for searches, such as Google Alert or Google Scholar are used by only a few Dutch journalists (Kemman et al. 2013). Our observational study found that journalism students relied heavily on search engines to find information, particularly Google, but more advanced tools, such as Google Scholar, were rarely used. Most interestingly, students often clicked on the first or second search result of the Google page. They also rarely moved

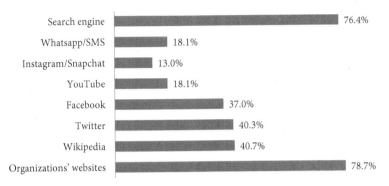

Figure 10.1 The use of digital news channels by Dutch journalists in percentages.

Note: Use of digital news channels was measured on a 5-point scale; the options "regularly" (3), "often" (4), and "always" (5) are combined, and this percentage is shown.

beyond the first page, which indicates that the students relied profoundly on the algorithms offered by Google.

Types of Channels Used

Regarding the channels that are used, it seems that more elite and legacy media platforms are consulted. When examining which sources were selected, our observational study found that journalism students often focus on elite and media sources (i.e., legacy media) when consulting the Internet for information. Thus journalism students follow traditional journalistic routines when searching for information online. Lastly, regarding social media, our study confirms that Twitter is often consulted to find more information, for example, about a well-known actor. Thus, altogether, these results indicate that digital sources are essential in the news production process. Yet, still more traditional sourcing patterns are followed, and elite sources remain dominant.

Verification of Digital Sources

More crucially, however, is the question to what extent Dutch journalists verify the information that they find online. Hermans et al. (2011) show that 66.3% of Dutch journalists claim that they use the Internet to check information. In line with this finding, Hermans et al. (2011) note that Dutch journalists often *claim* that they also verify online information: 79.4% of the Dutch journalists argue that they do so. One way to verify online information is by finding the "original source," which is done by 84.8% of the Dutch journalists. In our observational study, we refer to this as the circular verification strategy. We observed that a circular verification strategy, which is a form of hybrid verification strategy, was used frequently. This means that participants in our study verified by switching back and forth between various elite sources and a search engine (De Haan et al. 2017). However, another hybrid technique, background verification, was most often used. This strategy is characterized by, for example, checking social media account information or by employing website background checks (e.g., by checking the "About" section of a website). Besides the use of more hybrid forms of online verification, we found that available and thus more explicit automated tools to verify information online are rarely used. For instance, only LinkedIn was used to directly check the background of a source. Other forms, such as reverse image searches or other tools, were not consulted.

Taken together, these findings indicate that journalists verify information online. However, they do so using hybrid forms of verification. This means that the verification strategies online are present but have a more implicit than explicit character.

Journalists' Perception Regarding Verification of Digital Sources

Our survey confirms that journalists find it important to verify information, particularly regarding the digitalization of news in combination with the rise of commercialization in the media and the increased number of freelancers. While our observational study shows that journalists verify online sources and information, even though often implicit, time pressure, the fragmentation of news, and growth of social media puts pressure on the quality of news. One respondent of the survey argued, "Quantity is more important than quality: websites need to be filled quickly, and preferably with scoops. The accuracy of reporting, or the quality, is less relevant." Other journalists agreed, and mention that this is especially important online. "News is too often incorrect, especially on digital media, but also in newspapers. Claims are not checked." Therefore, journalists seem to see the verification of information as very important and as challenging. A journalist mentioned that "more and more [journalists] should take into account the verification and reliability of sources."

Concluding Remarks

This chapter aimed at providing a short introduction to how journalists use and verify online media sources during the news production process. "Good" journalism heavily depends on its claim to be accurate and provide truthful information. So, how has digitalization affected that claim? While the study of digital sources remains a moving target, where scholarship is outdated pretty much as soon as it is published, we believe that the literature allows for at least two initial conclusions.

First, while online sources are used, there is little indication that they have fundamentally changed issues such as elite bias in news journalism, nor do we see a complete change in the value journalists place on "traditional" techniques of news production through personal contact and on-site research. Besides, as many online sources are difficult to verify, it might also not be surprising that journalists stick with elite or formal sources, either online or offline. Short deadlines and less know-how about the verification of online sources may partly explain why journalists often select elite sources. Thus, journalists clearly access social media, for instance, during the research process. But, are they doing so to give a clearer voice to citizens, or are social media just quick access tools to the same sources that have always dominated journalistic reporting?

Second, there is a clear challenge to how online and social media sources should be verified. Our own research indicates that journalists have begun to intuitively develop hybrid forms of verification. How effective these forms really are in preventing misinformation or mistakes in reporting, however, remains a question for future research. Along these lines, we wonder if implicit or hybrid forms of verification should not be replaced with more explicit and testable verification techniques in future journalism generations. For instance, search engines often guide information search and verification. Search engines, however, are factors in their own right within the verification process, whose impact is not fully understood. They are our gateway to information, but should not journalists have somehow more "privileged" access, and how can newsrooms accomplish such access in a digital world? So, while there are many open questions yet to be answered, we are sure of one thing at this point; these questions form a foundation that may guide future inquiry into how journalists relate to their sources.

More concrete, we suggest several actions for journalists to guide the research production process in an online environment. First, it seems that journalists are not aware of the vast number of tools available to guide and facilitate their research process. Workshops and in-house training can motivate journalists to use search and verification tools in their daily working routine.

Second, while journalists are adapting verification strategies, the hybrid forms could be made more explicit. It seems that journalists verify their sources online, but it is not always clear if these verification actions are done consciously and explicitly, both for themselves and for their colleagues. Reflection on this process within the newsroom could enhance the awareness of online verification strategies.

Lastly, in this Internet era, journalists cannot imagine working without search engines such as Google. However, there is little awareness of how search engines can influence journalists' research process. While journalists might not have the power to influence algorithms, we suggest more knowledge and awareness on how the Internet works beyond the visible interface.

These suggestions might not immediately lead to more verified information or a better "truth" of what happens around us, but it is a first step of awareness in new research routines in a changing working environment.

Notes

1. Part of this chapter is based on Lecheler and Kruikemeier 2016, as well as De Haan, Kruikemeier, and Lecheler 2017.
2. Respondents chose the options regularly, often, or always.

References

AlMaskati, Nawaf Abdulnabi. 2012. "Newspaper Coverage of the 2011 Protests in Egypt." *International Communication Gazette* 74, no. 4: 342–366.

Bakker, Piet. 2014. "Mr. Gates Returns. Curation, community management and other new roles for journalists" *Journalism Studies* 15, no. 5: 1–11.

Brandtzaeg, Petter Bae, Marika Lüders, Jochen Spangenberg, Linda Rath-Wiggins, and Asbjørn Følstad. 2016. "Emerging Journalistic Verification Practices Concerning Social Media." *Journalism Practice* 10, no. 3: 323-342. doi: 10.1080/17512786.2015.1020331

Broersma, Marcel, and Todd Graham. 2012. "Social Media as Beat: Tweets as a News Source During the 2010 British and Dutch Elections." *Journalism Practice* 6, no. 3: 403–419.

Broersma, Marcel, and Todd Graham. 2013. "Twitter as a News Source: How Dutch and British Newspapers Used Tweets in Their News Coverage, 2007-2011." *Journalism Practice* 7, no. 4: 446-464.

Carlson, Matt. 2007. "Order Versus Access: News Search Engines and the Challenge to Traditional Journalistic Roles." *Media, Culture & Society* 29, no. 6: 1014–1030. doi: 10.1177/0163443707084346.

De Haan, Yael, Sanne Kruikemeier, and Sophie Lecheler. 2017. "Thank Google! Observing Journalistic Online Behaviour." Paper presented at ECREA Journalism Studies conference, Odense, Denmark. March.

Diakopoulos, Nicholas. 2014. "Algorithmic Accountability: Journalistic Investigation of Computational Power Structures." *Digital Journalism* 3, no. 3: 398–415.

Egelhofer, Jana, and Sophie Lecheler. 2017. "Conceptualizing 'Fake News' for Political Communication Research." Paper presented at the third annual International Journal of Press/Politics conference, Oxford. September.

Fink-Shamit, Noa, and Judit Bar-Ilan. 2008. "Information Quality Assessment on the Web: An Expression of Behaviour." *Information Research* 13, no. 4, paper 357. http://InformationR.net/ir/13-4/paper357.html.

Gillespie, Tarleton. 2014. "The Relevance of Algorithms." In *Media Technologies*, edited by Tarleton Gillespie, Pablo J. Boczkowski, and Kirsten A. Foot. Cambridge, MA: MIT Press.

Gulyas, Agnes. 2013. "The Influence of Professional Variables on Journalists' Use and Views of Social Media: A Comparative Study of Finland, Germany, Sweden and the United Kingdom." *Digital Journalism* 1, no. 2: 270–285.

Hallin, Daniel C., and Paolo Mancini. 2004. *Comparing Media Systems: Three Models of Media and Politics*. Cambridge: Cambridge University Press.

Hermans, E. A. H. M., M. R. M. Vergeer, and A. R. J. Pleijter. 2011. *Nederlandse journalisten in 2010: Onderzoek naar de kenmerken van de beroepsgroep, professionele opvattingen en het gebruik van digitale media in het journalistieke werk*. Nijmegen: RU.

Hermida, Alfred. 2013. "# JOURNALISM: Reconfiguring Journalism Research About Twitter, One Tweet at a Time." *Digital Journalism* 1, no. 3: 295–313.

Hermida, Alfred, Seth C. Lewis, and Rodrigo Zamith. 2014. "Sourcing the Arab Spring: A Case Study of Andy Carvin's Sources on Twitter During the Tunisian and Egyptian Revolutions." *Journal of Computer-Mediated Communication* 19, no. 3: 479–499.

Jordaan, Marenet. 2013. "Poke Me, I'm a Journalist: The Impact of Facebook and Twitter on Newsroom Routines and Cultures at Two South African Weeklies." *Ecquid Novi: African Journalism Studies* 34, no. 1: 21–35.

Kemman, Max, Martijn Kleppe, Bob Nieman, and Henri Beunders. 2013. "Dutch Journalism in the Digital Age." *Icono14* 11, no. 2: 163–181.

Knight, Megan. 2012. "Journalism as Usual: The Use of Social Media as a Newsgathering Tool in the Coverage of the Iranian Elections in 2009." *Journal of Media Practice* 13, no. 1: 61–74.

Lariscy, Ruthann Weaver, Elizabeth Johnson Avery, Kaye D. Sweetser, and Pauline Howes. 2009. "An Examination of the Role of Online Social Media in Journalists' Source Mix." *Public Relations Review* 35, no. 3: 314–316.

Lecheler, Sophie, and Sanne Kruikemeier. 2016. "Re-evaluating Journalistic Routines in a Digital Age: A Review of Research on the Use of Online Sources." *New Media & Society* 18, no. 1: 156–171. doi: 10.1177/1461444815600412.

Lewis, Justin, Andrew Williams, and Bob Franklin. 2008. "Four Rumours and an Explanation: A Political Economic Account of Journalists' Changing Newsgathering and Reporting Practices." *Journalism Practice* 2, no. 1: 27–45.

Lewis, Seth. 2015. "Journalism in the Era of Big Data: Cases, Concepts and Critiques." *Digital Journalism* 3, no. 3: 321–330.

Machill, Marcel, and Markus Beiler. 2009. "The Importance of the Internet for Journalistic Research: A Multi-method Study of the Research Performed by Journalists Working for Daily Newspapers, Radio, Television and Online." *Journalism Studies* 10, no. 2: 178–203.

Moon, Soo Jung, and Patrick Hadley. 2014. "Routinizing a New Technology in the Newsroom: Twitter as a News Source in Mainstream Media." *Journal of Broadcasting & Electronic Media* 58, no. 2: 289–305.

O'Sullivan, John, and Ari Heinonen. 2008. "Old Values, New Media: Journalism Role Perceptions in a Changing World." *Journalism Practice* 2, no. 3: 357–371.

Paulussen, Steve, and Raymond A. Harder. 2014. "Social Media References in Newspapers: Facebook, Twitter, and YouTube as Sources in Newspaper Journalism" *Journalism Practice* 8, no. 5: 1–10.

Reich, Zvi. 2011. "Source Credibility and Journalism: Between Visceral and Discretional Judgment." *Journalism Practice* 5, no. 1:51–67. doi: 10.1080/17512781003760519.

Schifferes, Steve, Nic Newman, Neil Thurman, David Corney, Ayse Göker, and Carlos Martin 2014. "Identifying and Verifying News Through Social Media: Developing a User-Centred Tool for Professional Journalists." *Digital Journalism* 2, no. 3: 406–418. doi:10.1080/21670811.2014.892747.

Sellers, Patrick J., and Brian F. Schaffner. 2007. "Winning Coverage in the U.S. Senate." *Political Communication* 24, no. 4: 377–391.

Shapiro, Ivor, C. Brin, I. Bédard-Brûlé, and K. Mychajlowycz. 2013. "Verification as a Strategic Ritual: How Journalists Retrospectively Describe Processes For Ensuring Accuracy. *Journalism Practice* 7, no. 6: 657–673.

Silverman, Craig. 2014. *The Verification Handbook: A Definitive Guide to Verifying Digital Content for Emergency Coverage.* Maastricht: European Journalism Centre. http://verificationhandbook.com/.

Thurman, Neil, and Anna Walters. 2013. "Live Blogging—Digital Journalism's Pivotal Platform? A Case Study of the Production, Consumption, and Form of Live Blogs at Guardian.co.uk." *Digital Journalism* 1, no. 1: 82–101.

Tylor, Julia. 2015. "An Examination of How Student Journalists Seek Information and Evaluate Online Sources During the Newsgathering Process." *New Media & Society* 17, no. 8: 1277–1298.

Usher, Nikki. 2014. *Making News at the New York Times.* Ann Arbor: University of Michigan Press.

Van Dalen, Arjen. 2012. "The Algorithms Behind the Headlines: How Machine-Written News Redefines the Core Skills of Human Journalists." *Journalism Practice* 6, no. 5–6: 648–658. http://dx.doi.org/10.1080/17512786.2012.667268.

Van der Kaa, H. A. J., and E. J. Krahmer. 2014. "Journalist Versus News Consumer: The Perceived Credibility of Machine Written News." In Proceedings of the Computation Journalism Conference, New York.

Van Leuven, Sarah, Annelore Deprez, and Karin Raeymaeckers. 2014. "Towards More Balanced News Access? A Study on the Impact of Cost-Cutting and Web 2.0 on the Mediated Public Sphere." *Journalism* 15, no. 7: 850–867.

11

Technological Affordances Can Promote Misinformation

What Journalists Should Watch Out for When Relying on Online Tools and Social Media

Maria D. Molina and S. Shyam Sundar

Introduction

Online tools and social media have changed the nature of news reporting and data collection, giving journalists new methods to uncover and contextualize news stories, as well as the opportunity to connect with new sources and different perspectives. It is not uncommon for a journalist to scour social media for leads on news stories and look at the number of likes or shares that an event has, or its novelty and uniqueness, to determine what to cover in their particular beat or segment. Although journalists benefit greatly from utilizing online tools, there are also risks that ensue from this practice, as evidenced by the increase in fake news and misinformation online.

A clear example of this occurred in late 2016, when CNBC reshared the following headline from the *Washington Post*: "Russian Hackers Penetrated U.S. Electricity Grid Through a Utility in Vermont, U.S." It turned out this news story was false; the utility company issued a statement explaining that a malware was found in one laptop, and this was not connected to the organization's grid system (Leetaru 2017). Nevertheless, the story went viral and was widely reshared. Although the original article was significantly altered in a matter of minutes, it took almost a full hour (after the utility company issued the statement) to update the headline. By that time, the genie was out of the bottle! This example is one of many where the reliance on online news networks, instead of old-fashioned reporting, backfired and hurt news credibility. CNBC was put in the unenviable position of retracting a story that it did not create in the first place, but it had to take responsibility for disseminating a false story published by the *Washington Post*. One can blame CNBC for sloppy journalism. But in the era of online news gathering and dissemination, it is common for journalists and news organizations—seeking to be ahead of the competition on a reporting a story—to disseminate information they have gathered from one source without independently verifying it. The journalistic tendency for rushing a story to one's audience is aided by technologies that afford quick sharing of social media information by way of tools that are quite easy to use. Just one click is sufficient to retweet a claim or story to millions of readers. Given the vast leverage power, it is important to understand the factors that motivate journalists to engage in such actions.

We argue that there are certain cues in the online interaction context that persuade journalists to rely on social media information for their news-gathering and dissemination activities. These cues are transmitted by the affordances (or action possibilities) of online media technology and can profoundly shape their perceptions of content they receive via this technology. The Modality-Agency-Interactivity-Navigability (MAIN) model identifies four categories of technological affordances that influence user perceptions of the medium and its content by triggering heuristics or "cognitive rules of thumb" about the nature and quality of the medium and its content (Sundar 2008).

While the cues generated by these affordances aid the general consumer in making quick decisions, relying on them can be risky for journalists, who are generally expected to report objectively, not simply further spread what is trending on social media. We think that journalists and scholars should be aware of the cues triggered by the MAIN variables and consider them while making decisions regarding what and how to report. Awareness of the psychological mechanisms underlying interface cues and the heuristics they trigger can allow journalists to avoid falling for such heuristics, minimizing the chances of selecting a fake event online to cover or reshare, like the above example of CNBC sharing a *Washington Post* headline. In this chapter, we provide recent examples of misinformation, and evaluate how the different cues in social media, as delineated by MAIN model, could have played a role in journalistic decision-making.

Modality

Modality, or the different types of content presentation, is a clear and noticeable affordance in an interface and includes elements related to our sensory processing (Sundar 2008). For example, the use of print is related to a textual modality where the audience has to decode the written content reported by the journalist. Radio, on the other hand, is related to our aural senses, and television appeals audio-visually. Both require less interpretation compared to text as they include specific depictions and imagery about the event being covered. With digital technologies, content creators are able to mix various text, audio, and visual cues when presenting information to their audiences and thus trigger the *realism* heuristic ("seeing is believing"). For example, in Appiah's (2006) study comparing audio-visual testimonies versus text/picture testimonies in a website, audio-visual testimonies were rated more favorably. The author attributes this to the vividness and realism of the modality. The realism heuristic predicts that individuals will be more likely to believe content they can see than that which they can only read about; after all, it is easier to lie through text than deceive through a visual feature such as an image or video. But, is this true? Can we actually detect visual deception?

Nightingale, Wade, and Watson (2017) studied this phenomenon and tested if individuals can identify real photos from fake photos in real-world scenes and discovered that our ability to detect and locate manipulations is generally poor. When participants did detect the exact manipulation, it was due to disruptions of pixel structure and distortions that altered the perspective and realism of the image. In other words, they spotted them largely only when the manipulations were not subtle. The practice of fake photos is not new, indeed, manipulated images have been used for propagandistic and exploitative purposes since shortly after photography was invented. To wit, Chen (2016) shows how European colonial powers manipulated photographs to frame the Arab and Asian worlds in a way that supported colonial rule.

Rather than solving the problems, computer technologies have increased the use of fake images (Klein and Wueller 2017) because they made it easier and cheaper to create well-manipulated images that can evade detection. For instance, in July 2014, the website Uncle Sam's Misguided Children shared a manipulated image dated 1998 showing Barack Obama as a young Black Panther member (see figure 11.1). Although the origin of the photo

Figure 11.1 *Left*: Manipulated image of Barack Obama as member of the Black Panthers. *Right*: Unaltered image showing two individuals of the New Black Panther Party.
Credit: Snopes.

is unknown, several versions have circulated on the Internet, spreading false rumors about the former president. According to LaCapria (2017), the original unaltered picture was published online in 2009 and illustrates two members of the New Black Panther Party, a more recent militant group that bears little relationship to the original Black Panthers.

Photo manipulation is not the only way that the realism heuristic can work. Real photos are easier to take out of context in the current information environment where a simple web search will yield pictures from a variety of contexts that an individual can select for their own use. For example, during Hurricane Harvey, Katie Couric, an American journalist, who has been a television host and anchor on the three major networks of the United States, posted a picture that a friend had sent her (Willingham 2017). The picture was of an alligator in the friend's driveway (see figure 11.2). This image, however, was from an earlier, unrelated event. In a follow-up post, Couric called this instance a "double punk" as a friend had sent this image to her friend, who in turn sent it to Couric.

Upon looking at breaking events on social media, journalists may possibly be persuaded by such realism and thus become convinced that an event being shared is indeed true. After all, an image of an alligator from your close friend is more believable than her texting you about it. This realism heuristic is particularly important with the rise of citizen journalism

Figure 11.2 *Left*: Katie Couric's original twitter post with a picture of an alligator supposedly at a friend's driveway. *Right*: Kate Couric's follow-up Twitter calling the situation a double punk.
Credit: Willingham, 2017.

and live feeds, where citizens are provided online access to broadcast an event. Given the ease with which citizens can digitally manipulate images and video, and then broadcast them on the Internet, journalists must be aware of their susceptibility to the realism heuristic and therefore investigate further before sharing or writing about events appearing online in the form of pictures and videos. Journalists can follow several strategies to avoid falling for such modality-related heuristics. A simple reverse Google search would have informed Couric that the picture of the alligator was used before. Couric would have also benefited by resisting the urge to rush to publish and calling her source to verify the information she received. Following the basic journalistic principle of verification can go a long way in combating the misinformation arising from deceptive use of modern modalities of communication. That said, caution when using online searches is necessary, as misinformation and wrong fact checks have been the bane of even diligent journalists seeking to uncover the accuracy of claims.

Agency

The agency affordance relates to the source of media content (Sundar 2008). In traditional media, it is easy to identify who is the source of a news article;

however, this difference is not as distinguishable in digital media where the audience can act as disseminators, creators, and curators of content. For instance, although some might get news directly from a news organization (e.g., its newspaper, TV channel, or website), others might use news aggregator sites, which are customized to individual users' preferences, or get information from their Facebook or Twitter feeds. Consequently, it is not uncommon to hear the phrase "I read in Twitter," "according to Google," or "a friend from Facebook shared it." In a study by Pew, news consumers could only recall the original sources of news 56% of the time. As many as 10% of participants responded "Facebook" when asked for the specific news outlet of their news (Mitchell et al. 2017). Further, in a study by Sundar and Nass (2001), when participants were told news stories were selected by a computer or other users (vs. news editors or themselves), they rated the stories as higher in quality. Taken together, these findings reveal that in the online environment the concept of sources becomes murky and is broadened to include not only traditional news organizations but also other users, the users themselves, and technology (be it the computer, a website, or a social media feed).

To disambiguate sources and assess the credibility of information encountered online, users utilize heuristic cues available on the interface. For example, in the CNBC case described earlier, the original tweet as of this writing (mid-2018) had over 4,000 retweets. Perhaps interface cues displaying the number of "retweets," "shares," or "likes" triggered the *bandwagon* heuristic (i.e., if a lot of people are talking about it, then it must be true), where audiences serve as indirect gatekeepers of information, unwittingly boosting the credibility of a breaking news story by sharing it with others. Perhaps the high number of retweets played a role in CNBC's decision to retweet the news story and engage in a public conversation. After all, CNBC cannot fall behind in covering such an important event. Also, the *Washington Post* is a reputable news source, cueing the *authority* heuristic, or the sense of experience and source credibility, giving further assurance to the reporter about the credibility of the published story.

Coming back to the bandwagon heuristic, the hashtag culture of modern social media has made it easy for new bandwagons to form and grow quickly. The bandwagon heuristic was clearly in action amid the flooding that devastated Houston after Hurricane Harvey when fake twitter accounts were used to instill fear and racial hatred. Through the hashtag #harveylootcrew these accounts gave the false impression that massive looting followed the hurricane while the Houston Police Department said otherwise (Emery 2017). Through such tweets, these group of individuals spoke about looting stores owned by white people and Trump supporters (see figure 11.3). The proliferation of these tweets was aided by the use of the hashtag and retweet feature, through which dozens of similar stories were disseminated. Importantly, research on Twitter dissemination reveals that "any retweeted tweet reaches an average of 1,000 users no matter what the number of followers is on the original tweet," implying, that once retweeted, the diffusion of the content is even faster (Kwak et al. 2010, 600). In the case of #harveylootcrew, the fast dissemination and retweet numbers might have increased the bandwagon perception, giving the impression that if others are retweeting this content, then it must be true. As such, some mainstream media including Click2Houston, as well as right-leaning blogs such as *Think Americana* and *Pacific Pundit*, reported on these tweets as if they were real. Upon further investigation, Emery (2017) identified that not only was this information being shared by fake accounts but that none of the photos in these post took place in Houston or in 2017.

The bandwagon effect is exacerbated by the layering of information that occurs in social media, where seeing something that a friend shared

Figure 11.3 *Left*: The image in this false tweet traces back to a 2013 report by the *Daily News* about cops in New York using social networking sites to track gang members. *Right*: Tweet by a fake account (since deleted) speaking about looting Trump supporters' properties.

Credit: Snopes.

can further conceal the original source of the information (Sundar 2016). A study examining source cues (Kang et al. 2011) reveals the more proximate the user perceives the source to be, "the greater its influence on perceived credibility of the message" (731). This is particularly important given the increasing use of news aggregator sites (that personalize based on user's preferences) and social media (where friends share information important to them) for news consumption. For journalists receiving information through several layers of sources, this is especially problematic because their credibility evaluations are based on the most proximate source, i.e., the one that delivered the information to them, rather than the original source of that information.

Relatedly, agency can trigger the *identity* heuristic, or a sense of identification and similitude with the content being presented (Sundar 2008). For example, customization and personalization options allow the user to tailor their information environment so that it elicits a feeling of resemblance and belonging. Such tailoring facilitates the development of echo chambers (Sunstein 2002) and reduces exposure to counter-attitudinal messages (Dylko et al. 2017). In the journalism context, when searching for new information and sources, journalists should be aware of the tailoring algorithms that are present, which in turn construct a biased information environment where they might be exposed primarily to information according to their "likes," "follows," and previous browsing behavior.

During the 2016 election cycle, when most journalists collectively believed in a Hillary Clinton victory, they ignored indicators of the grassroots support for Donald Trump and were therefore responsible for the "bubble" that blinded them and thus their readers to the reality of voters' attitudes toward the candidates. A likely reason is the operation of identity cues, allowing for extreme tailoring of incoming information, dividing the country into two realities—a fact that was not evident until after the elections. Although reporters generally place more value on Twitter than Facebook due to its broader network and fostering of weaker ties, they still use Facebook as a tool to query friends and conduct background research (Santana and Hopp 2016), a practice that can be a double-edge sword because users of social media generally receive content based on algorithm-driven efforts to serve content that aligns with their personal biases. In fact, Bakshy, Messing, and Adamic (2015) analyzed exposure to news on Facebook and revealed that friends share less diverse and cross-cutting news, contributing to users encountering approximately 15% less opposing content in news feeds, and clicking approximately 70% less of this cross-cutting content because of algorithm-based ranking. The 2016 elections were no different. Regardless of political ideology, users were 15% more likely to believe ideologically aligned headlines, a relationship that grew stronger when users had a highly segregated social media (Allcott and Gentzkow 2017). Importantly, the algorithms used in Facebook and other social networking sites apply to all users, including journalists. In social media, we typically "like" "friend" or "follow" individuals in our circle of friends and acquaintances, or others whom we deem as important sources of content. In this case, the self becomes the source, as we are given the ability to gatekeep our information environment. As we do this, however, we unconsciously shield ourselves from information and opinions that might not be common in our online network. This kind of echo chamber does not foster the diversity of content and opinions necessary for producing objective, unbiased journalism.

Interactivity

Interactivity affordances refer to the back-and-forth activity provided by an interface technology. It can trigger the *activity* heuristic (a mental shortcut equating higher activity with higher credibility; Sundar 2008), where the presence of certain features, such as discussion forums and commenting features, can be perceived as fostering interaction, and thus lead to more favorable perceptions and evaluations concerning the content. Before the advent of digital media, users were largely passive consumers of news. You could either pick up a newspaper to read or watch the evening news, and conversations about the news were typically at the dinner table and with your family, friends, and acquaintances. Nowadays, many news sites provide users a space to comment, which allows the possibility of reading an opinion from someone from the other side of the country or the world. This functionality enables users to receive different perspectives of events and occurrences or even additional or contravening information. Social networking sites such as Facebook and Twitter provide heightened levels of interactivity, as users can not only comment on news pieces but also converse about a piece of information with their network of friends and followers. In this way, interactivity offers users the possibility of being interactive participants and contributors.

Relatedly, the *contingency* heuristic, or the thread of messages reflecting a sequence of interaction, triggers a perception of reciprocity (Sundar 2008). An interactive message is contingent on not just the message immediately before it but also on the thread of messages previously displayed. The commenting functions provided in digital technologies allows for the perception of dialogue and discourse, easing communication between users. Reciprocity enhances participation intention in online communities (Wise, Hamman, and Thorson 2016) in such a way that a journalist may decide to engage in a particular conversation, like the CNBC reporter on Twitter in the case mentioned in the chapter's beginning, where, in light of the back-and-forth conversation that ensued, he decided to share a piece of news from another source in an attempt to participate in the conversation. In this light, journalists should remember that just because a post sparked conversation, it does not mean that the content is worth attention.

Additionally, although the Internet has facilitated the spread of information, it has also contributed to unprecedented pressure on journalists to not only report with accuracy and timeliness but also contribute to online engagement. An interview with 50 journalists at four metropolitan newspapers in the United States found that all four newsrooms provided staff with the latest smartphones to encourage Twitter use, particularly when reporting from the front lines (Swasy 2016). Journalists have embraced this new requirement. Fifty-four percent of US journalists said they used microblogs such as Twitter during their reporting and information gathering, and 23.6% indicated using blogs by other journalists (Willnat and Weaver 2014). The interactivity provided by these digital technologies changes the way that audiences interact with news outlets, allowing citizens to have direct dialogue with reporters. For example, in an analysis of social media interactivity in two UK newspapers, Canter (2013) found that "journalists are making individual decisions to share information that will not be published in their print newspaper or website, and they are engaging in open conversation with their readers" (492). Nowadays it is often the individual journalist who engages with readers in an informal and reciprocal manner.

As an example, in December 2017 CNN aired a story (later followed by other media organizations such as MSNBC and CBS) reporting on having proof that Wikileaks had offered the Donald Trump presidential campaign access to emails from the Democratic National Committee before they were published online and publicly available (Greenwald 2017). This story was based on an email to which CNN claimed to have exclusive access. This email was sent to the media outlet by Michael J. Erickson, self-described president of an aviation company. However, as the *Washington Post* (Helderman and Hamburger 2017) clarified, the date of the email was incorrect. In reality, it was sent a day after the documents had become public, indicating that Mr. Erickson might have been informing the Trump campaign administrator about the existence of now publicly available information from Wikileaks (Helderman and Hamburger 2017; Greenwald 2017). Despite correcting the misinformation, CNN stated that the dates were provided by multiple sources, without identifying them. This example illustrates the closeness that traditional gatekeepers have with their audiences, where audiences can use technology to communicate with news organizations directly, setting the agenda of the media, rather than the other way around, all facilitated by interactive features of technology that afford two-way communication.

Upon deciding what content to cover, it is important for reporters to ask themselves the reasons why this content is worth paying attention to, and if the reason is that others are talking about it or because of its exclusive nature, it is incumbent to fact-check and further investigate before making it a part of their conversation or that of their media organization. This holds especially true when the primary source of such information is an unknown user.

Navigability

Finally, navigability refers to the movement across the online environment. The structural component of digital media "allows the interface designer to mimic the nature of the human memory system, particularly the processing of information through associative links" (Sundar 2008, 89). One way that digital media accomplishes this is by providing cues regarding the perceived importance of content. These cues elicit the *prominence* heuristic, which in this case is the belief that results that appear first in a search engine are the best results. In day-to-day journalistic practice, it is common for a journalist to use Internet searches to contextualize a story or get background for an event. For instance, in Willnat and Weaver's (2014) survey, 22.2% of journalists expressed using crowd-sourcing websites, such as Wikipedia, for gathering information and reporting. Although the Internet has facilitated the ability to investigate and acquire information about historical and current events, there are important cognitive decisions when selecting information. For example, using the Google search engine, Pan et al. (2007) found that users are more influenced by the order of yielded results than the summary abstract presented with each search result. Oftentimes, journalists "google" to find information to contextualize their news stories, typically utilizing information from the first page without exploring subsequent pages of the search results. The reality is that the algorithms used by search engines are trade secrets and depend on more than 500 million factors (Hariri 2011), including previous browsing behaviors. The order in which information appears after a search will be different among users, automated based on prior browsing to maximize personal utility and liking of the content, thus triggering the *similarity* heuristic (the promised information is similar to one's objectives, therefore it is credible). This means that the information that a journalist encounters when searching background information may be that which aligns with their previous browsing behavior, excluding other information and points of view which might also be relevant. Interestingly, when comparing the relevance ranking of Google with the user's point of view, Hariri (2011) found that users judged the first document of a search as more relevant only in 16 of 34 searches. Additionally, even in the fourth page of results, documents were still perceived as relevant. This means that journalists might be missing out on relevant information that was ranked by the system as less important.

This problem was compounded when Google incorporated feature snippets, providing answers to user's questions displayed on top of the Google results page. These answers come from high-ranking websites that are not necessarily correct (Cellan-Jones 2017). Another navigationally salient feature utilized by journalists is Google Trends, a tool that shows "how heavily a topic is being Googled" relative to other topics (Shoorbajee 2016). Here, the *prominence* heuristic can also be influential and warrants attention. For example, after 52% of voters in the United Kingdom voted for leaving the European Union (Brexit), international media, including the *Washington Post*, NPR, and *Fortune*, covered the event questioning British citizens' knowledge about the unfolding events. These media outlets referenced Google Trends and its tweet illustrating the top Google searches in the UK after the elections. The top searches included "What does it mean to leave the E.U.?" and "What is the E.U.?" Inspired by this tweet, the *Washington Post* headline "The British Are Frantically Googling What the E.U. Is, Hours After Voting to Leave It" made it to the top of the list of the news-aggregating site Memorandum (Shoorbajee 2016). Such stories gave the impression that the British were just now, after the elections, learning about the event they were voting for. However, this is not quite true. Google Trends, as its name indicates, presents trends and patterns, providing journalists a means to get a sense of public interest. However, its data does not provide enough information to draw conclusions in large populations because it works in an index format such that it specifies a topic's search relative to other topics and not how many people searched for a term (Shoorbajee 2016). Furthermore, it does not indicate who these people were, whether they were, for instance, mostly registered voters or merely tourists, and in general, how representative they may be of the voting population.

Although the Internet and big data provide impressive tools for journalists to get information previously inaccessible to them, it is advisable to be aware of the mechanisms, strengths, and limitations of technologies, and especially of typical human cognitive processing when selecting and interpreting a topic based on prominence placement and similarity metrics. This is all the more advisable considering the many mechanisms that can be used to alter these metrics. One example is Google-bombing where a group of individuals can artificially increase the ranking of a website through strategies such as linking their site to popular words or phrases even though they may be off-topic or irrelevant to the site's content.

Summary

When using the Internet as a tool for data collection, journalists should be equipped with the necessary knowledge to combat misinformation and use social media to their advantage. To this effect, journalists are trained to look at the characteristics of the content being shared and are encouraged to look at the material presented, leaving aside their own biases. Journalists should additionally consider the role that technology plays during data collection. The examples we presented illustrate major heuristics that journalists might use during their journalistic endeavors, and their attendant consequences.

Affordances pertaining to modality, agency, interactivity, and navigability shed light on the three themes of this book—media and technology, abstract notions of truth, and politics. First, this chapter elucidates the role of technology, specifically heuristic cues, on user's assessment of content online, and how these can impact journalistic decision-making. Second, we highlighted the role of agency cues in facilitating an information environment personalized to each person's desires, attitudes, and beliefs. In this online world, we tend to encounter information from our network of friends and followers, which often aligns with our own biases. We also discussed the role of prominence and similarity heuristics as a consequence of navigability affordances in online searches, revealing how the relevance ranking of our web searches limits our information retrieval, missing out on other important information that might be located further down the list, or in the third or fourth pages of our search. Truth and reality are, thus, in the eye of the beholder, which is often held hostage to personalization algorithms. Finally, the different affordances highlighted in this chapter can play a role in journalists' coverage of information of any genre, be it sports, entertainment, or politics. The latter is particularly important given the role of journalists as the fourth estate. An informed citizenry is imperative for democracy, and the news media are key in this process. However, as examples from this chapter illustrate, fake news can disrupt this process. The Internet provides new tools and features that journalists can successfully use, but advances in technology also bring with them affordances that have hidden meanings, in that they trigger cognitive heuristics among users for facilitating efficient decisions. Awareness of these hidden heuristics among journalists can alert them to potential cues that may negatively influence their decisions in information gathering and reporting processes.

Lessons for Practitioners

The MAIN model offers some key lessons for journalists in the digital age. When using technology for journalistic practices, we should be cautious about the following affordances:

- Modality can trigger the realism heuristic (seeing is believing). Individuals are likely to readily believe visual information compared to textual information. We encourage journalists to verify the images and videos they come across by conducting a reverse Google search and go the extra step of verification before taking further action.
- Agency can trigger the bandwagon heuristic (if a lot of people are talking about it, then it must be true, and certainly important) and identity heuristic (a sense of similarity and belonging) biasing our exposure toward content that others deem as important and that which

often aligns well with our own predispositions. Practitioners should be aware of these heuristics and analyze information based on its inherent newsworthiness rather than on the degree to which it reflects self-agency or crowd support.

- Interactivity can trigger activity and contingency heuristics enabling interaction and engagement with audiences. Although this engagement is a positive tool for maintaining an informed citizenry and for journalists to be in touch with citizens, it can be a double-edge sword in that it privileges interaction over proper vetting, thereby allowing greater room for misinformation.
- Navigability can trigger the similarity and prominence heuristics where content that is trending or first in the search list are considered more important than others. Journalists should be aware that search algorithms are based on maximizing the common denominator of audience interest rather than on potential newsworthiness of information. Therefore, when contextualizing and searching for background information, journalists are encouraged to look beyond the first search results in the list, as they might be missing out on important and relevant information hidden in lower ranked results.

References

Allcott, Hunt, and Matthew Gentzkow. 2017. "Social Media and Fake News in the 2016 Election." *Journal of Economic Perspectives* 31, no. 2: 211–236. doi: 10.1257/jep.31.2.211.

Appiah, Osei. 2006. "Rich Media, Poor Media: The Impact of Audio/Video vs. Text/Picture Testimonial Ads on Browsers' Evaluations of Commercial Web Sites and Online Products." *Journal of Current Issues and Research in Advertising* 28: 73–86. doi:10.1080/10641734.2006.10505192.

Bakshy, Eytan, Solomon Messing, and Lada A. Adamic. 2015. "Exposure to Ideologically Diverse News and Opinion on Facebook." *Science* 348, no. 6239: 1130–1132. doi: 10.1126/science.aaa1160.

Canter, Lily. 2013. "The Interactive Spectrum: The Use of Social Media in UK Regional Newspapers." *Convergence* 19, no. 4: 472–495. doi: 10.1177/1354856513493698.

Cellan-Jones, Rory. 2017. "Google's Fake News Snippets." BBC, August 29. http://www.bbc.com/news/technology-39180855#.

Chen, Angus. 2016. "Long Before There Was 'Fake News,' There Were 'Fake Photos.'" NPR, February 5. http://www.npr.org/sections/goatsandsoda/2017/02/05/513252650/long-before-there-was-fake-news-there-were-fake-photos.

Dylko, Ivan, Igor Dolgov, William Hoffman, Nicholas Eckhart, Maria Molina, and Omar Aaziz. 2017. "Dark Side of Technology: An Experimental Investigation of

Customizability Technology on Political Selective Exposure." *Computers in Human Behavior* 73: 181–190. http://dx.doi.org/10.1016/j.chb.2017.03.031.

Emery, David. 2017. "Racist Twitter Trolls Pose as Houston Looters." September 1. https://www.snopes.com/2017/09/01/harvey-looting-troll-tweets/.

Greenwald, Glenn. 2017. "The U.S. Media Suffered Its Most Humiliating Debacle in Ages and Now Refuses All Transparency Over What Happened." *The Intercept*, December 9. / https://theintercept.com/2017/12/09/the-u-s-media-yesterday-suffered-its-most-humiliating-debacle-in-ages-now-refuses-all-transparency-over-what-happened.

Hariri, Nadjla. 2011. "Relevance Ranking on Google." *Online Information Review* 35, no. 4: 598–610. doi:10.1108/14684521111161954.

Helderman, Rosalind S., and Tom Hamburger. 2017. "Email Pointed Trump Campaign to Wikileaks Documents That Were Already Public." *Washington Post*, December 8. https://www.washingtonpost.com/politics/email-offering-trump-campaign-wikileaks-documents-referred-to-information-already-public/2017/12/08/61dc2356-dc37-11e7-a841-2066faf731ef_story.html?utm_term=.1a42a389608e.

Kang, Hyunjin, Keunmin Bae, Shaoke Zhang, and S. Shyam Sundar. 2011. "Source Cues in Online News: Is the Proximate Source More Powerful than Distal Sources?" *Journalism & Mass Communication Quarterly* 88, no. 4: 719–736.

Klein, David O., and Joshua R. Wueller. 2017. "Fake News: A Legal Perspective." *Journal of Internet Law* 20, no. 1 (Apr.): 1–13.

Kwak, Haewoon, Changhyun Lee, Hosung Park, and Sue Moon. 2010. "What Is Twitter, a Social Network or a News Media?" *19th International Conference on World Wide Web* (Apr.): 591–600. doi:10.1145/1772690.1772751.

LaCapria, Kim. 2017. "Was Barack Obama a Black Panther?" November 24. https://www.snopes.com/obama-black-panther-photo/.

Leetaru, Kalev. 2017. "'Fake News' and How the *Washington Post* Rewrote Its Story on Russian Hacking of the Power Grid." *Forbes*, January 1. https://www.forbes.com/sites/kalevleetaru/2017/01/01/fake-news-and-how-the-washington-post-rewrote-its-story-on-russian-hacking-of-the-power-grid/#41f5bed97ad5

Mitchell, Amy, Jeffrey Gottfried, Elisa Shearer, and Kristine Lu. 2017. "How Americans Encounter, Recall and Act Upon Digital News." Pew Research. February 9.http://www.journalism.org/2017/02/09/how-americans-encounter-recall-and-act-upon-digital-news/.

Nightingale, Sophie J., Kimberley A. Wade, and Derrick G. Watson. 2017. "Can People Identify Original and Manipulated Photos of Real-World Scenes?" *Cognitive Research: Principles and Implications* 2, no. 1: 1–21. doi:10.1186/s41235-017-0067-2.

Pan, Bing, Helene Hembrooke, Thorsten Joachims, Lori Lorigo, Geri Gay, and Laura Granka. 2007. "In Google We Trust: Users' Decisions on Rank, Position, and Relevance." *Journal of Computer-Mediated Communication* 12, no. 3: 801–823.

Santana, Arthur D., and Toby Hopp. 2016. "Tapping into a New Stream of (Personal) Data: Assessing Journalists' Different Use of Social Media." *Journalism & Mass Communication Quarterly* 93, no. 2: 383–408. doi: 10.1177/1077699016637105.

Shoorbajee, Zaid. 2016. "What Journalists Should Know About Using Google Trends." *Media File*, August 29. http://www.mediafiledc.com/google-trends-a-reporting-tool-but-not-a-perfect-one/

Sundar, S. Shyam. 2008. "The MAIN Model: A Heuristic Approach to Understanding Technology Effects on Credibility." In *Digital Media, Youth, and Credibility*, edited by Miriam. J. Metzger and Andrew. J. Flanagin, 72–100. Cambridge: MIT Press.

Sundar, S. Shyam. 2016. "Why Do We Fall for Fake News?" *The Conversation*, December 7. https://theconversation.com/why-do-we-fall-for-fake-news-69829.

Sundar, S. Shyam, and Clifford Nass. 2001. "Conceptualizing Sources in Online News." *Journal of Communication* 51, no.1: 52–72. doi: 10.1111/j.1460-2466.2001.tbO2872.x

Sunstein, Cass R. 2002. "The Law of Group Polarization." *Journal of Political Philosophy* 10, no. 2: 175–195. http://dx.doi.org/10.1111/1467-9760.00148.

Swasy, Alecia. 2016. *How Journalists Use Twitter: The Changing Landscape of U.S. Newsrooms*. Lanham: Lexington Books.

Willingham, A. J. 2017. "5 Reasons Why People Share Fake Photos During Disasters." CNN, September 8. http://www.cnn.com/2017/09/08/health/fake-images-posts-disaster-trnd/index.html.

Willnat, Lars, and David H. Weaver. 2014. *The American Journalist in the Digital Age*. Bloomington: School of Journalism, Indiana University.

Wise, Kevin, Brian Hamman, and Kjerstin Thorson. 2006. "Moderation, Response Rate, and Message Interactivity: Features of Online Communities and Their Effects on Intent to Participate." *Journal of Computer-Mediated Communication* 12, no. 1: 24–41. doi: 10.1111/j.1083-6101.2006.00313.x.

PART IV
RECEPTION AND PERCEPTION

12

Fake News Finds an Audience

Erik P. Bucy and John E. Newhagen

Social media were never intended to be news platforms. Facebook, in particular, has long presented itself as a neutral platform for user-generated content that does not have traditional journalistic responsibilities (Levin 2018). As a conduit and amplifier for others' information, the company could claim that it did not control what users posted, including fake news and other suspect content—and merely benefited incidentally when a piece of misinformation went viral and attracted advertising revenue. This is consistent with Section 230 of the Communications Decency Act, which holds that networked platforms cannot be liable for content users post on their sites (Levin 2018). Since the 2016 US presidential election, however, Facebook has come under sharp criticism for its role in proliferating misinformation and, after initially denying any culpability, has attempted to stem the spread of false information over its network by alerting users to signs of fake news, experimenting with forms of censorship, and allowing fact-checkers to debunk articles and label them as "disputed." Both Facebook and Google have also agreed to block or remove suspected fake news accounts from their advertising platforms (Frenkel 2018). These well-intentioned efforts to curb fake news have met with moderate success—and a begrudging realization of the problem's magnitude.

Some might say the warning signs were there all along. Clifford Stoll, in *Silicon Snake Oil*, a widely debated jeremiad against online communication, cataloged the many "disappointing realities" of digital message flows, including their susceptibility to spreading rumor and valorizing trivia, lending credibility to extreme opinions, and circulating false information around the globe at cybernetic speeds (Stoll 1995a). An early, high-profile example of conspiracy endorsement occurred in November 1996 when Pierre Salinger held a press conference insisting that the downing of TWA flight 800 three months earlier was by an errant US Navy missile; Salinger had been misled by false claims circulating on the Internet (Devaney 2013).

In the pre-bot era, such instances of wholesale gullibility were rare and did not spark widespread public concern. Though online engagement was never without its problems, as concerns over pornography and Internet addiction underscored, in the nascent days of mobile communication and social media, networked connectivity was more likely to be hailed for its revolutionizing potential to upend established orders and empower collective movements (Grossman 1995; Rheingold 2002).

Academic accounts of network power prior to 2016 were more measured in their optimism, highlighting the ways digital communication technologies were simultaneously empowering but also exposing users. Castells (2009) highlighted online mobilization and citizen organizing via mobile media and autonomous communication networks as evidence of a new phase of counter-power in the network society, later describing social movements as "networks of outrage and hope" (Castells 2012). Papacharissi (2015) documented the emotional and discursive dimensions of networked political action, tracing how they foster rhetorical solidarity and the formation of affective publics among users. At the same time, the growing surveillance and data collection regime fed by this participatory ethos was raising red flags (see Andrejevic 2007; Rosen 2001), and policy scholars drew attention to the inconvenient fact that most users do not possess the requisite skills for succeeding in digital environments (van Dijk 2005). Hopes for citizen empowerment via social media, encouraged by the campaign and election of Barack Obama in 2008 (Katz, Barris, and Jain 2013), were dimmed by the infiltration of social media by strategic actors intent on manipulating public opinion in the years following that historic election.

Then along came the 2016 Brexit vote in the UK, the 2016 US presidential contest, and the French presidential election of 2017, each of which witnessed multilayered, and at times weaponized (i.e., automated, sophisticated, harmful in intent) use of the very social media platforms that were considered individually empowering just a few years prior. In one of the industry's biggest data breaches to date, the now-defunct political consulting firm Cambridge Analytica harvested information from the Facebook profiles of up to 87 million US citizens and 1 million Britons without their consent, then used the information in an effort to predict and influence voting behavior (Cadwalladr and Graham-Harrison 2018; Lapowsky 2018). At issue was the firm's ability to access data through an online "personality test," both from users who were being paid as part of a supposed academic study—and from each user's network of unsuspecting Facebook friends.

The data were collected through an app called "thisisyourdigitallife," which upon downloading asked for permission to scrape users' personal information, then automatically harvested the data from Facebook friends (Cadwalladr and Graham-Harrison 2018).

As social media have matured, their porousness has been penetrated and leveraged by opportunists in the United States and beyond, to exploit social fault lines, vilify political targets, and peddle false information as true (European Commission 2018). While still facilitating network empowerment in certain circumstances (see Bennett and Segerberg 2014), social media are increasingly utilized as tools for coordinated confusion and mass deception, culminating in the curious circumstance that by the close of the 2016 US presidential election fake news stories from hoax sites and hyperpartisan blogs (e.g., *End the Fed, The Denver Guardian*) received more shares, reactions, and comments on Facebook than legitimate election coverage (Silverman 2016).[1] To the extent that Facebook has become a global phenomenon, so too has fake news become a world problem (European Commission 2018; Grillo 2018).

In this chapter we argue that the vulnerabilities exposed by attacks on truth from fake news and computational propaganda, which came into widespread public view in 2016, should be considered in light of the characteristics and concerns surrounding big data, especially the volume and velocity of messages delivered over social media platforms that tax the individual user's capacity to determine their truth value in anything approximating real time. For reasons explained by the psychology of information processing, a high percentage of fake news that reaches audiences is accepted as true (see Silverman and Singer-Vine 2016), particularly when distractions and interruptions typify user experiences with technology (Ophir, Nass, and Wagner 2009).

Message features, including sensational headlines and news-like formatting, and qualities of social media that promote bandwagon effects and an absence of close scrutiny (Tandoc, Lim, and Ling 2018), further intensify the problem that fake news presents to users attempting to distinguish fact from fiction. Fake news thrives in environments lacking editorial policing and epistemological vigilance (Nielsen 2015), making the social media milieu ideally suited for spreading false information. Fake news is also embraced—and more readily believed—by users who know the least about newsgathering and legitimate news production (Amazeen and Bucy, 2019), suggesting the value of an educational strategy to combat the dilemma that digital disinformation poses to democracy. We proceed by considering fake news in light of big data.

Fake News as a Big Data Problem

The steady stream of "news" items on social media feeds may not seem like a big data problem because individual users generally only see one news feed at a time—their own—and the real-time procession of updates and postings appears superficially manageable, or at least ignorable. But aggregated, the propagation of user-generated content across billions of accounts worldwide on a 24/7/365 basis adds up, making the scope of activity vast but difficult to quantify, let alone verify. In these interconnected and only partially monitored environments, "content can be relayed among users with no significant third-party filtering, fact-checking, or editorial judgment [and users] with no track record or reputation can in some cases reach as many readers" as major media (Allcott and Gentzkow 2017, 211). The porousness of the two largest social media networks, Facebook and Twitter, to bot-generated activity by scammers, operatives, and propagandists (Timberg and Dwoskin 2018) greatly magnifies the circulation of wrong and misleading information—and the potential for unsuspecting users to encounter it (more on this later). After intense pressure by civic organizations, academics, and activists, Facebook and Google have moved to block or remove suspected fake news accounts from their advertising platforms—and also to rank mainstream news sources as credible—but the effort is far from perfect and doesn't always succeed (see Frenkel 2018; Wingfield, Isaac, and Benner 2016).

Rather than enhancing accuracy, the speedy exchange and spread of information over social media detracts from it, turning information sharing into something akin to a digitized rumor mill. The amount of attention a post receives in the form of shares, likes, and comments becomes a proxy for its truth value, as if repetition and amplification make it so, but empirical research has found that users "seldom verify the information that they share" (Tandoc et al. 2018, 139). Data scientists who initially identified three dimensions, or "V's" of big data (volume, velocity, and variety), soon found themselves adding an important fourth dimension—veracity—when it became apparent that much of the data they were extracting and parsing had a tenuous relationship with the truth (Lukoianova and Rubin 2014). Veracity is, of course, the reason why fake news poses such a problem for democratic systems that rely on a fair and full accounting of the day's events as well as coherent coverage of social and political developments to successfully navigate the way forward (see Schudson 2008).

Since Frankfurt (2005) declared "bullshit" to be a defining characteristic of our age, researchers across disparate domains have found purchase in the concept's application. Nielsen (2015) argues that social media are prone to generating bullshit (in the technical, not normative, sense)[2] because they continuously present opportunities for users, whether commenting on prom photos or important breaking news developments, to talk without knowing what they are talking about. Popularity, not expertise, is the common currency. While the volume and velocity of social media message flows facilitate the former, they undermine the latter. Likes and shares beget more likes and shares, becoming a "self-fulfilling cycle, one that lends well to the propagation of unverified information" (Tandoc et al. 2018, 139). Veracity requires verification, but confirming—and fixing—the truth of something across the diverse set of technologies and practices that make up the social media universe in a way that is not immediately challenged is nigh impossible. Social media are not scientific societies with agreed upon terminology, accepted frameworks for analysis, and forms of justification (Nielsen 2015).

That content in such an environment would trend toward the sensational and emotive to generate more likes and shares, and the emergent stars of this system clever storytellers rather than truth purveyors, should not be surprising. Trending topics are rarely dull news. As well, it is important to appreciate the structural biases and built-in affordances of social media that promote particular uses and favor outlandish claims. They are popularity engines that reward spreadability (Jenkins, Ford, and Green 2013). In this sense, the interactive tools of social media—the likes, shares, comments, and retweets—serve as forms of precision feedback that allow strategic operators to fine-tune the appeal of their persuasive messaging in a form of pseudo-polling. In such a milieu, emotional truth and trending sentiment are all that matter and messages that carry emotional resonance are likely to spread.

Beyond concerns about veracity, there is a fifth "V" of big data that characterizes social media platforms and helps explains their deceptive complexity and tendency to distort, which is their lack of transparency or network visibility (see Bucy 2018; Kanellos 2016; Zelenkauskaite and Bucy

2016). Like other software platforms, social media obscure as much as they illuminate. Users are not privy to the overall size of the network, the scope of activity on the network, or the amount of *genuine* (i.e., human) activity on the network; although Twitter and other platforms now offer "verified" accounts that confirm identities for celebrities and other public figures who are at risk of impersonation. It just seems as if each user is harmlessly communicating with their friends and followers—and the occasional ideologue, be they bot or troll, who somehow infiltrates their news feed.

Social media are also opaque in the sense that they obscure the routine collection of data from users (anything posted is also generally recorded on network servers, even if the user attempts to delete it later) while generating copious amounts of "covert data" that are available only to system operators and those granted permission to access deeper system tiers and data stores (Zelenkauskaite and Bucy 2016). Facebook has come under considerable criticism for granting inappropriate access to user data, first for allowing information from the profiles of more than 50 million users to be shared with the consulting firm Cambridge Analytica for personality profiling and behavioral influence in the run-up to the 2016 US presidential election (Rosenberg, Confessore, and Cadwalladr 2018) and, more recently, for granting "deep access" to data of users and their friends to over 60 device makers and electronics firms, including a Chinese telecommunications company (Huawei) flagged by American intelligence as a national security threat (Dance, Confessore, and LaForgia 2018; LaForgia and Dance 2018). The ensuing furor has led to calls for Facebook's break up and downsizing using antitrust laws, similar to AT&T's forced retrenchment in the 1980s (Editorial Board, *NYT* 2018).

Since the value on social media platforms is on sharing and spreading (in other words, on traffic generation), and not on authenticating, assessing the pedigree of a piece of circulated information is not an affordance built into the system design. In his prescient warnings, Stoll (1995b) highlighted the crucial distinction between unstructured and unconfirmed "data" on the one hand—suspect content "lacking editors, reviewers, or critics," which he argued the Internet was full of—and vetted "information" on the other, which has a pedigree and traceable history. For fake news items that appear on social media, the onus of verification and fact-checking, including authentication that the posted or shared item is indeed from a legitimate source, is on the individual. For reasons explained below, this outsourcing of editorial labor traditionally performed by news organizations quickly overwhelms the typical user, who is not only uninterested but also ill-equipped to handle the volume, velocity, variety, and (in)visibility of social media data flows just to gauge their veracity.

Descartes, Spinoza, and the Acceptance of False Information

Beyond sensational headlines, fake news finds an audience on social media because users have difficulty identifying and rejecting false information. A survey conducted in the aftermath of the 2016 US presidential election by the news and entertainment site Buzzfeed found that 75% of American adults who were familiar with a political fake news headline also believed it was accurate (Silverman and Singer-Vine 2016). Respondents who cited Facebook as a major source of news were more likely to report fake news as true than people who did not rely on the platform for information—and at the same rate that actual news headlines were judged accurate by the sample overall (83%). Setting aside the political implications of these findings for a moment (most of the headlines tested were about Donald Trump, and Republican partisans had a higher rate of acceptance than Democrats), such willingness to believe phony information would seem startling were it not for the fact that psychological research has convincingly demonstrated the ease with which made-up claims are believed.

Daniel Gilbert and colleagues tested the acceptance of false information in a series of elegant experiments run in the pre-online era, contrasting the assertions of Renaissance philosophers Rene Descartes and Baruch Spinoza (Gilbert, Krull, and Malone 1990). Ever the rationalist, Descartes ([1641] 1984) was convinced that upon exposure to an idea or proposition, the listener could hold the information in suspended equilibrium without judging it to be true or false (that is, without reference to its veracity), until such time that it could be subjected to systematic analysis. Upon hearing new information, Descartes would have us suspend judgment, decide whether we agree or not first, then render a judgment about its truth value. By contrast, Spinoza ([1677] 1982) suggested that all ideas are accepted in the mind as true *prior* to rational analysis (even if only briefly), as a condition of comprehension, and that some ideas or assertions are later rejected upon further reflection. In other words, the mental representation of an idea, even if absurd, has a truth value associated with it, and the default value is *true*—only to be changed if and when the idea is subsequently assessed as false (Gilbert et al. 1990).

Participants in the studies were presented with a series of true, false, and meaningless linguistic propositions and, on some trials, their processing of that information was interrupted. Telling for our times, interruptions increase the likelihood of considering false propositions as true (but not true propositions as false), and, as Spinoza's model predicts, merely comprehending a false proposition increases the likelihood of regarding it as true (Gilbert et al. 1990). Two background factors help explain the tendency to accept new propositions as true—cognitive economy and survival. Humans by design are both limited capacity processors and cognitive misers, and veer toward strategies that conserve resources (Fiske and Taylor 1991). Entertaining false statements requires not only more time but more *cognitive capacity* than processing true statements, simply because false propositions must be accepted first as Spinoza asserted and then unaccepted.[3] Since rejection requires more effort than acceptance, it happens less. And when false claims carry political content, as they often do on social media, partisan motivated reasoning may come into play, where information processing shifts to conform to pre-existing attitudes and beliefs.

Even if efforts are made to verify suspect content, another psychological tendency grounded in evolutionary theory supports the acceptance of initial claims as true because doing so places one in a heightened state of action readiness, thereby maximizing survival. "Imagine the moment when some prehistoric ancestor out on a hunt encountered a sudden rustling in the bush. From an information processing perspective, the challenge . . . is to pay attention to the novel event, classify it based on limited information, and reach a behavioral decision about how to respond" (Newhagen and Levy 1998, 10). The more menacing and apocalyptic a fake news headline sounds—i.e., the more it resembles a rustling in the bush—the more it likely triggers an analogous response, as negatively valenced information crowds out less urgent material and even retroactively inhibits memory for information that preceded it (Newhagen and Reeves 1992). Indeed, emotional arousal generated by a message increases its chances of being shared (Berger 2011), and stories likely to evoke fear and disgust spread more readily, and widely, on social media than neutral reports (Cotter 2008).

Not surprisingly, then, an analysis of viral hoaxes in 2017 found that the most circulated categories concerned crime and politics (Silverman, Lytvynenko, and Pham 2017). So bogus information with a high threat value, which strikes an emotional chord and resonates as if it were real news (e.g., "WikiLeaks confirms Hillary sold weapons to ISIS . . . Then drops another bombshell"), often wins out over well-intentioned but insufficient efforts to correct false claims. This is a politically astute though unfortunate hallmark of populist discourse, which aims to disrupt the established order without concern for the truth (Engesser, Fawzi, and Larsson 2017). For social media users inundated by a continuous flow of postings and updates, the incentives and wherewithal necessary to dedicate the time and attention needed to determine the veracity of each new posting that appears in a news feed is low, and there are cognitive and evolutionary biases at work that mitigate against the rejection of false information.

Distractions and multitasking, hallmarks of the contemporary digital lifestyle, compound the problem. The acontextual way in which fake news items suddenly appear in social media news feeds, seeming to have but lacking in credibility, and the likelihood of encountering them on a small screen one isolated story at a time, also increases the likelihood of acceptance because the user can't see, for example, that they really belong in a supermarket tabloid amid other hoaxes and tall tales (Allcott and Gentzkow 2017). Fragmentation of the media landscape by new apps and mobile devices is thus "an important contributor to misinformation's particular resilience to correction" (Lewandowsky et al. 2012, 108). Finally, there are characteristics of fake news messages themselves, both their content and form, that contribute to their virality and spreadability over social media. These issues are discussed next.

Dimensions of Fake News

Before the rise of social media and its propagation of misinformation, the term "fake news" was used in a mostly playful sense to denote political satire and parody on television shows like *Saturday Night Live, The Daily Show*, and *Colbert Report*—programs descended from the pioneering televised satire of the 1960s, including *Rowan & Martin's Laugh-In, That Was the Week That Was*, even *Monty Python's Flying Circus*. From a review of the academic literature on fake news over the past 15 years, Tandoc and colleagues (2018) developed a typology of scholarly definitions, identifying six ways the term has been used in research: as news satire, news parody, news fabrication, manipulation, (native) advertising, and propaganda.

For classification, these categories of fake news can be arrayed across two dimensions of message content and purpose—level of facticity and the author's intent to deceive, whether low or high—forming a 2 × 2 matrix that facilitates grouping of different fake news genres by their level of veracity and deceptive intent (Tandoc et al. 2018, 148).

Native advertising and propaganda populate the high level of facticity but also high intent to deceive quadrant, while news satire is recognized as having a high level of facticity and low intent to deceive. The lighthearted yet arousing manner in which *The Daily Show* and other political entertainment formats address current events helps explain why frequent viewers of these shows, particularly younger audiences, experience considerable learning effects and other civically beneficial outcomes (Delli-Carpini 2012). News parody, such as the *Onion* newspaper/website, falls just outside this sweet spot of entertaining delivery, with low deceptive intent but also a low level of facticity (i.e., hilarious but divorced from reality). News fabrication and manipulation, perhaps the most sinister forms of fake news because they seem real but aren't, are grouped into the low level of facticity and high intent to deceive cell. Current definitions and analyses of fake news focus largely on these two types, given their problematic relationship with the truth and prominence in public discourse (Tandoc et al. 2018).

Along these lines, Allcott and Gentzkow (2017, 213) conceptualize misinformation as distorted signals about the world that are uncorrelated with the truth, defining fake news as "articles that are intentionally and verifiably false, and could mislead readers." Intentionality is a key discriminating factor between real news reports that carry honest mistakes—an inevitable byproduct of breaking news and other modes of newsgathering under tight deadlines—and fake news reports that deliberately deceive, whether for ideological or pecuniary purposes. Figure 12.1 presents a continuum of fake news that arrays different forms of news by their truth value, from nonexistent to extremely high. On the right are the two most problematic genres of fake news identified in research—manipulation and outright fabrication (Tandoc et al. 2018). Whereas fabricated stories invent news-like claims out of whole cloth (e.g., "FBI Agent Suspected in Hillary Email Leaks Found Dead in Apartment Murder-Suicide"), circulating what would be shocking if true, manipulated news spins dark narratives around real news to proffer the illusion of something sinister, often referencing tragic events (e.g., "Las Vegas: Video Footage Confirms Multiple Shooters, Co-ordinated Attack").[4] Neither fabricated nor manipulated fake news offers any substantiation for

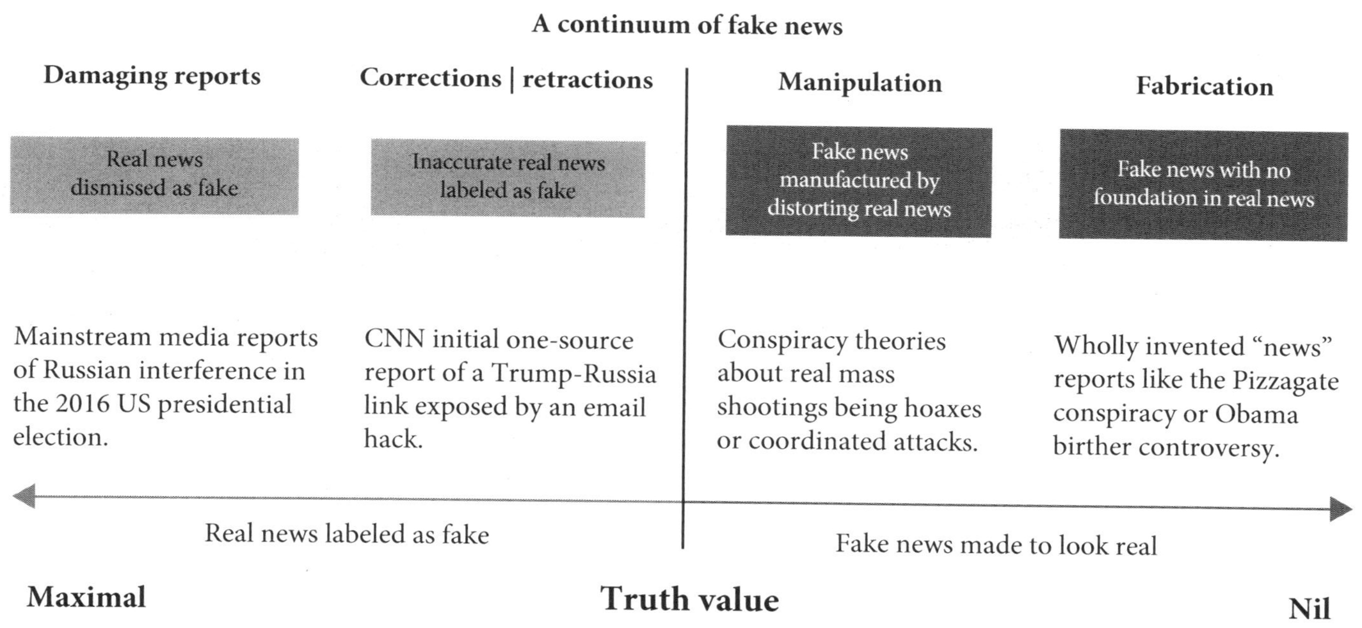

A continuum of fake news

Damaging reports	Corrections | retractions	Manipulation	Fabrication
Real news dismissed as fake.	Inaccurate real news labeled as fake	Fake news manufactured by distorting real news	Fake news with no foundation in real news
Mainstream media reports of Russian interference in the 2016 US presidential election.	CNN initial one-source report of a Trump-Russia link exposed by an email hack.	Conspiracy theories about real mass shootings being hoaxes or coordinated attacks.	Wholly invented "news" reports like the Pizzagate conspiracy or Obama birther controversy.

Real news labeled as fake

Fake news made to look real

Truth value

Maximal   **Nil**

Figure 12.1 A continuum of fake news.

its claims, and many of these stories and host sites are taken down shortly after surfacing to avoid legal action once their monetary worth as clickbait has passed.

As a cultural form, fake news gains impetus from two powerful motivations: profit and persuasion, or social influence. Both depend on the potential for fake news stories to go viral and provide content producers with clicks that convert to advertising revenue and social media traffic (Tandoc et al. 2018). As these motivations mix with the fake news purveyor's lack of concern about facticity, they generate different levels of information taintedness or degree of compromised status. Figure 12.2 illustrates these dimensions graphically, with fabricated stories (in the outer ring) appearing at the lowest point of facticity and highest level of profit motivation, and manipulated news (in the inner ring) slightly higher in facticity and more closely aligned with the persuasion motive. But author motivation and fake news accuracy do not tell the whole story.

News can be distinguished by its structural appearance and content characteristics, as well (Barnhurst and Nerone 2002). Structure has to do with the stylistic appearance of a story, where prominence on a page, physical layout of a news article (e.g., nameplate, masthead, headline, byline, lede paragraph), or position in a newscast signal an item's importance. An obvious but sometimes overlooked factor concerning social media's challenge to journalistic truth is that new apps and distribution platforms have stripped news interfaces of the physical cues necessary for

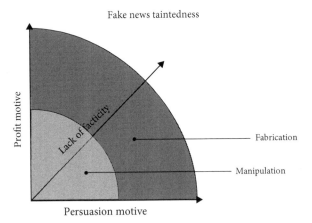

Figure 12.2 Fake news taintedness.

audiences to effectively parse news content from opinion, advertising, and other non-news content. Markers such as section and story location on the page allowed readers to make sense out of a large amount of information with little effort because the news had been pre-processed by journalists (Newhagen and Levy 1998). Emerging media interfaces, particularly on mobile devices, have largely obliterated these traditional sign posts. Add this to the growing list of reasons why separating the editorial wheat from the fake news chaff for users of social media, particularly on smart phones, remains a daunting task.

Native advertising, which resembles a publication's editorial content but is underwritten by sponsors intending to promote a product or service, thrives in this ambiguous context (see Amazeen and Muddiman 2018), as does fake news. A similarity between native ads and fake news postings, which are both deceptive in intent, is their authoritative, news-like packaging. Fake news posts are made to look just like news but are devoid of original reporting or empirical verification, a feature that makes their production virtually cost-free compared with the more precise social signals generated by real news practices (Allcott and Gentzkow 2017). Newsgathering and verification are highly labor and resource intensive; storytelling is not.

Fake news also grabs viewer attention with the newspaper hawker's promise of jaw-dropping content, with the intent to titillate or persuade, an outrageous quality that contributes to their spreadability (Tandoc et al. 2018). But if the user looks for precise signals from fake news and unwittingly relies on misinformation because it somehow feels right, then the outcome is propaganda. At this point, the intent is no longer to persuade—but to confuse. Here, communication introduces instability because confusion is not a functional psychological state. If widely disseminated, fake news exacts a high social cost because belief in lies, untruths, and manipulative assertions promotes actions that are not in an individual's, or a society's, best interest (Lewandowsky et al. 2012).

Another facilitator of fake news dissemination on social media is the blurred status of the originating information source. In networked systems, a news item might "reach an individual through a dedicated news site, via the news organization's Facebook site, or through a 'shared' posting of their social network. Social media users, therefore, have to navigate through a multitude of information [layers] shared by multiple sources" (Tandoc et al. 2018, 139). On social media, determining news authorship and authenticity arguably takes a back seat to assessing the social proximity of who forwards or retweets a piece of news; indeed, the simple act of receiving information from friends can help legitimate the perceived veracity of information that is shared (Tandoc et al. 2018). In this way, social media foreground what Sundar (2008) has identified as a bandwagoning heuristic, with each new post accompanied by popularity ratings in the form of shares, likes, comments, or retweets, giving widely shared items ever more viral momentum.

Figure 12.3 presents a conceptual model of fake news virality, showing the assumed synergistic effects of story outrageousness, news-like formatting, and digital bandwagoning on the spread of fake news. As a piece of fake news ascends along each dimension, the likelihood of it moving from mere circulation (the inner ring) to widely shared and viral in nature (the outer ring) increases proportionally.

On the other side of the facticity ledger are flawed news reports by legitimate news organizations that require correction or retraction, which are then seized upon by the alt.media universe and Trump White House as examples of fake news in mainstream media more generally (see figure 12.1). Some of CNN's reporting on purported links between the Trump presidential campaign and Russian operatives or WikiLeaks fall into this category (see Ember and Grynbaum 2017; Grynbaum and Ember 2017). Stories of this type, labeled "corrections | retractions," are often flawed not because they are completely factually incorrect but because they get a name, date, or other isolated piece of information wrong that needs to be

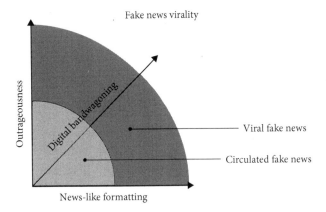

Figure 12.3 Fake news virality.

corrected, or rely on a single anonymous source so the information cannot be verified. The story may be materially true but suffer from a lack of clarity and proper editorial vetting. Finally, there are wholly accurate but critical accounts of power holders or any administration, repeatedly labeled "fake news" by Trump, that represent journalism in the public interest. We label these "damaging reports" because they have high truth value but are dismissed by extreme partisans as fake.

While politically useful for rallying followers, attempts to discredit mainstream media by labeling them fake news are socially costly because they further weaken the credibility of an already beleaguered press and foster an "us versus them" mentality. Trump has not only accused the legitimate press of telling lies, he has also cast the news media as an "enemy of the American people" (Grynbaum 2017)—a line he temporarily toned down following a deadly newsroom shooting at the *Capital Gazette* newspaper in Annapolis, Maryland in June 2018 that killed five people (Landler 2018). Such rhetoric gives his supporters reason for discounting factual reporting and sets up the press as an oppositional faction rather than impartial observer of the day's events. The repeated accusations also give adversaries a strategic opening, allowing Russian President Vladimir Putin, for instance, to claim that the "fake news" media and "deep state" bureaucrats are conspiring against Putin and Trump from becoming closer friends (Jaffe, Dawsey, and Leonnig 2018). By obsolescing the traditional gatekeeping function of journalism, facilitating the spread of false information, and allowing an impetuous president to repeatedly bash legitimate news, social media make the search for truth more difficult than it might be.

A Modest Proposal

The situation that news purveyors and news audiences now find themselves in, besieged by digital entrepreneurs and strategic propagandists without any commitment to the truth, seems nothing short of dire. Even in the European Union, which has developed a strong tradition of privacy laws and individual control over personal information, regulatory efforts to control content and data flows of the biggest social media players are fraught with difficulty, even as pressure to do so mounts (Hern 2018). And counterpropaganda efforts won't stop the influx of digital disinformation even if early warnings from intelligence agencies and active counter-measures can sometimes neutralize its worst effects (see Nossiter, Sanger, and Perlroth 2017). However, there is a simpler, less costly, and easily implemented solution with the potential to inoculate audiences from the pernicious influence of digital disinformation: build societal resilience by requiring journalism training—news reporting, writing, and editing—as a core requirement of any secondary, post-secondary (college), or adult education program.

The benefits of a journalism education are well established. First, like composition courses, news writing teaches students how to communicate effectively in writing and structure evidence in a coherent fashion, putting the most important information first and saving less urgent context for later in the story. Similar to fiction, quotes are used in news reports to bring the main characters to life and give the reporting narrative appeal. Unlike composition and fiction writing, however, journalism requires that news writing be based not on the reporter's imagination, opinion, or interpretation (although there is a place for opinion on the op-ed page and news analysis is increasingly seeping into hard news reporting) but on some empirically observable or verifiable facts. For legitimate news organizations, the golden rule of verification is that no piece of information should be published unless it can be independently confirmed by at least two different sources. Crucially, all editorial copy then undergoes review and revision by the assignment editor or news desk to improve accuracy through a rigorous process of editing and correction. At major magazines, verification via an intensive process of fact-checking at the sentence level is also *de rigueur*—and has been for decades.

The upshot of learning the discipline that news reporting requires, and in working within a system of close review and editing feedback, is that norms of representing reality as faithfully and accurately as possible are internalized and the skills for "bullshit detection" (see Nielsen 2015) cultivated. Studying and practicing journalism also makes one a more perceptive consumer of mainstream media and enhances motivation to engage with actual news. Gleaning both story-related and process-oriented information *from* and *about* the news then becomes more likely, turning otherwise casual audiences into more motivated and sophisticated consumers of news. Such talk isn't just idle speculation. Large-scale studies employing media literacy measures tapping the procedures and hallmark qualities of legitimate news show that respondents with increased knowledge about the workings of the press consume news from a wider range of sources and rely on a broader range of credibility cues when deciding whether to click through to a story than those with lower levels of news literacy (Fletcher 2018).

In basic training for World War II, US military recruits were shown Frank Capra's "Why We Fight" anti-propaganda films to overcome resistance to American involvement in the war and educate the troops about the Axis powers' use of biased and misleading messaging to undermine morale. The films were deemed necessary as a form of inoculation because the chance of exposure to enemy propaganda once deployed was considered high. Today, the chance that social media users will encounter fake news or bot-generated propaganda is similarly high. Facebook and Twitter, which now find themselves exploited by pranksters, political ideologues, data analytics firms, and even foreign governments, are making some remedial efforts to rectify the situation (Levin 2017), but blocking users and deleting accounts en masse goes against their commercial self-interest to show continuous growth. Even if all bot-generated activity could be filtered out, bad actors (at least in the US context) will continue to cite First Amendment protections to disseminate lies and misinformation as commentary or political perspective, so much fake news will continue to get through. Governments, moreover, have shown reluctance to regulate digital media with the same heavy hand as broadcast media—and definitional debates about whether social media firms are technology companies or publishers, which bear on regulation, remain in flux.

In these circumstances, new educational requirements that treat mainstream media as important civic institutions worthy of understanding and respect, including the practice of legitimate newsgathering itself, could go a long way toward mitigating some of the damage that will inevitably ensue from the next all-out disinformation campaign.

Notes

1. Even though truth in news and politics is more tenuous than truth in less charged contexts, such as math instruction or botany, the level of distortion and use of propaganda techniques in current public discourse, including on cable news and partisan blogs in addition to social media, is arguably unprecedented in peacetime (see Bard 2017; Conway, Grabe, and Grieves 2007). For the biggest fake news headlines of 2016, see https://www.cnbc.com/2016/12/30/read-all-about-it-the-biggest-fake-news-stories-of-2016.html.

2. Understood as "statements made with little or no concern for their truth-value" that have no epistemological grounding, verifiability, or satisfying and generally acceptable answer to the question "How do you know?" (Nielsen 2015, 1; see Frankfurt 2005).

3. More recent research has shown that suspension of belief is possible, but requires "a high degree of attention, considerable implausibility of the message, or high levels of distrust at the time the message is received. So, in most situations, the deck is stacked in favor of accepting information rather than rejecting it" (Lewandowsky et al. 2012, 112; see also Hasson, Simmons, and Todorov 2005).

4. The most aggressive fake news sites and associated YouTube channels, such as Infowars, The Gateway Pundit, and Daily Stormer, are routinely sued by victims of these published reports for libel and defamation (Ohlheiser 2018; Tani 2018). Alex Jones, a prominent conspiracy theorist whose audience now rivals that of major cable news networks, characterizes his accusatory posts and radio show assertions as "commentary" but has on occasion apologized to the targets of his attacks when compelled by lawsuits (Rosenberg 2017).

References

Allcott, Hunt, and Matthew Gentzkow. 2017. "Social Media and Fake News in the 2016 Election." *Journal of Economic Perspectives* 31, no. 2: 211–236.

Amazeen, Michelle A., and Bucy, Erik P. 2019. "Conferring Resistance to Digital Disinformation: The Inoculating Influence of Procedural News Knowledge." *Journal of Broadcasting and Electronic Media*.

Amazeen, Michelle A., and Ashley R. Muddiman. 2018. "Saving Media or Trading on Trust? The Effects of Native Advertising on Audience Perceptions of Legacy and Online News Publishers." *Digital Journalism* 6, no. 2: 176–195.

Andrejevic, Mark. 2007. *iSpy: Surveillance and Power in the Interactive Era.* Lawrence: University Press of Kansas.

Bard, Mitchell T. 2017. "Propaganda, Persuasion, or Journalism? Fox News' Prime-Time Coverage of Health-Care Reform in 2009 and 2014." *Electronic News* 11, no. 2: 100–118.

Barnhurst, Kevin G., and John Nerone. 2002. *The Form of News: A History.* New York: Guilford Press.

Bennett, W. Lance, and Alexandra Segerberg. 2014. *The Logic of Connective Action: Digital Media and the Personalization of Contentious Politics.* New York: Cambridge University Press.

Berger, Jonah. 2011. "Arousal Increases Social Transmission of Information." *Psychological Science* 22, no. 7: 891–893.

Bucy, Erik P. 2018. "The Calibration Problem: ICT Complexity and Average User Competencies." *Journal of Communication Technology*, 1 no. 1: article 3. http://www.joctec.org/volume-1-issue-1-article-3/.

Cadwalladr, Carole, and Emma Graham-Harrison. 2018. "Revealed: 50 Million Facebook Profiles Harvested for Cambridge Analytica in Major Data Breach." *The Guardian*, March 17. https://www.theguardian.com/news/2018/mar/17/cambridge-analytica-facebook-influence-us-election.

Castells, Manuel. 2009. *Communication Power.* Oxford: Oxford University Press.

Castells, Manuel. 2012. *Networks of Outrage and Hope: Social Movements in the Internet Age.* Cambridge: Polity Press.

Conway, Mike, Maria Elizabeth Grabe, and Kevin Grieves. 2007. "Villains, Victims and the Virtuous in Bill O'Reilly's 'No-Spin Zone.'" *Journalism Studies* 8, no. 2: 197–223.

Cotter, Ellen M. 2008. "Influence of Emotional Content and Perceived Relevance on Spread of Urban Legends: A Pilot Study." *Psychological Reports* 102, no. 2: 623–629.

Dance, Gabriel J. X., Nicholas Confessore, and Michael LaForgia. 2018. "Facebook Gave Device Makers Deep Access to Data on Users and Friends." *New York Times*, June 3. https://www.nytimes.com/interactive/2018/06/03/technology/facebook-device-partners-users-friends-data.html.

Delli-Carpini, Michael X. 2012. "Entertainment Media and the Political Engagement of Citizens." In *The SAGE Handbook of Political Communication*, edited by Holly Z. Semetko and Margaret Scammel, 9–21. London: SAGE.

Descartes, René. (1641) 1984. "Fourth Meditation." In *The Philosophical Writings of Descartes,* trans. and ed. John Cottingham, Robert Stoothoff, and Dugald Murdoch, vol. 2, 37–43. Cambridge: Cambridge University Press.

Devaney, Robert. 2013. "Salinger's Accusations About TWA Flight 800 Resurface in New Documentary." *The Georgetowner*, July 22. https://georgetowner.com/articles/2013/07/22/salingers-accusations-about-twa-flight-800-resurface-new-documentary.

Editorial Board. 2018. "Can Facebook Be Cut Down to Size?" *New York Times*, op-ed section, June 5. https://www.nytimes.com/2018/06/05/opinion/facebook-china-privacy-data-security.html.

Ember, Sydney, and Michael M. Grynbaum. 2017. "At CNN, Retracted Story Leaves an Elite Reporting Team Bruised." *New York Times*, September 5. https://www.nytimes.com/2017/09/05/business/media/cnn-retraction-trump-scaramucci.html.

Engesser, Sven, Nayla Fawzi, and Anders Olof Larsson. 2017. "Populist Online Communication: Introduction to the Special Issue." *Information, Communication, & Society* 20, no. 9: 1279–1292.

European Commission. 2018. "A Multi-Dimensional Approach to Disinformation: Report of the Independent High-Level Group on Fake News and Online Disinformation." Directorate-General for Communication Networks, Content and Technology. Luxembourg: Publications Office of the European Union, March. https://ec.europa.eu/digital-single-market/en/news/final-report-high-level-expert-group-fake-news-and-online-disinformation.

Fiske, Susan T., and Shelley E. Taylor. 1991. *Social Cognition*. 2nd ed. New York: McGraw-Hill.

Fletcher, Richard. "The Impact of Greater News Literacy." In *Reuters Institute Digital News Report 2018*, edited by Nic Newman, 34–37. Oxford: Reuters Institute for the Study of Journalism, University of Oxford. http://www.digitalnewsreport.org.

Frankfurt, Harry G. 2005. *On Bullshit*. Princeton, NJ: Princeton University Press.

Frenkel, Sheera. 2018. "Facebook Tried to Rein in Fake Ads. It Fell Short in a California Race." *New York Times*, June 3. https://www.nytimes.com/2018/06/03/technology/california-congressional-race-facebook-election-interference.html.

Gilbert, Daniel T., Douglas S. Krull, and Patrick S. Malone. 1990. "Unbelieving the Unbelievable: Some Problems in the Rejection of False Information." *Journal of Personality and Social Psychology* 59, no. 4: 601–613.

Grillo, Ioan. 2018. "Fake News Crosses the Rio Grande." *New York Times*, May 3. https://www.nytimes.com/2018/05/03/opinion/fake-news-mexico-election.html.

Grossman, Lawrence K. 1995. *The Electronic Republic: Reshaping Democracy in the Information Age*. New York: Viking.

Grynbaum, Michael M. 2017. "Trump Calls the News Media the 'Enemy of the American People.'" *New York Times*, February 17. https://www.nytimes.com/2017/02/17/business/trump-calls-the-news-media-the-enemy-of-the-people.html.

Grynbaum, Michael M., and Sydney Ember. 2017. "CNN Corrects a Trump Story, Fueling Claims of 'Fake News.'" *New York Times*, December 8. https://www.nytimes.com/2017/12/08/business/media/cnn-correction-donald-trump-jr.html.

Hasson, Uri, Joseph P. Simmons, and Alexander Todorov. 2005. "Believe It or Not: On the Possibility of Suspending Belief." *Psychological Science* 16, no. 7: 566–571.

Hern, Alex. 2018. "Privacy Policies of Tech Giants 'Still Not GDPR-Compliant.'" *The Guardian*, July 5, 2018. https://www.theguardian.com/technology/2018/jul/05/privacy-policies-facebook-amazon-google-not-gdpr-compliant.

Jaffe, Gregg, Josh Dawsey, and Carol D. Leonnig. 2018. "Ahead of NATO and Putin Summits, Trump's Unorthodox Diplomacy Rattles Allies." *Washington Post*, July 6. https://www.washingtonpost.com/politics/ahead-of-nato-and-putin-summits-trumps-unorthodox-diplomacy-rattles-allies/2018/07/06/16c7aa4e-7006-11e8-bd50-b80389a4e569_story.html.

Jenkins, Henry, Sam Ford, and Joshua Green. 2013. *Spreadable Media: Creating Value and Meaning in a Networked Culture*. New York: New York University Press.

Kanellos, Michael. 2016. "The Fourth 'V' for Big Data." *Forbes*, October 11. https://www.forbes.com/sites/michaelkanellos/2016/10/11/the-fourth-v-for-big-data/#318e50cd5909.

Katz, James, Michael Barris, and Anshul Jain. 2013. *The Social Media President: Barack Obama and the Politics of Citizen Engagement*. New York: Palgrave Macmillan.

LaForgia, Michael, and Gabriel J. X. Dance. 2018. "Facebook Gave Data Access to Chinese Firm Flagged by U.S. Intelligence." *New York Times*, June 5. https://www.nytimes.com/2018/06/05/technology/facebook-device-partnerships-china.html.

Landler, Mark. 2018. "Condemning Deadly Newsroom Shooting, Trump Tempers Hostility Toward Media." *New York Times*, June 29. https://www.nytimes.com/2018/06/29/us/politics/donald-trump-newsroom-shooting.html.

Lapowsky, Issie. 2018. "Facebook Exposed 87 Million Users to Cambridge Analytica." *Wired*, April 4. https://www.wired.com/story/facebook-exposed-87-million-users-to-cambridge-analytica.

Levin, Sam. 2017. "Facebook Promised to Tackle Fake News. But the Evidence Shows It's Not Working." *The Guardian*, May 16. https://www.theguardian.com/technology/2017/may/16/facebook-fake-news-tools-not-working.

Levin, Sam. 2018. "Is Facebook a Publisher? In Public It Says No, But in Court It Says Yes." *The Guardian*, July 3. https://www.theguardian.com/technology/2018/jul/02/facebook-mark-zuckerberg-platform-publisher-lawsuit.

Lewandowsky, Stephan, Ullrich K. H. Ecker, Colleen M. Seifert, Norbert Schwarz, and John Cook. 2012. "Misinformation and Its Correction: Continued Influence and Successful Debiasing." *Psychological Science in the Public Interest* 13, no. 3: 106–131.

Lukoianova, Tatiana, and Victoria L. Rubin. 2014. "Veracity Roadmap: Is Big Data Objective, Truthful and Credible?" *Advances in Classification Research Online* 24, no. 1: doi:10.7152/acro.v24i1.14671.

Newhagen, John E., and Mark R. Levy. 1998. "The Future of Journalism in a Distributed Communication Architecture." In *Rumor, Reputation, and Reporting in the New Online Environment*, edited by Diane L. Borden and Kerric Harvey, 10–21. Mahwah, NJ: Lawrence Erlbaum.

Newhagen, John E., and Byron Reeves. 1992. "This Evening's Bad News: Effects of Compelling Negative Television News Images on Memory." *Journal of Communication* 42, no. 2: 25–41.

Nielsen, Rasmus Kleis. 2015. "Social Media and Bullshit." *Social Media and Society* 1, no. 1: 1–3.

Nossiter, Adam, David E. Sanger, and Nicole Perlroth. 2017. "Hackers Came, but the French Were Prepared." *New York Times*, May 20. https://nyti.ms/2ptwWSf.

Ohlheiser, Abby. 2018. "Here's Why Sandy Hook Parents and Others Are Suing Alex Jones." *Washington Post*, April 17. https://www.washingtonpost.com/news/the-intersect/wp/2018/04/17/heres-why-sandy-hook-parents-and-others-are-suing-alex-jones.

Ophir, Eyal, Clifford Nass, and Anthony D. Wagner. 2009. "Cognitive Control in Media Multitaskers." *PNAS* 106, no. 37: 15583–15587.

Papacharissi, Zizi. 2015. *Affective Publics: Sentiment, Technology, and Politics.* New York: Oxford University Press.

Rheingold, Howard. 2002. *Smart Mobs: The Next Social Revolution.* New York: Basic Books.

Rosen, Jeffrey. 2001. *The Unwanted Gaze: The Destruction of Privacy in America.* New York: Vintage Books.

Rosenberg, Eli. 2017. "Alex Jones Apologies for Promoting 'Pizzagate' Hoax." *New York Times*, March 25. https://www.nytimes.com/2017/03/25/business/alex-jones-pizzagate-apology-comet-ping-pong.html.

Rosenberg, Matthew, Nicholas Confessore, and Carole Cadwalladr. 2018. "How Trump Consultants Exploited the Facebook Data of Millions." *New York Times*, March 17. https://www.nytimes.com/2018/03/17/us/politics/cambridge-analytica-trump-campaign.html.

Schudson, Michael. 2008. *Why Democracies Need an Unlovable Press.* Cambridge: Polity Press.

Silverman, Craig. 2016. "This Analysis Shows How Viral Fake Election News Stories Outperformed Real News on Facebook." Buzzfeed, November 16. https://www.buzzfeed.com/craigsilverman/viral-fake-election-news-outperformed-real-news-on-facebook.

Silverman, Craig, Jane Lytvynenko, and Scott Pham. 2017. "These Are 50 of the Biggest Fake News Hits on Facebook in 2017." Buzzfeed, December 28. https://www.buzzfeed.com/craigsilverman/these-are-50-of-the-biggest-fake-news-hits-on-facebook-in.

Silverman, Craig, and Jeremy Singer-Vine. 2016. "Most Americans Who See Fake News Believe It, New Survey Says." *Buzzfeed*, December 6, 2016. https://www.buzzfeed.com/craigsilverman/fake-news-survey

Spinoza, Baruch. (1677) 1982. *The Ethics and Selected Letters.* Edited by Seymour Feldman. Translated by Samuel Shirley. Indianapolis: Hackett.

Stoll, Clifford. 1995a. *Silicon Snake Oil: Second Thoughts on the Information Highway.* New York: Anchor Books.

Stoll, Clifford. 1995b. "Why the Web Won't Be Nirvana." *Newsweek*, February 26. http://www.newsweek.com/clifford-stoll-why-web-wont-be-nirvana-185306.

Sundar, Shyam S. 2008. "The MAIN Model: A Heuristic Approach to Understanding Technology Effects on Credibility." In *Digital Media, Youth, and Credibility*, edited by Miriam J. Metzger and Andrew J. Flanagin, 73–100. Cambridge, MA: MIT Press.

Tani, Maxwell. 2018. "Infowars and The Gateway Pundit Slapped with Lawsuit for Spreading Charlottesville Conspiracy." *The Daily Beast*, March 13. https://www.

thedailybeast.com/infowars-and-the-gateway-pundit-slapped-with-lawsuits-for-spreading-charlottesville-conspiracies.

Tandoc, Edson C., Jr., Zheng Wei Lim, and Rich Ling. 2018. "Defining 'Fake News': A Typology of Scholarly Definitions." *Digital Journalism* 6, no. 2: 137–153.

Timberg, Craid, and Elizabeth Dwoskin. 2018. "Twitter Is Sweeping Out Fake Accounts Like Never Before, Putting User Growth at Risk." *Washington Post*, July 6. https://www.washingtonpost.com/technology/2018/07/06/twitter-is-sweeping-out-fake-accounts-like-never-before-putting-user-growth-risk.

Van Dijk, Jan A. G. M. 2005. *The Deepening Divide: Inequality in the Information Society.* Thousand Oaks, CA: SAGE.

Wingfield, Nick, Mike Isaac, and Katie Benner. 2016. "Google and Facebook Take Aim at Fake News Sites." *New York Times*, November 14. https://www.nytimes.com/2016/11/15/technology/google-will-ban-websites-that-host-fake-news-from-using-its-ad-service.html.

Zelenkauskaite, Asta, and Erik P. Bucy. 2016. "A Scholarly Divide: Social Media, Big Data, and Unattainable Scholarship." *First Monday* 21, no. 5: http://dx.doi.org/10.5210/fm.v21i5.6358.

13

Truth at Large

When Social Media Investigations Get It Wrong

Edson C. Tandoc Jr.

After two bombs went off near the finish line of the Boston Marathon in the morning of April 15, 2013, online users quickly sprang into action. While police officers were on the hunt for the bombers, online users were examining photos and sorted through social media posts to help investigators identify the perpetrators. The online manhunt, particularly on the social news aggregation and discussion site Reddit, led some users to 22-year-old Sunil Tripathi, a Brown University student who had been reported missing for almost a month. Scrutinizing grainy CCTV images the police had released that showed a suspect, they noted his physical similarities to Sunil, whose photos were available online.

Sunil's family had created a Facebook page while searching for him. The page included video messages from family and friends as well as Sunil's recent photos. But hours after the release of the CCTV images, the page was bombarded by threatening messages, asserting that Sunil was one of the two Boston Marathon bombers. These messages prompted Sunil's family to remove the Facebook page, which only further fueled speculations about Sunil's role in the attack. Several journalists also tweeted about the removal of the page. Hours later, reporters from news organizations such as NBC and BuzzFeed posted tweets that specifically named Sunil as one of the bombers (Gourarie 2015; J. C. Kang 2013).

Sunil's body was found on April 23, 2013. He had killed himself on the day he went missing. The Reddit-inspired manhunters, the reporters who tweeted and identified Sunil as a suspect based on Reddit posts, and the journalists who subsequently phoned Sunil's family for interviews had gotten it wrong.

This chapter examines the intersection between journalism and social media. Specifically, it argues that social media platforms are changing the relationship between journalists and their audiences. This has important implications on what versions of truth ultimately reach the public.

The Changing Audience

Social media have drastically altered the relationship between journalists and their audiences. While theories of news construction have always considered audiences as important influences on journalists (Boczkowski 2005; Gans 1979; Shoemaker and Reese 2014), news audiences were traditionally assumed to play only a minor role. News audiences were conceptualized as either consumers or commodities (Webster and Phalen 1994). They were valued as buyers of journalistic outputs that emerged from news production processes solely controlled by journalists as well as for their media attention that could be sold to advertisers (Napoli 2011). The audience is an institutional construction (Butsch 2000; Turow 2005). For example, Napoli (2011, 3) said the "institutionalized audience" is "socially constructed by media industries, advertisers, and associated audience measurement firms." This is plausibly why traditional definitions of the audience referred to passive media consumers, whose media consumption can be measured quantitatively, in terms of ratings and circulation rates, among others. But today's news audiences are no longer the passive media consumers that traditional definitions had referred to, especially with the technological innovations that are now at their disposal.

The changing relationship between journalists and their audiences can be seen in the three different ways that news audiences now figure in the news construction process: through (1) content tailoring, (2) news dissemination, and (3) information generation (adapted from Tandoc and Vos 2016). First, news audiences provide journalists with detailed feedback, both intentional and unintentional. They can actively leave comments on news organizations' websites or social media accounts, or engage in media criticism by posting on their personal social media pages (Craft, Vos, and Wolfgang 2016). They can like and share news articles and follow news organizations' accounts on social media. But news audiences also leave their digital footprints that are tracked, recorded, and stored by web and social media analytics (Tandoc 2014). These different forms of feedback can influence journalists' editorial decisions, such as tailoring content to audience preferences.

Second, news audiences have become influential players in news dissemination. The digitization of news allowed journalism to play catch up with the changing audience, but it also confronted journalism with more competition. Thus, news publication does not automatically mean reaching an audience. To a large extent, news audiences now determine the reach of particular news items by emailing links or sharing them on their social media accounts (Thorson 2008). News items can spread not only geographically but also across time, with old news articles becoming viral after a few months or even years. This means journalists also have to be active in promoting and distributing their own work on social media (Tandoc and Vos 2016), something they never had to do in the past.

Third, news audiences upload and share bits of information, photos, videos, and even their commentaries about newsworthy events they witness firsthand. While these are often publicized for other news audiences to directly see, jumping the journalists' gates so to speak (Hermida 2011), they also sometimes end up in journalists' news outputs. News organizations have recognized citizen journalists and user-generated content and have since started efforts to provide spaces for audience contributions within their respective news sites (Singer 2010). Crowdsourcing became a buzzword in journalism, referring to the process of soliciting and obtaining ideas and information from non-journalists (Akagi and Linning 2013). These contributions have provided newsrooms with usually free content, but they also had to be subjected to the newsrooms' editorial processes (Tandoc and Vos 2016).

These three ways in which audiences now figure in news construction via social media have important implications on the versions of truth that ultimately reach the public. While content tailoring can be considered an indirect effect on the news items that ultimately reach public consciousness, as audience preferences are communicated to journalists who decide the extent to which such feedback is incorporated into editorial decisions, audiences' role in news dissemination and generation of information can be argued as more direct, as these processes can operate outside the control of traditional journalists and affect the range of news content that reaches the public.

Audiences and Journalists

Journalists have always been exposed to different forms of audience feedback. In the past, feedback from the news audience came in the form of letters to the editor and phone calls to the newsroom (Schlesinger 1978). Later, quantified and aggregated forms were used, such as readership surveys and television ratings (Beam 1995; Butsch 2000). However, these traditional forms of feedback came from only a subgroup of the actual audience and were often disregarded by journalists trying to protect their editorial autonomy (Gans 1979). Thus, in the past, how journalists imagined their audience—rather than their actual audiences—was what affected journalistic work (de Sola Pool and Shulman 1959; Ettema and Whitney 1994).

New forms of audience feedback, however, seem to be increasing audiences' indirect and direct impact on journalistic work. Social media platforms, for example, provide journalists with numerous forms of audience feedback. Social media feedback can be individual or aggregated, as well as qualitative or quantitative. Facebook and Twitter, for example, provide platforms for news audiences to comment or post about news articles or news organizations. They also provide journalists with lists of trending topics. Social media platforms also aggregate audience metrics, in the form of number of likes, shares, and comments. Compared with earlier forms of audience feedback, social media feedback is (1) faster, as data collection can be in real time; (2) more automatic, as intentional and unintentional feedback can be tracked and recorded; (3) more inclusive, as they can come from larger segments of the actual audience; (4) more comprehensive, as they come in both qualitative and quantitative forms; and (5) more public, as these forms of feedback can also be visible to other audiences, possibly putting more pressure on journalists to not ignore them (Lee and Tandoc 2017).

Studies have examined the impact these new forms of audience feedback have on journalists, particularly on journalistic routines, role orientations, and even newsroom culture. For example, a study found that newsrooms usually start their morning meetings by looking at trending topics on social media to guide subsequent coverage (Tandoc and Vos 2016). Individual journalists are also now expected to promote their articles on social media to drive social media engagement and traffic to the site, giving rise to what seems like a "marketing" function (Tandoc and Vos 2016, 958). They are also encouraged to interact with audiences by sharing their opinions or posting about stories they are working on (Canter 2013). News selection also seems to operate differently for social media. A study found that the range of topics that news organizations promote on their social media accounts tend to be different from the distribution of topics on their respective websites (Bastos 2015).

These changes in newsroom routines also seem to be leading to adjustments in how journalists conceive of their social roles. A survey of journalists in Australia found that frequency of reading comments from news audiences increased journalists' perception of how important both civic and consumer orientations are, while dependency on audience analytics increased perception of the importance of consumer orientation (Hanusch and Tandoc 2017). While civic orientation refers to providing news that "audiences need to know to act as responsible citizens," consumer orientation is often associated with providing entertainment (Hanusch and Tandoc 2017, 4).

Embedding social media into news routines is also associated with organizational culture. For example, the news and entertainment site BuzzFeed closely monitors social media engagement. While traditional news sites focus on analytics from their websites, BuzzFeed values social media metrics more. It keeps track of "social lift," which measures how viral a post gets on social media (Tandoc and Foo 2017). This is consistent with the prevailing newsroom culture at BuzzFeed that is "marked by a close attention to the audience" (Tandoc and Foo 2017, 13).

The economic uncertainty confronting journalism across different media contexts can help explain journalists' increased attention to audience feedback. Trending topics, social media comments, and audience metrics provide journalists many clues to what audiences want. They provide journalists with more clues about who the actual audiences are. But while they now have more clues about the audience than in the past, journalists still need to engage in some level of editorial guesswork to guide their subsequent editorial decisions (Tandoc and Vos 2016). And editorial guesswork might not always turn out to be correct. For example, many journalists think that most news audiences are interested in non-public affairs topics, such as celebrity and sports news. However, a study that looked at the *New York Times* and *The Guardian* found that while these news organizations indeed published a lot of sports and celebrity articles, social media users actually shared opinion and hard news articles more frequently (Bastos 2015). There is also the danger of considering audience metrics as a goal rather than as a means to do responsible journalism (Tandoc and Thomas 2014). Knowing what audiences want, and giving what they want, might get in the way of providing what audiences need (Tandoc and Thomas 2014). Informing audiences might be compromised by too much focus on entertaining them.

Audiences in Journalism

But aside from influencing journalists through their feedback that has become almost omnipresent in most newsrooms, news audiences also now directly influence which news articles get distributed and consumed. Social media platforms are increasingly becoming the main sources of news for a growing number of people across different media systems (Gottfried and Shearer 2016; Nielsen and Schrøder 2014). As news consumption becomes more and more incidental, especially among younger people (Antunovic, Parsons, and Cooke 2018), social media have become important platforms for users to come across news (Nielsen and Schrøder 2014). Thus, news organizations are becoming more aggressive in distributing their content through social media. But while news organizations and individual journalists now routinely disseminate links to their news articles on social media (Ju, Jeong, and Chyi 2014; Molyneux 2015), social media users seem to depend more on their own social networks for their news consumption.

Studies have found that social endorsements based on number of likes and comments (Messing and Westwood 2014) and recommendations by friends or family members (Anspach 2017) are more influential than news organizations in social media users' decisions on which news articles to read. Social recommendations also influence perceptions of source and message credibility, so that news organizations are perceived more trustworthy when their stories are recommended by friends (Turcotte et al. 2015), and news articles are perceived more credible when they are shared by friends than by news outlets (H. Kang et al. 2011). News consumption on social media is increasingly driven by social media users—more than news organizations—who share and recommend news articles to their social networks.

But aside from disseminating news content produced by traditional news organizations, social media users also share firsthand information, including details about newsworthy events, to a potentially mass audience without having to go through traditional media organizations. This gives rise to what Castells (2007) referred to as mass self-communication. Indeed, studies have documented instances when social media users shared details about or photos of newsworthy events—ahead of journalists—because they happened to be on the scene (Hermida 2010; Jewitt 2009), such as during disasters (Tandoc and Takahashi 2017). Social media users are now engaged in breaking the news to other audiences, sometimes even to journalists.

Stories that become viral on social media, catching traditional news organizations unaware, subsequently get journalists' attention, giving rise to what can be described as a reversed agenda-setting process (Ragas, Tran, and Martin 2014). For example, news about the shooting that killed an unarmed African American teenager in Ferguson, Missouri, in 2014, which sparked violent protests in the United States, was first reported on Twitter before it was carried by traditional news organizations (Groshek and Tandoc 2017; Hitlin and Vogt 2014). This capability of non-journalists to engage in acts of journalism, facilitated by social media, helps expand the reach of journalism to places, times, issues, and events that journalists, who are confronted by the numerous limits of their increasingly demanding jobs, cannot attend to. But traditional news construction processes are marked by routines that have evolved over time to ideally ensure responsible and accurate reporting. When news is produced outside these traditional processes, some norms might be compromised.

For example, on November 9, 2016, a 35-year-old Twitter user with only about 40 followers tweeted photos of buses he saw in Austin, Texas, that he said were carrying paid protesters against then newly elected US President Donald Trump. His tweet was later posted on Reddit and was subsequently shared by Republican supporters (Maheshwari 2016). Soon, the tweet was shared more than 16,000 times on Twitter and more than 350,000 times on Facebook (Maheshwari 2016). This is an example of mass communication, as Twitter allowed the user to reach a potentially "global audience" and yet the original tweet was "self-generated in content, self-directed in emission, and self-selected in reception" (Castells 2007, 248). For a larger group of people, the tweet was an act of journalism, reporting about an important development. However, the tweet turned out to be wrong—the buses were not carrying paid protesters but rather delegates to a local conference (Maheshwari 2016).

The online world, marked by a seemingly limitless supply of information, has created impatient information consumers. If they encounter a paywall and cannot get a news article for free, they search for the same news story elsewhere. If they hear about an event and don't see it from a traditional news source, they search for information elsewhere. Speed seems to trump other considerations, occasionally even source credibility. In the past, journalists just had to keep an eye on one another when competing to break a story first. Now, competition comes from different sources, even from those who do not claim to be journalists. Sometimes, competition comes from newsmakers themselves, who would make newsworthy announcements on their social media accounts, bypassing the news media to directly reach the public (Vis 2012). Speed has always been essential for journalists—news had to be current. But in the age of social media, speed has become more paramount, sometimes at the expense of accuracy. A "tweet first, verify later" approach to reporting breaking news on social media is spreading, often privileging speed over verification (Bruno 2011). While the use of social media can help diversify sourcing and enrich coverage, too much focus on speed is also "very dangerous for one of journalism's golden rules: each news story must be verified first" (Bruno 2011, 66).

Verification on Social Media

Verification is at the core of responsible journalism. It is "what separates journalism from entertainment, propaganda, fiction, or art" (Kovach and Rosenstiel 2007, 71). Verification refers to the "skilled determination of the accuracy or validity of both the source and the content itself" (Brandtzaeg et al. 2016, 325). It can be tedious, but it is a necessary process to fulfill the social functions of journalism. Over the years, journalists have developed a system of practices to maintain journalism as a discipline of verification (Hermida 2012). For example, journalists interview multiple news sources to verify a piece of information (Brandtzaeg et al. 2016). But as social media platforms are changing the traditionally linear flow of news from journalists to news audiences, others argue that journalism is heading toward "collaborative verification," in which the discipline of verification that originated from traditional journalism is merged with literacies related with social media network systems (Hermida 2012, 663).

However, the digitization of news that brought along a never-ending news cycle has created new routines and roles for journalists that can leave them with almost no time to pause and reflect on every single editorial decision they make, such as verifying information they come across on social media (Tandoc 2014). Indeed: "As journalists spend more time trying to synthesize the ever-growing stream of data pouring in through the new portals of information, the risk is they can become more passive, more receivers than gatherers" (Kovach and Rosenstiel 2007, 76). Thus, verifying information going viral on social media might become secondary to reporting about that information quickly (Bruno 2011). Merely retweeting or sharing someone else's viral post becomes a way out of the responsibility and task of verification. This is consistent with the twisted notion of balance in journalism as an end in itself rather than as a tool to uncover truth—some journalists would just quote different newsmakers disagreeing on an issue to keep coverage balanced, despite knowing for a fact that one side is lying or presenting false claims (Boykoff and Boykoff 2004; Kovach and Rosenstiel 2007). But this is more dangerous when done on social media, where a multitude of information—and misinformation—spreads fast and where source credibility is confounded.

This brings us back to the unfortunate case of Sunil Tripathi. Many of the users on Reddit who engaged in an online manhunt for the Boston Marathon bombers were searching for truth. But their eagerness, insufficient training on conducting investigations, and unfamiliarity with (or disregard for) the discipline of verification brought them to wrong conclusions and brought a family already distressed about a missing loved one yet more anguish. What made it worse was that some journalists—trained and expected to engage in verification in their routine pursuit for truth—also fell for the wrong conclusion and even propagated the error on social media (Gourarie 2015), becoming complicit not only in spreading disinformation but also in hurting an already grieving family.

Conclusion

Journalism refers to the "business or practice of producing and disseminating information about contemporary affairs of general public interest and importance" (Schudson 2003, 11). It occupies an important place in society, for it is a source of "independent, reliable, accurate, and comprehensive information that citizens require to be free" (Kovach and Rosenstiel 2007, 11). Social media platforms can help journalists fulfill this role, as they provide journalists (1) opportunities to understand, reach, and engage with the news audience; and (2) access to a steady supply of sources and information related to events and issues that can be potentially newsworthy.

But social media platforms also bring challenges to the search for truth. Focusing too much on audience feedback can distract journalists from balancing giving what audiences want and what they need. Relying heavily on user-generated content can also lead journalists to erroneous conclusions. While news consumption on social media is increasing, journalists must be careful about being enslaved by the rules of social media (Tandoc and Maitra 2018). These external rules must always be scrutinized and compared with journalism's internal rules. For example, many news organizations in the United States increased their native videos when Facebook adjusted its algorithms to favor native videos to keep users within the confines of Facebook (Tandoc and Maitra 2018). However, an increased number of native videos did not translate into increased audience engagement for the news organizations—or at least not in the short term (Tandoc and Maitra 2018).

Many journalists are aware of the pitfalls of relying too heavily on social media. Interviews with journalists found that some of them try to balance offering what audiences want and what audiences need (Tandoc 2014) as well as combine traditional verification strategies with new verification tools online when they encounter information on social media (Brandtzaeg et al. 2016). Considering both what audiences want and what they need will help guide journalists in providing the public a more complete version of reality. Engaging in the discipline of verification amid the pressure for speed and the barrage of information on social media will also help journalists protect their work and the public from disinformation. But in a period when many acts of journalism—and acts claiming to be journalism—are done by nonjournalists who have access to an audience through social media, journalists must rethink how they ought to fulfill their traditional social functions.

References

Akagi, Katie, and Stephanie Linning. 2013. "Crowdsourcing Done Right." *Columbia Journalism Review*, April 29. http://www.cjr.org/between_the_spreadsheets/crowdsourcing_done_right.php.

Anspach, Nicolas M. 2017. "The New Personal Influence: How Our Facebook Friends Influence the News We Read." *Political Communication* 34, no. 4: 590–606. doi:10.1080/10584609.2017.1316329.

Antunovic, Dunja, Patrick Parsons, and Tanner R Cooke. 2018. "'Checking' and Googling: Stages of News Consumption among Young Adults." *Journalism* 19, no. 5: 632–648. doi:10.1177/1464884916663625.

Bastos, Marco Toledo. 2015. "Shares, Pins, and Tweets: News Readership from Daily Papers to Social Media." *Journalism Studies* 16, no. 3: 305–325. doi:10.1080/1461670X.2014.891857.

Beam, Randal A. 1995. "How Newspapers Use Readership Research." *Newspaper Research Journal* 16, no. 2: 28–38. doi:10.1177/073953299501600204.

Boczkowski, Pablo J. 2005. *Digitizing the News: Innovation in Online Newspapers.* Cambridge, MA: MIT Press.

Boykoff, Maxwell T., and Jules M. Boykoff. 2004. "Balance as Bias: Global Warming and the US Prestige Press." *Global Environmental Change* 14, no. 2: 125–136.

Brandtzaeg, Petter Bae, Marika Lüders, Jochen Spangenberg, Linda Rath-Wiggins, and Asbjørn Følstad. 2016. "Emerging Journalistic Verification Practices Concerning Social Media." *Journalism Practice* 10, no. 3: 1–20.

Bruno, Nicola. 2011. "Tweet First, Verify Later? How Real-Time Information Is Changing the Coverage of Worldwide Crisis Events." Reuters Institute for the Study of Journalism. http://reutersinstitute.politics.ox.ac.uk/our-research/tweet-first-verify-later.

Butsch, Richard. 2000. *The Making of American Audiences from Stage to Television, 1750–1990.* Cambridge Studies in the History of Mass Communications. New York: Cambridge University Press.

Canter, Lily. 2013. "The Interactive Spectrum: The Use of Social Media in UK Regional Newspapers." *Convergence* 19, no. 4: 472–495. doi:10.1177/1354856513493698.

Castells, Manuel. 2007. "Communication, Power, and Counter-Power in the Network Society." *International Journal of Communication* 1, no. 1: 238–266.

Craft, Stephanie, Tim P. Vos, and J. David Wolfgang. 2016. "Reader Comments as Press Criticism: Implications for the Journalistic Field." *Journalism* 17, no. 6: 677–693. doi:10.1177/1464884915579332.

de Sola Pool, Ithiel, and Irwin Shulman. 1959. "Newsmen's Fantasies, Audiences, and Newswriting." *Public Opinion Quarterly* 23, no. 2: 145–158.

Ettema, James S., and D. Charles Whitney. 1994. "The Money Arrow: An Introduction to Audiencemaking." In *Audiencemaking: How the Media Create the Audience*, edited by James S. Ettema and D. Charles Whitney, 1–18. New York: Sage.

Gans, Herbert. 1979. *Deciding What's News: A Study of* CBS Evening News, NBC Nightly News, Newsweek, *and* Time. 1st ed. New York: Pantheon Books.

Gottfried, Jeffrey, and Elisa Shearer. 2016. "News Use Across Social Media Platforms 2016." Pew Research Center. http://www.journalism.org/2016/05/26/news-use-across-social-media-platforms-2016/.

Gourarie, Chava. 2015. "A Closer Look at the Man Wrongfully Accused of Being the Boston Bomber." *Columbia Journalism Review.* October 9. https://www.cjr.org/analysis/sunil_tripathi_was_already_dead.php.

Groshek, Jacob, and Edson Tandoc. 2017. "The Affordance Effect: Gatekeeping and (Non)Reciprocal Journalism on Twitter." *Computers in Human Behavior*, 66, no. C: 201–210. doi: http://dx.doi.org/10.1016/j.chb.2016.09.020.

Hanusch, Folker, and Edson Tandoc. 2017. "Comments, Analytics, and Social Media: The Impact of Audience Feedback on Journalists' Market Orientation." *Journalism.* doi:10.1177/1464884917720305.

Hermida, Alfred. 2010. "Twittering the News." *Journalism Practice* 4, no. 3: 297–308. doi:10.1080/17512781003640703.

Hermida, Alfred. 2011. "Fluid Spaces, Fluid Journalism: The Role of the 'Active Recipient' in Participatory Journalism." In *Participatory Journalism: Guarding Open Gates at Online Newspapers*, edited by Jane B. Singer, David Domingo, Ari Heinonen, Alfred Hermida, Steve Paulussen, Thorsten Quandt, Zvi Reich, and Marina Vujnovic, 177–191. Malden, MA: John Wiley and Sons.

Hermida, Alfred. 2012. "Tweets and Truth: Journalism as a Discipline of Collaborative Verification." *Journalism Practice*, 6, no. 5–6: 1–10. doi:10.1080/17512786.2012.667269.

Hitlin, Paul and Nancy Vogt. 2014. "Cable, Twitter Picked up Ferguson Story at a Similar Clip." *Factank: News in the Numbers*, Pew Research Center, August 20. http://www.pewresearch.org/fact-tank/2014/08/20/cable-twitter-picked-up-ferguson-story-at-a-similar-clip/.

Jewitt, Rob. 2009. "The Trouble with Twittering: Integrating Social Media into Mainstream News." *International Journal of Media & Cultural Politics* 5, no. 3: 233–246. https://doi.org/10.1386/macp.5.3.233_3.

Ju, Alice, Sun Ho Jeong, and Hsiang Iris Chyi. 2014. "Will Social Media Save Newspapers?" *Journalism Practice* 8, no. 1: 1–17. doi:10.1080/17512786.2013.794022.

Kang, Hyunjin, Keunmin Bae, Shaoke Zhang, and S. Shyam Sundar. 2011. "Source Cues in Online News: Is the Proximate Source More Powerful than Distal Sources?" *Journalism & Mass Communication Quarterly* 88, no. 4: 719–736. doi:10.1177/107769901108800403.

Kang, Jay C. 2013. "Should Reddit Be Blamed for the Spreading of a Smear?" *New York Times*, July 25. http://www.nytimes.com/2013/07/28/magazine/should-reddit-be-blamed-for-the-spreading-of-a-smear.html?pagewanted=all&_r=1.

Kovach, Bill, and Tom Rosenstiel. 2007. *The Elements of Journalism: What Newspeople Should Know and the Public Should Expect*. 1st rev. ed. New York: Three Rivers Press.

Lee, Eun-Ju, and Edson C. Tandoc. 2017. "When News Meets the Audience: How Audience Feedback Online Affects News Production and Consumption." *Human Communication Research* 43, no. 4: 436–449. doi:10.1111/hcre.12123.

Maheshwari, Sapna. 2016. "How Fake News Goes Viral: A Case Study." *New York Times*. November 21. https://www.nytimes.com/2016/11/20/business/media/how-fake-news-spreads.html?_r=0.

Messing, Solomon, and Sean J. Westwood. 2014. "Selective Exposure in the Age of Social Media: Endorsements Trump Partisan Source Affiliation When Selecting News Online." *Communication Research* 41, no. 8: 1042–1063. doi:10.1177/0093650212466406.

Molyneux, Logan. 2015. "What Journalists Retweet: Opinion, Humor, and Brand Development on Twitter." *Journalism* 16, no. 7: 920–935. doi:10.1177/1464884914550135.

Napoli, Philip. 2011. *Audience Evolution: New Technologies and the Transformation of Media Audiences*. New York: Columbia University Press.

Nielsen, Rasmus Kleis, and Kim C. Schrøder. 2014. "The Relative Importance of Social Media for Accessing, Finding, and Engaging with News." *Digital Journalism* 2, no. 4: 472–489. doi:10.1080/21670811.2013.872420.

Ragas, Matthew W., Hai L. Tran, and Jason A. Martin. 2014. "Media-Induced or Search-Driven?" *Journalism Studies* 15, no. 1: 48–63. doi:10.1080/1461670X.2013.793509.

Schlesinger, Philip. 1978. *Putting "Reality" Together*. Beverly Hills, CA: Sage.

Schudson, Michael. 2003. *The Sociology of News*. New York: W.W. Norton.

Shoemaker, Pamela J., and Stephen D. Reese. 2014. *Mediating the Message in the 21st Century: A Media Sociology Perspective*. 3rd ed. New York: Routledge.

Singer, Jane B. 2010. "Quality Control: Perceived Effects of User-Generated Content on Newsroom Norms, Values and Routines." *Journalism Practice* 4, no. 2: 127–142. doi:10.1080/17512780903391979.

Tandoc, Edson C. 2014. "Journalism Is Twerking? How Web Analytics Is Changing the Process of Gatekeeping." *New Media & Society* 16, no. 4: 559–575. doi:10.1177/1461444814530541.

Tandoc, E., and Cassie Foo. 2017. "Here's What BuzzFeed Journalists Think of Their Journalism." *Digital Journalism, Online First*: 1–17. doi:10.1080/21670811.2017.1332956.

Tandoc, Edson C., and Julian Maitra. 2018. "News Organizations' Use of Native Videos on Facebook: Tweaking the Journalistic Field One Algorithm Change at a Time." *New Media & Society* 20, no. 5: 1679–1696. doi:10.1177/1461444817702398.

Tandoc, Edson C., and Bruno Takahashi. 2017. "Log in If You Survived: Collective Coping on Social Media in the Aftermath of Typhoon Haiyan in the Philippines." *New Media & Society* 19, no. 11: 1778–1793. doi:10.1177/1461444816642755.

Tandoc, Edson, and Ryan J. Thomas. 2014. "The Ethics of Web Analytics: Implications of Using Audience Metrics in News Construction." *Digital Journalism* 3, no. 2: 243–258. doi:10.1080/21670811.2014.909122.

Tandoc, Edson, and Timothy P. Vos. 2016. "The Journalist Is Marketing the News: Social Media in the Gatekeeping Process." *Journalism Practice* 10, no. 8: 950–966. doi:10.1080/17512786.2015.1087811.

Thorson, Emily. 2008. "Changing Patterns of News Consumption and Participation." *Information, Communication and Society* 11, no. 4: 473–489. doi:10.1080/13691180801999027.

Turcotte, Jason, Chance York, Jacob Irving, Rosanne M. Scholl, and Raymond J. Pingree. 2015. "News Recommendations from Social Media Opinion Leaders: Effects on Media Trust and Information Seeking." *Journal of Computer-Mediated Communication* 20, no. 5: 520–535. doi:10.1111/jcc4.12127.

Turow, Joseph. 2005. "Audience Construction and Culture Production: Marketing Surveillance in the Digital Age." *Annals of the American Academy of Political and Social Science* 597: 103–121.

Vis, Farida. 2012. "Twitter as a Reporting Tool for Breaking News." *Digital Journalism* 1, no. 1: 27–47. doi:10.1080/21670811.2012.741316.

Webster, James G., and Patricia Phalen. 1994. "Victim, Consumer, or Commodity? Audience Models in Communication Policy." In *Audiencemaking: How the Media Create the Audience*, edited by James S. Ettema and David Charles Whitney, 19–37. New York: Sage.

14

Emotional Characteristics of Social Media and Political Misperceptions

Brian E. Weeks and R. Kelly Garrett

Introduction

Social media have in many ways been a boon to journalists by providing new avenues to conduct, promote, and disseminate their work, thereby reaching new or expanded audiences. Yet social media also pose a threat to a core mission of journalism: to deliver to the public facts and truths citizens need to be accurately informed. Social media allow any person—not just journalists—the ability to create, comment on, or distribute information related to politics or public affairs. These changes suggest that gatekeeping power has in some ways shifted from the journalism industry toward the public. As a result, journalists today have less control over information in the public sphere, their work and legitimacy are being called into question, and they are no longer considered by many to be the primary bearers of political truth. What is particularly problematic for journalists is that their work, which is meant to be obligated to the truth, competes with non-credible political misinformation, rumors, conspiracy theories, and innuendo for public attention online. As social media have become engrained in the lives of a majority of the American public, there are growing concerns that these platforms also promote exposure to and acceptance of misleading, inaccurate, and fictitious claims about politics, all of which undermine journalism's fundamental values and purpose.

However, it is not simply the existence or presence of social media that may promote political misperceptions and threats to the truth; it is unlikely that social media create echo chambers that isolate people from facts entirely (Garrett 2017, 370). Instead, we argue that the highly emotional characteristics of information and interactions on social media help create conditions ripe for the spread of political misinformation. Interactions on social media run the gamut of politically related emotions, from negative emotions like fear, anger, and anxiety to positive emotions like hope or enthusiasm. These emotional experiences—particularly negative ones—can become problematic because they encourage psychologically biased responses to political information. In this chapter we build on the three cross-cutting themes of this volume and argue that social media platforms (media/technology) are highly charged, emotional political spaces that can increase the likelihood that users will be exposed to, engage with, and believe in political misinformation (politics). As a result, the emotional nature of social media can undercut journalists' work and make it harder for people to accept facts and arrive at the truth (i.e., abstract notion of truth).

Political Misperceptions and Emotions

Determining the nature of truth in politics can be difficult, as facts are often contentious and debated among interested parties. For example, the unemployment rate may vary depending on which criteria are used in its calculation. The resulting jobless rate taken as a "fact" for some may not be for others. Despite these hurdles, disagreements over political truths do not mean there are no truths in politics. Truth and facts are determined by verification and evidence, such as relevant physical evidence or the conclusions of experts in a particular area. Misinformation, which includes misleading, false, or deceitful content, challenges this notion of political truth by introducing doubt or uncertainty about the nature of reality or by encouraging inaccurate beliefs based on political falsehood. Political misperceptions exist when people's political beliefs are inconsistent with the facts and the best available evidence (Kuklinski et al. 1998, 147).

The presence of emotions in politics can make it even harder for people to arrive at the truth. Emotions are short-lived, valenced psychological feeling states that occur in response to external stimuli (Nabi 2010, 153–154). In politics, emotions are abundant and are often a strong undercurrent in political news, debates, and discussions. Politically driven emotions can emerge in any number of instances, from anger in response to a politician's social media post, to anxiety about how a proposed bill might affect one's family, to enthusiasm about an inspiring new candidate. These emotions evoked from politics are meaningful in determining how people respond to political information and situations. They help guide how people think and behave politically, affecting what types of information they seek out, how they process political content, and whether they become more engaged.

As Nabi (2010, 154) notes, the study of emotion in communication (and elsewhere) generally takes one of two approaches, either the dimensional or discrete model of emotions. The dimensional model generally suggests that emotions can be conceptualized along the two dimensions of arousal (high to low) and valence (positive to negative). Under this approach, the influence of an emotional response on cognitions and behaviors depends on the degree of physiological responses triggered by positive or negative feelings. In contrast, the discrete model examines unique and categorical emotional states. According to this model, different emotional states—even those of the same valence—can be distinguished by different situational cognitive appraisals and behavioral tendencies. This model would argue, for example, that two negative emotions—fear and anger—are distinct and should be associated with different thought patterns, motivations, and behaviors (Nabi 2010, 154). Different emotions of the same valence often work differently, especially when considering how people respond to, process, and engage with political information (MacKuen et al. 2010, 441). Although there is a robust discussion among scholars about which approach to emotion is most valuable, in this chapter we consider how both approaches can offer important insights about the interplay between social media, emotion, and political misperceptions.

The Emotional Characteristics of Social Media

Although politics has always been tinged with emotional elements, the role of emotion in the American political environment has been increasing steadily. Over the last five decades, members of the Republican and Democratic parties in the United States have grown more hostile and loathing toward individuals who belong to the opposing political party, a process that has been labeled affective polarization (Iyengar, Sood, and Lelkes 2012, 407). At the same time, individuals in the United States increasingly identify with one political party or the other, and that party affiliation creates stronger political identities that facilitate emotional responses (like anger) to political content (Mason 2016, 369). Whether it is a cause or consequence (or both) of partisans' increased negative feelings toward the other side, contemporary media also focus on emotional elements of politics. Political news often promotes political discourse that is replete with incivility and outrage that further trigger negative emotional responses in the audience, and this is especially true with partisan news (Sobieraj and Berry 2011, 19).

This influx of emotions in politics has carried over to online spaces and social media. Political discussions and interactions online are increasingly uncivil and disrespectful (Coe, Kenski, and Rains 2014, 673), and these emotional elements make it hard for people to find common ground and can promote polarization of attitudes about political issues (Anderson et al. 2014, 381). In general, expression of emotional sentiment on social media tends to increase in response to important political and social events (Bollen, Mao, and Pepe 2011, 450). Social media also serve as a conduit for the flow of emotion between individuals. Users who are exposed to less positive content in their social media feeds are more likely to post negatively valenced content (Kramer, Guillory, and Hancock 2014, 8789). This suggests that emotional content and expression thrive on social media, making these platforms ripe for the flow of political misinformation.

Emotion and Exposure to Misinformation on Social Media

The emotional elements of social media interactions can influence how people subsequently search for political news, promoting exposure to information sources with less journalistic credibility and adherence to the truth. People often respond to emotional situations by searching for information that can help them either alleviate or channel that emotion. This emotionally driven information seeking can lead people to information that is of questionable quality or reinforces their existing political beliefs. In doing so, various emotions may promote exposure to political information that is unverified, false, or misleading.

One way emotions can encourage exposure to less reputable sources of information is by creating a strong need to manage social or political uncertainty. Fear and anxiety can arise from situations where the outcome is unknown or where credible explanations from traditional sources are lacking or not trusted (like mainstream media or government officials) (DiFonzo 2008, 86). One of the most effective ways to cope with anxiety in these ambiguous situations is to find information that helps reduce it by filling in gaps or answering lingering questions. This anxiety-reducing information provides an explanation for negative events and helps people regain a sense of control over the situation. If government sources, politicians, or legacy media fail to offer a convincing explanation for such events, individuals will seek answers elsewhere and may turn to alternative sources of information online—including disreputable sources on social media—to reduce their anxiety and help make sense of uncertain times. Sources that provide plausible explanations for situations are attractive because they can lower anxiety, even if they are not empirically supported. As a result, people often unwittingly use inaccurate information to diminish these negative feelings (DiFonzo 2008, 47).

The emotional nature of contemporary politics may increase the possibility that people will lose faith in well-established sources of information, abandoning them in favor of more politically palatable outlets or individuals on social media. The noted increase in the American public's negative feelings toward members of the opposed political has been accompanied by increasing distrust in the news media and established channels of information. In 2017, only 11% of Republicans and 34% of Democrats say they trust news they get from national news organizations, and a majority from both parties believe the media favors one side in the presentation of news (Barthel and Mitchell 2017). In other words, most Americans are suspicious of mainstream news outlets. President Trump's repeated use of the term "fake news" to describe much of the legacy press is a notable example. Research has shown that such distrust is driven at least in part by emotional arousal, particularly negative emotions like anger. Individuals who experience negative emotional reactions in response to a news story or political issue are more likely to report bias in the media (Arpan and Nabi 2011, 12; Matthes 2013, 378). Such distrust can lead them to seek out information from sources that reinforce the party line but offer less credible information.

Social media exacerbate the problem of growing distrust in legacy media by providing easy access to alternative news or information outlets that are trusted by like-minded others. These alternative sites often question the legitimacy of mainstream sources of information and explicitly encourage distrust of established outlets that promote politically inconvenient facts (Kata 2012, 3783). On both the political left and right, there is a profusion of political information sites that offer a very different perspective on the day's news than from established media. While many of these sites resemble legitimate news sites in appearance, they are not bound by the same journalistic standards and ethics. As a result, they can publish conjecture or outright false information with little consequence. Audiences have trouble distinguishing the credibility of these political information sources online and tend to base assessments of trustworthiness and expertise more on socially derived factors like the number of likes, followers, or retweets and less on the long-standing reputation of the outlet (Flanagin and Metzger 2017, 421). This suggests that people who feel some level of distrust toward mainstream media may be more inclined to turn to these alternative outlets on social media to fulfill their need for information, thus increasing the chance of exposure to political misinformation.

Distrust is not the only factor by which emotion encourages the use of more partisan, less reliable sources. Interpersonal political conflict, as well as the widespread use of politically charged content and evocative headlines, can also promote anger, which can influence exposure to political misinformation. Social media can provoke political anger in several ways. First, social media platforms are spaces for emotionally laden political expression in the form of posts and comments. Although social media may encourage interactions among politically heterogeneous individuals, engagement with disagreeable others can trigger strong feelings of anger when the discussions turn uncivil (Gervais 2015, 176). Second, these sites are also filled with emotional headlines and posts designed to attract users' attention (i.e., clickbait). These types of posts seem to be effective, as news articles with headlines that contain more emotional sentiment—particularly negative sentiment—are more likely to be clicked and commented on (Reis et al. 2015). Although the experience of negative emotions can be alleviated in a number of ways, one documented way people manage anger is to revert back to what is familiar and comforting. In the case of political information exposure, this means angry people are more inclined to exhibit a confirmation bias by seeking out attitude-consistent information that helps them reaffirm their existing political views and bolster their identity (Arpan and Nabi 2011, 12; MacKuen et al. 2010, 443). When users are exposed to highly charged political content on these sites, they are more likely to experience anger, which makes them more inclined to seek out attitude-consistent information. This can take many forms, including following like-minded news and political pages or prominent individuals (e.g. politicians, celebrities, media personalities) who subscribe to a similar political or worldview.

If anger drives engagement with like-minded partisans on social media, the concern next becomes whether consumption of partisan content promotes exposure to misinformation. There is evidence to suggest that it does. Partisan news outlets offer content that is highly critical of political opponents and parties, particularly in their opinion-based coverage that may deviate from well-established facts, which may ultimately encourage exposure to false or misleading information (Budak, Goel, and Rao 2016, 261; Feldman et al. 2012, 12). Partisan news outlets from each end of the political spectrum also cover political actors and events in ways that can be misleading or inaccurate, thereby promoting exposure to outlet-favored misinformation (Garrett, Weeks, and Neo 2016, 343). In fact, individuals who use partisan political sites online are more likely to be exposed to political misinformation (Garrett 2011, 266), and audiences of partisan news outlets demonstrate higher levels of false beliefs, suggesting that exposure to these outlets promotes familiarity with false claims (Meirick and Bessarabova 2016).

The tendency of angry individuals to use like-minded social media may further increase exposure to inaccurate political information. Misinformation tends to spread more rapidly within homogeneous clusters on sites like Facebook, suggesting that following similar others may promote exposure to false claims (Del Vicario et al. 2016, 558). Similarly, following politicians or political commentators on social media can lead to exposure to false claims. Social media allow politicians or political party members to communicate directly with the public without having the truth behind those messages vetted by journalists. For example, President Trump made 350 false or misleading claims on Twitter during his first year in office, or nearly one per day (Kessler, Kelly, and Lewis 2017). All told, exposure to political misinformation remains relatively low, as the average American saw one explicitly false news story during the 2016 election (Allcott and Gentzkow 2017, 227). Yet, partisan selective exposure online that stems from emotional experiences may enhance familiarity with misinformation.

Emotions and the Dissemination of Political Misinformation on Social Media

There is growing evidence that social media introduce a multiplicity of "truths" that make it more difficult for people to arrive at accurate conclusions. While journalists and experts were once the primary source of facts about public affairs, they now must compete with crowd-sourced and user-generated versions of truth that are based on personal experience, interpretation, or opinion rather than evidence. Some have argued that so-cial media create a new paradigm of truth in which the perspective of those with authority is viewed with suspicion, the credibility of legitimate experts is continually questioned, and anyone can claim expertise on any topic. As a result, the power to shape the truth has shifted away from reporters and experts toward non-expert citizens (Kata 2012, 3779). One problem with this shift is that on social media, non-experts' positions are presented alongside those of recognized experts, which lends a degree of legitimacy to lay opinions, making it harder for people to distinguish credibility between the two (Flanagin and Metzger 2017, 421; Kata 2012, 3779).

Although debates about politically important facts are inevitable (Kuklinski et al. 1998, 147), the range of claims that are disputed and the alternatives put forth have changed significantly over the past decade, in part because of social media. Indeed, empirical evidence is regularly dis-puted on social media. For example, despite no supporting evidence, claims of voter fraud circulate widely on social media and are endorsed by President Trump (Berman 2017). Conspiracy theories asserting that surviving students of the high school shooting in Parkland, Florida, were "crisis actors" were quickly debunked, yet evidence dispelling the theo-ries was widely reinterpreted and disputed on social media (Timberg and Harwell 2018). These and other disputes are not merely disagreements over the interpretation of political facts but rather the validity of empirical evi-dence and expertise.

The presence of multiple "truths" and disputes over empirical evidence may be further promoted by the emotional nature of social media. Political misinformation on social media is unlikely to thrive unless users of these platforms actively post, share, and disseminate false information to their so-cial networks. Many of the false claims and challenges to established truths are highly emotional and thus shared more widely.

Emotions can motivate people to engage with and distribute political content on social media, thus widening the reach of political informa-tion, including inaccuracies. Content that contains more physiologically arousing emotions like anger, anxiety, and awe is more likely to be shared on social media and tends to spread throughout social networks more fre-quently and quickly than emotionally neutral content (Berger and Milkman 2012, 199; Stieglitz and Dang-Xuan 2013, 235–236). Individuals are also more likely to share political information when experiencing emotions like anger (Hasell and Weeks 2016, 652). Emotional misinformation may therefore spread widely.

Emotionally evocative misinformation thrives in part because emotions create a need for understanding and a desire to manage threat. As noted, this desire can promote acceptance of plausible, though inaccurate explanations; it also makes sharing such information with others more likely (DiFonzo 2008, 84–85). Sharing information with others is a way for people to work collectively to meaningfully interpret an ambiguous situation, a process that has been described as "improvising" news (Shibutani 1966, 17). The interaction of social media and emotion, however, might introduce more falsehoods into this process. The emotionally extreme content on social media could jump-start this process by providing both the impetus and opportunity for individuals to try to make sense of the world, often by sharing false information. This process may help explain why a conspiracy theory like Pizzagate or the false story that the pope endorsed Donald Trump's presidential campaign may have spread so widely. The stories likely triggered feelings of anxiety and uncertainty in some, who may have subsequently shared it to make sense of the situation. In doing so, they (inadvertently) increased the reach of the falsehood.

Emotion and Belief in Misinformation

Emotions not only play a pivotal role in facilitating exposure to misinformation on social media, they may also alter cognitive processing of that information, making it more likely to be accepted under certain circumstances. In particular, emotions can exacerbate existing psychological biases related to information processing and message credibility that can encourage beliefs in false claims encountered on social media.

Political partisans often do not process information in an unbiased way. Instead, partisans are motivated to evaluate incoming information in a directional manner with the goal of affirming their existing beliefs to avoid cognitive dissonance and maintain consistency with prior attitudes or beliefs. This partisan motivated reasoning leads individuals to rate attitude-consistent information as more persuasive, credible, and convincing, while dismissing and discrediting disagreeable information (Taber and Lodge 2006, 756). In the case of political misinformation, this means that people are more likely to believe claims that reflect favorably on their preferred party or are consistent with their ideology or worldview, while rejecting those that may be unfavorable toward their prior attitudes or beliefs.

The pull to process political information in a partisan way is strong, and emotions can further exacerbate this motivated reasoning. In particular, anger may drive individuals to evaluate political claims in a partisan manner. Anger leads people to rely more on prior attitudes and beliefs in their evaluation of new information. Angry people are more dismissive of information that is disagreeable, and they are more likely to become defensive. As a result, they are less open to considering new information (MacKuen et al. 2010, 443). These processing tendencies associated with anger have important implications for political beliefs. Partisans who are angry should be most likely to consider information in a way that is consistent with existing attitudes or beliefs. When people are angry and are exposed to false information that is favorable to their preferred political party, they are more likely to accept the misinformation as true (Weeks 2015). Angry people are more likely to fall back on prior attitudes when considering new information, augmenting the influence of political affiliation on misperceptions. This is especially problematic given that individuals with strong partisan identities tend to experience the greatest degree of political anger (Mason 2016, 369).

Importantly, the effects of emotion need not stem from the stimuli or message itself (e.g., news article, social media post, politician's statement). The incidental experience of emotions—or emotions unrelated to the topic at hand—can also be used in assessments of the truth. Emotional experiences can be used as heuristic information in the evaluation process, much as any other piece of information would. Thus, affect can serve as information that can lead people to frequently make judgments that are congruent with their specific emotional state (Schwarz 2001, 159). When an individual's incidental emotional state matches the emotional framing of a message, that message should become more convincing and persuasive. For example, the incidental experience of an emotion like anger makes messages using anger-framed appeals more persuasive (DeSteno et al. 2004, 51). This congruence between one's emotional state and emotions induced by a message promotes acceptance of misinformation; individuals who feel angry when receiving a message are more likely to believe anger-inducing rumors (Na, Garrett, and Slater 2018, 791).

This has important consequences for what people believe following exposure to misinformation on social media. It suggests that false claims on these platforms that play on anger are more likely to be believed. If people are angry when they are exposed to false political information, or if that information makes them angry, they are more prone to think it is true if it is in line with their prior beliefs. It is likely not a coincidence that many of the most-believed fake news stories that circulated on social media during the 2016 US election were anger inducing for some individuals.

Conclusion

The highly emotional nature of social media offers a space for political misinformation to thrive. This poses a challenge for journalists, fact-checkers, educators, and others who work to combat political misinformation. Although emotions may make it more difficult to find the truth in politics, encouraging recent developments suggest there are ways to limit emotions' influence. First, corrections and fact-checks to misinformation can be effective and rarely backfire—even in emotional contexts—especially for less prominent political issues (Flynn, Nyhan, and Reifler 2017, 130; Weeks, 2015, 712; Wood and Porter 2018, 26). Some promising corrective strategies include finding ways to reduce partisan cues, for example by providing corrections from in-group members (Berinsky 2017, 258), which may help mitigate negative emotional reactions, or using algorithms to put misinformation in context, presenting more accurate coverage alongside it (Bode and Vraga 2015, 633). Although hopeful, more research is needed on how corrections can reduce the effect of emotions and misinformation and what type of messages are most successful in doing so. Second, new methods of reducing political divides online may also be the first step in lowering the rancor and incivility that set the emotional processes outlined above in motion. Civil interventions such as including a "Respect" button along with the standard "Like" and "Recommend" buttons in social media can reduce hostility and partisan behavior, which may also diminish negative emotions (Stroud, Muddiman, and Scacco 2017, 1738). Similarly, interventions that promote (civil) interactions and contact between dissimilar individuals or groups online can lower negative emotions and increase positive attitudes toward an out-group (Kim and Wojcieszak 2018, 69). A related approach may be effective with partisan groups, so long as these interactions avoid the incivility that often polarizes political factions online (Gervais 2015, 176). In the context of political misperceptions, finding ways for Republicans and Democrats to find common ground may help reduce the affective divide between these groups and lead to less falsehoods being circulated or believed. Doing so may help improve the value of truth in our political system.

Lessons for Journalism Practitioners and News Consumers

- Be aware of emotional biases: Emotions bias the type of political information we seek, what we believe, and what information we share on social media. Highly emotional political content may promote exposure to, belief in, and engagement with false information.
- Recognize that news consumers' emotions shape their engagement with news: An emotionally evocative headline or lede can promote engagement, but it is also likely to alter what news consumers take away from the story and may make consumers more vulnerable to future misinformation.
- Social media provide alternative sources of information that seek to challenge conventional notions of truth and fact by promoting distrust in journalists and more mainstream media organizations, especially for emotional issues or topics.
- Minimizing unnecessarily emotional content in news on social media may promote more accurate beliefs and reduce the dissemination of misinformation.

References

Allcott, Hunt, and Matthew Gentzkow. 2017. "Social Media and Fake News in the 2016 Election." *Journal of Economic Perspectives* 31, no 2: 211–236. https://doi.org/10.1257/jep.31.2.211.

Anderson, Ashley A., Dominique Brossard, Dietram A. Scheufele, Michael A. Xenos, and Peter Ladwig. 2014. "The 'Nasty Effect': Online Incivility and Risk Perceptions of Emerging Technologies." *Journal of Computer-Mediated Communication* 19, no. 3: 373–387. https://doi.org/10.1111/jcc4.12009.

Arpan, Laura M., and Robin L. Nabi. 2011. "Exploring Anger in the Hostile Media Process: Effects on News Preferences and Source Evaluations." *Journalism and Mass Communication Quarterly* 88, no. 1: 5–22. https://doi.org/10.1177/107769901108800101.

Barthel, Michael, and Amy Mitchell. 2017. "Americans' Attitudes About the News Media Deeply Divided Along Partisan Lines." *Pew Research Center*. http://www.journalism. org/2017/05/10/americans-attitudes-about-the-news-media-deeply-divided-along-partisan-lines/

Berinsky, Adam J. 2017. "Rumors and Health Care Reform: Experiments in Political Misinformation." *British Journal of Political Science* 47, no. 2: 241–262. https://doi. org/10.1017/S0007123415000186

Berger, Jonah, and Katherine L. Milkman. 2012. "What Makes Online Content Viral?" *Journal of Marketing Research* 49, no. 2: 192–205. http://www.jstor.org/stable23142844,

Berman, Ari. 2017. "The Man Behind Trump's Voter-Fraud Obsession." *The New York Times*, June 13, 2017. https://www.nytimes.com/2017/06/13/magazine/the-man-behind-trumps-voter-fraud-obsession.html

Bode, Leticia and Emily K. Vraga. 2015. "In Related News, That Was Wrong: The Correction of Misinformation Through Related Stories Functionality in Social Media." *Journal of Communication* 65, no. 4: 619–638. https://doi.org/10.1111/jcom.12166.

Bollen, Johan, Huina Mao, and Alberto Pepe. 2011. "Modeling Public Mood and Emotion: Twitter Sentiment and Socio-Economic Phenomena." *Proceedings of the Fifth International AAI Conference on Weblogs and Social Media*. 2009arXiv0911.1583B.

Budak, Ceran, Sharad Goel, and Justin M. Rao. 2016. "Fair and Balanced: Quantifying Media Bias Through Crowdsourcing Content Analysis." *Public Opinion Quarterly* 80, no. S1: 250–271. https://doi.org/10.1093/poq/nfw007.

Coe, Kevin, Kate Kenski, and Stephen A. Rains. 2014. "Online and Uncivil? Patterns and Determinants of Incivility in Newspaper Website Comments." *Journal of Communication* 64, no. 4: 658–679. https://doi.org/10.1111/jcom.12104.

Del Vicario, Michela, Allessandro Bessi, Fabiano Zollo, Fabio Petroni, Antonio Scala, Guido Caldarelli, H. Eugene Stanley, and Walter Quattrociocchi. 2016. "The Spreading of Misinformation Online." *Proceedings of the National Academy of Sciences of the United States of America* 113, no. 3: 554–559. https://doi.org/10.1073/pnas.1517441113.

DeSteno, David, Richard E. Petty, Derek D. Rucker, Duane T. Wegener, and Julia Braverman. 2004. "Discrete Emotions and Persuasion: The Role of Emotion-Induced Expectancies." *Journal of Personality and Social Psychology* 86, no. 1: 43–56. https://doi.org/10.1037/0022-3514.86.1.43.

DiFonzo, Nicholas. 2008. *The Watercooler Effect: A Psychologist Explores the Extraordinary Power of Rumors*. New York: Penguin Group.

Feldman, Lauren, Edward W. Maibach, Connie Roser-Renouf, and Anthony Leiserowitz. 2012. "Climate on Cable: The Nature and Impact of Global Warming Coverage on Fox News, CNN, and MSNBC." *International Journal of Press/Politics* 17, no. 1: 3–31. https://doi.org/10.1177/1940161211425410

Flanagin, Andrew J., and Miriam J. Metzger. 2017. "Perceptions of Source Credibility in Political Communication." In *The Oxford Handbook of Political Communication,* edited by Kate Kenski and Kathleen Hall Jamieson, 417–435. New York: Oxford University Press.

Flynn, D. J., Brendan Nyhan, and Jason Reifler. 2017. "The Nature and Origins of Misperceptions: Understanding False and Unsupported Beliefs About Politics." *Political Psychology* 38, no. S1: 127–150. https://doi.org/10.1111/pops.12394.

Garrett, R. Kelly. 2017. "The 'Echo Chamber' Distraction: Disinformation Campaigns Are the Problem, Not Audience Fragmentation." *Journal of Applied Research in Memory and Cognition* 6, no. 4: 370–376. https://doi.org/10.1016/j.jarmac.2017.09.011.

Garrett, R. Kelly. 2011. "Troubling Consequences of Online Political Rumoring." *Human Communication Research* 37, no. 2: 255–274. https://doi.org/10.1111/j.1468-2958.2010.01401.

Garrett, R. Kelly, Brian E. Weeks, and Rachel L. Neo. 2016. "Driving a Wedge Between Evidence and Beliefs: How Online Ideological News Exposure Promotes Political Misperceptions." *Journal of Computer-Mediated Communication* 21, no. 5: 331–348. https://doi.org/10.1111/jcc4.12164.

Gervais, Bryan T. 2015. "Incivility Online: Affective and Behavioral Reactions to Uncivil Political Posts in a Web-based Experiment." *Journal of Information Technology & Politics* 12, no. 2: 167–185. https://doi.org/10.1080/19331681.2014.997416.

Hasell, A., and Brian E. Weeks. 2016. "Partisan Provocation: The Role of Partisan News Use and Emotional Responses in Political Information Sharing in Social Media." *Human Communication Research* 42, no. 4: 641–661. https://doi.org/10.1111/hcre.12092.

Iyengar, Shanto, Gaurav Sood, and Yphtach Lelkes. 2012. "Affect, Not Ideology: A Social Identity Perspective on Polarization." *Public Opinion Quarterly* 76, no. 3: 405–431. https://doi.org/10.1093/poq/nfs038.

Kata, Anna. 2012. "Anti-Vaccine Activists, Web 2.0, and the Postmodern Paradigm—An Overview of Tactics and Tropes Used Online by the Anti-Vaccination Movement." *Vaccine* 30, no. 25: 3778–3789. https://doi.org/10.1016/j.vaccine.2011.11.112.

Kessler, Glenn, Meg Kelly, and Nicole Lewis. 2017. "President Trump Has Made 1,950 False or Misleading Claims Over 347 days." *Washington Post*, January 2. https://www.washingtonpost.com/news/fact-checker/wp/2018/01/02/president-trump-has-made-1949-false-or-misleading-claims-over-347-days/?utm_term=.299e88ed07b8.

Kim, Nuri, and Magdalena Wojcieszak. 2018. "Intergroup Contact Through Online Comments: Effects of Direct and Extended Contact on Outgroup Attitudes." *Computers in Human Behavior* 81: 63–72. https://doi.org/10.1016/j.chb.2017.11.013.

Kramer, Adam D. I., Jamie E. Guillory, and Jeffrey T. Hancock. 2014. "Experimental Evidence of Massive-Scale Emotional Contagion Through Social Networks." *Proceedings of the National Academy of Sciences of the United States of America* 111, no. 24: 8788–8790. https://doi.org/10.1073/pnas.1320040111.

Kuklinski, James H., Paul J. Quirk, David Schwieder, and Robert F. Rich. 1998. "Just the Facts, Ma'am: Political Facts and Public Opinion." *The ANNALS of the American Academy of Political and Social Science* 560, no. 1: 143–154. https://doi.org/10.1177/0002716298560001011.

MacKuen, Michael, Jennifer Wolak, Luke Keele, and George E. Marcus. 2010. "Civic Engagements: Resolute Partisanship or Reflective Deliberation." *American Journal of Political Science* 54, no. 2: 440–458. https://doi.org/10.1111/j.1540-5907.2010.00440.x.

Matthes, Jörg. 2013. "The Affective Underpinnings of Hostile Media Perceptions: Exploring the Distinct Effects of Affective and Cognitive Involvement." *Communication Research* 40, no. 3: 360–387. https://doi.org/10.1177/0093650211420255.

Meirick, Patrick C., and Elena Bessarabova. 2016. "Epistemic Factors in Selective Exposure and Political Misperceptions on the Right and Left." *Analyses of Social Issues and Public Policy* 16, no. 1: 36–68. https://doi.org/10.1111/asap.12101.

Mason, Lilliana. 2016. "A Cross-Cutting Calm: How Social Sorting Drives Affective Polarization." *Public Opinion Quarterly* 80, no S1: 351–377. https://doi.org.10.1093/poq/nfw001.

Na, Kilhoe, R. Kelly Garrett, and Michael D. Slater. 2018. "Rumor Acceptance During Public Health Crises: Testing the Emotional Congruence Hypothesis."

Journal of Health Communication 23, no. 8: 791–799. https://doi.org/10.1080/10810730.2018.1527877.

Nabi, Robin L. 2010. "The Case for Emphasizing Discrete Emotions in Communication Research." *Communication Monographs* 77, no. 2: 153–159. https://doi.org/10.1080/03637751003790444.

Reis, Julio, Fabricio Benevenuto, Pedro O. S. Vaz de Melo, Raquel Prates, Haewoon Kwak, and Jisun An. 2015. "Breaking the News: First Impressions Matter on Online News." In *ICWSM-15: Proceedings of the International Conference on Weblogs and Social Media*. arXiv: 1503.07921.

Schwarz, Norbert. 2001. "Feeling as Information: Implications for Affective Influences on Information Processing." In *Theories of Mood and Cognition: A User's Handbook*, edited by Leonard L. Martin and Gerald L. Clore, 159–176. Mahwah, NJ: Erlbaum.

Shibutani, Tamotsu. 1966. *Improvised News: A Sociological Study of Rumor*. New York: Bobbs-Merrill.

Sobieraj, Sarah, and Jeffrey M. Berry. 2011. "From Incivility to Outrage: Political Discourse in Blogs, Talk Radio, and Cable News." *Political Communication* 28, no. 1: 19–41. https://doi.org/10.1080/10584609.2010.542360.

Stieglitz, Stefan, and Linh Dang-Xuan. 2013. "Emotions and Information Diffusion in Social Media—Sentiment of Microblogs and Sharing Behavior." *Journal of Management Information Systems* 29, no. 4: 217–248. https://doi.org/10.2753/MIS0742-122290408.

Stroud, Natalie Jomini, Ashley Muddiman, and Joshua M. Scacco. 2017. "Like, Recommend, or Respect? Altering Political Behavior in News Comments Sections." *New Media & Society* 19, no. 11: 1727–1743. https://doi.org/10.1177/1461444816642420.

Taber, Charles S., and Milton Lodge. 2006. "Motivated Skepticism in the Evaluation of Political Beliefs." *American Journal of Political Science* 50, no. 3: 755–769. https://doi.org/10.1111/j.154-5907.2006.00214.x.

Timberg, Craig, and Drew Harwell. 2018. "We Studied Thousands of Anonymous Posts About the Parkland Attack—and Found a Conspiracy in the Making." *Washington Post*, February 27. https://www.washingtonpost.com/business/economy/we-studied-thousands-of-anonymous-posts-about-the-parkland-attack---and-found-a-conspiracy-in-the-making/2018/02/27/04a856be-1b20-11e8-b2d9-08e748f892c0_story.html?utm_term=.fd318ed9056d.

Weeks, Brian E. 2015. "Emotions, Partisanship, and Misperceptions: How Anger and Anxiety Moderate the Effect of Partisan Bias on Susceptibility to Political Misinformation." *Journal of Communication* 65, no. 4: 699–719. https://doi.org/10.1111/jcom.12164.

Wood, Thomas, and Ethan Porter. 2018. "The Elusive Backfire Effect: Mass Attitudes' Steadfast Factual Adherence." *Political Behavior*. https://doi.org/10.1007/s11109-018-9443-y

15

Conclusion

Kate K. Mays and James E. Katz

Since 2016, there has been skyrocketing awareness of the term "fake news." Writing in 2018, Britain's *Daily Telegraph* noted that the term was not one "many people used two years ago, but it is now seen as one of the greatest threats to democracy, free debate and the Western order" (Carson 2018).

The absence of truthfulness in journalistic accounts has been long been asserted, even by the father of the free press, Thomas Jefferson. In 1807, he wrote, "Nothing can now be believed which is seen in a newspaper. Truth itself becomes suspicious by being put into that polluted vehicle" (Jefferson 1807). Despite the rich history of such potshots, how was it that "fake news," something practically unheard of at least in terms of the public consciousness, so suddenly became perceived as a great threat to democracy, public health, the social order, and the planet's survival?

In fact, this shouldn't be entirely surprising, given the events in 2016: the "Brexit" vote for Britain to leave the European Union and the US election of President Trump shocked many people across the ideological spectrum. How could these two votes have gone in such an unexpected way, and ones so contrary to the expectations of the respective elites? Perhaps it was due to false information, and perhaps the false information was intentionally spread by domestic and foreign malefactors. Worries about plantings and the spread of fake news stories were reinforced by the 2017 French presidential election, won by Emmanuel Macron, which was also marred by vicious false stories of dubious provenance. (Although we are deeply concerned about fake news and attempts to use such stories to alter elections and sow civil discord, we cannot help but wonder if there would be as much concern as there is currently if the outcomes of these elections had gone the way preferred by the respective national elites.)

Further, though the absence of evidence is not evidence of absence (i.e., no effect), certainly in the US context there does not seem to be much empirical evidence that the election outcome was swayed by intentionally malicious fake news (Boxell, Gentzkow, and Shapiro 2018); indeed, many other factors were at play. This is partly revealed by a recent study's finding that Trump supporters in critical electoral areas were not heavy Internet users and were unlikely to be exposed to intentional fake news (Boxell et al. 2018). Though on balance conservative-leaning, fake news was promulgated against both Democrats and Republicans during the election (Hindman and Barash 2018), presumably seeking to sow discord among the electorate regardless of the result (but whose propagators, like most, were presumably expecting the conservatives to be the losers).

Still, fake news looms as a significant problem. According to a 2018 report by the Knight Foundation, on Twitter specifically, about 80% of the disinformation accounts that operated during the 2016 US election were still active two years later, publishing about 1 million tweets per day and form what is described as an incredibly dense "fake news network." Despite Twitter's promises to crack down on bot-like and spamming activity, a vast majority of these accounts remain active as of this writing (Hindman and Barash 2018). So, we cannot rely on the platforms themselves to solve this problem, not only because technically it may be difficult but also because their priorities may ultimately lie elsewhere.

And despite the uncertainty over past effects of fake news, there is no uncertainty that the problem is viewed with alarm by many foundations and governments that, in turn, are pumping many millions of dollars to study the problem and sponsoring a variety of research programs, educational initiatives, and technological interventions by scholars (including one of the authors of this chapter).

Moreover, it is likely that fake news attacks will grow increasingly sophisticated in coming years, both in terms of content that seems real and the ability of bad faith actors to infiltrate media systems, and thus may be more of a profound threat in the future. Hence, dealing with fake news is a major challenge that journalism faces as it pursues the truth; the situation is exacerbated by the onslaught of digital and social media. As noted above and throughout the chapters, there has been fake and misleading news throughout the history of journalism and the history of political campaigns. Nonetheless, there is both the qualitative and quantitative change in the nature of fake news today, as is amply demonstrated in the earlier chapters.

In essence, we see that there is a distinct tendency to perceive a crisis in the current wave of fake news, but, despite the exaggerated impact, it does not mean the problem is unimportant—it is important. Indeed, we believe that with advances in technology the ability to propagate destructive fake news will outstrip the ability of algorithms to staunch it. Moreover, fake news producers will get better at their work, meaning that the opportunities for impact will grow. What this means in practice is that journalists need to be highly effective in their efforts to not fall prey to false news. Media outlets also need to do a better job of bringing their efforts into a clearer alignment with truth in both the theoretical and practical senses of the word. To foster insight into current conditions, and suggest a roadmap for needed developments, we offer in this volume a variety of studies of what truth means in a journalistic world and how journalists produce their working relationship with the truth. And as an important complement to these processes, our contributors have looked at how audiences come to perceive the truthfulness of the journalistic products they consume. As a unifying thread, we had all contributors bring forward insights in these areas, with special attention to technology, social media, and policy.

Major Conclusions by Chapter Authors

As we explored these topics, we did not aim in this volume to write a sociology of the newspaper industry or of newspaper reporting; nor are we trying to offer exhaustive instruction about good journalistic practices. There are many great works on these topics. Rather, we seek to characterize how the arrival of social media has affected the production and consumption of journalism and how these changes have influenced what is perceived as truth. In this volume, we consider this question from multiple perspectives, including the technical, political, and social media aspects. The following synthesis highlights some of the more salient findings and points of connection between chapters, though our areas of emphasis are more selective than they are exhaustive. For an encyclopedic view, we invite the reader to (re)consider the arguments presented in the preceding chapters.

Politics

Lest we become too nostalgic for a "golden age" of journalism and truth in politics, the chapters in this book make clear that political misinformation and manipulation are not new. As Michael Schudson puts it in his chapter, "politics inspires lying," and there is a historical precedent for what we see today. Edward Schiappa also asserts that "truth-deficient political discourse is nothing new," and John Maxwell Hamilton and Heidi Tworek outline some of the ways in which foreign correspondents historically have been manipulated by foreign governments to propagate their versions of events or frame issues in strategic ways abroad. Peppino Ortoleva takes us back to mid-19th-century France, where *canards* (invented narrative tidbits to enliven dull copy or a slow news day) flourished. These pieces of fiction were employed for entertainment or as a useful distraction for elites to redirect the attention of the masses away from actual civic and political matters and instead toward "spectacular hoaxes." In this way, "invented information [served as] a currency exchanged between journalists and politicians, or high-ranking bureaucrats" (p. 123).

To that end, then, fake news has tended to prosper more in times of crisis or uncertainty, Ortoleva observes. This is illustrated in the ways that fabricated news and conspiracy theories took hold in the 20th century. What is important here is how these theories and pieces of information acted not as factual truth but as "oracles" (e.g., signs) that filled a deeper need for people to understand their realities. All this was prior to the advent of social media, of course. In the current polarized political climate, fake news has not just surfaced as a response to crisis but has also thrived in the Trump era. As Nicole Krause and colleagues argue, in an increasingly polarized climate there is a tendency for close ties (one's circle of immediate friends and family) to become more like-minded. Relating this to networked news consumption, social media users become more likely to trust and engage with news shared with them by ties they trust. Therefore, combating misinformation may be ever more difficult as it circulates within users' social and political milieu, never challenged by opposing information from diverse sources.

Brian Weeks and Kelly Garrett present evidence that compounds the problem further in their chapter about emotional reasoning. Politics has become increasingly emotional, as evidenced by the "affective polarization" that characterizes much of the political landscape that individuals must navigate if they are to be civically informed. Moreover, self-declared partisans are staking out increasingly extreme positions consistent with their respective parties' activist base, and these purified-issue stances lead to ever-more amplified emotional responses to political messaging. To pile on, political news coverage tends to focus on the uncivil and outrageous, which triggers negative emotional responses in news consumers. This emotionally charged, negative political content is ripe fodder for liking and sharing on social media, where "emotional content and expression thrive" (p. 239).

In their chapter, Lucas Graves and Chris Wells consider how the larger social and civic context has given rise to a political sphere rife with polarization, negativity, and cynicism. The decay in civil and democratic norms may be attributed in part to the overall disillusionment and distrust in government that has been observed over time. Additionally, social fragmentation and partisanship may also be blamed for the weakening of these norms: whereas once in politics being a good and civil actor took precedence over party divides (one is reminded of the time John McCain stood up for Barack Obama's character against a constituent's virulent attack at a town hall meeting during the 2008 presidential campaign), now the weighting of norms has shifted such that party loyalty may actually *justify* violations of civility.

Part and parcel of the breakdown of democratic norms is what Graves and Wells call a corrosion of "factual accountability," which they define as "the regulating functions binding actors in the public sphere to truth-telling" (p. 42), and the subset of the public, civil sphere that is most pertinent to journalism. The issue for journalists today is not that there is a dearth of information available, but that the normal, self-regulating mechanisms of civility have malfunctioned, rendering the truth impotent. Drawing on the work of others, they note that this has come about from a "breakdown in epistemic solidarity," which arises as a culmination of the public's growing polarization and subsequent disillusionment with our social and governing systems: today, supporters may view political leaders more favorably *because* they lie, resting on their belief of the illegitimacy of politics and media, which have also thrived on the extreme fear-mongering and divisiveness. To partisan audiences, "lying represents a just violation of unjust norms," Graves and Wells comment: "Partisanship has overcome adherence to civil norms as the basis of solidarity" (p. 48). Ortoleva describes how people, especially in times of crisis, have tolerated untruths in service of what may be perceived as the larger truth or "disturbingly coherent representation of the world." Narratives whose meaning is entirely free-floating (think of the Pizzagate conspiracy here, or wild accusations that Hillary Clinton killed people) "may be credible even though spectacularly unreal" (p. 129), precisely because they may contribute to individuals' perceptions of reality. Thus, attempts to refute this kind of information may only serve to enforce people's belief in it.

Truth

Given these degraded norms of factual accountability, Graves and Wells suggest that there is little journalists can do alone to improve their situation—a more rigorous reporting of the truth does not accomplish much if the audiences (and/or a politician's constituents) disregard the information or fail to hold the *mis*leaders to account for their deception. Moreover, there are historical roots for misinformation's lure and appeal, as Ortoleva shows us, which suggests its staying power over time. This paints a bleak picture indeed. Schiappa reminds us, however, that there is a silver lining in this current era of fake news, which is that we do still, on the whole, appear to care about the truth. We have simply reached a more nuanced understanding of truth, what he terms "Sophisticated Modernism," as a more contingent concept but one that does indeed exist.

The chapters in this volume present considerations of how truth in society operates at both a larger social level and in the narrower context of how journalists perform their job, though these are not mutually exclusive considerations. Clearly, social-level discourses and approaches to truth affect how journalists may conceive of their role as truth-tellers. Further, as Schudson sets forth, truth requires a set of "shared definitions" and the ability to agree on them. As he and others in this book have noted, however, the information overload that citizens currently experience from myriad sources online, through social media, over the air waves, in newspapers, and on their smartphones makes it more difficult to reach any kind of social consensus about what is an objective reality—or even an objective fact.

Of course, journalists' work does a great deal to contribute to a "social consensus" about reality. This is a large part of their influence, and in his mini-chapter David Swartz, following Bourdieu, lays out how the power to define reality is at the center of journalism's ability to determine and convince others what is newsworthy and "true" about society. In this, journalists struggle with each other for various forms of "capital" that may aid in the acquisition and assertion of cultural power. They also compete with other disciplinary fields, such as politics and economics, over "the power to define what is legitimate knowledge for the society as a whole" (p. 37). Schudson examines the definitional field more broadly, citing Hannah Arendt on how any group with enough power may control the narrative or set of facts about what is true (as we see in Russia and North Korea today): with enough of a power monopoly, one might successfully argue that the precipitating cause of World War II was Belgium's invasion of Germany, as an extreme example.

As described above, Graves and Wells suggest that partisanship and power only define what is true in contexts where norms and institutions for factual accountability have been degraded. Thus the standard academic and journalistic approach to truth that is based on "information availability"—which focuses on correcting falsehoods, setting the record straight, and tracking the spread of misinformation—is less useful in today's climate than an approach to truth based on factual accountability. It is more important now to discern how facts "make a difference for public life," not just whether facts are available for the public's consumption. This distinction seems particularly pertinent in today's age when, as Erik Bucy and John Newhagen point out, information overload makes the task of discerning fact from fiction increasingly difficult. It may well be that fiction is dwarfing the facts as it is, but if the public and their institutions care little about believing truth claims and holding those to account for telling the truth, then journalists' efforts to track down the truth would be in vain. Just as Schudson defines truth as a "social consensus . . . constrained by conditions of reality" (p. 24), Graves and Wells assert that there needs to be a social and institutional consensus not just about what truth is but also that it matters in public life.

Juliet Floyd pushes back on notions of truth as a social construction, asserting that there can be no actual truth (which she refers to as "The True") if it is determined by people's power and cunning to mold reality for their own purposes. While there certainly are such attempts, Floyd optimistically defends "The True" as an aim for every journalist, a norm that must be upheld in the pursuit of covering news. The professional realities journalists face—wide and varied audiences, and other new challenges from technology that this volume explores—do not require a new norm, simply a doubling-down on the norm of truth: what we need, Floyd argues, is new respect for the difficulty and ideality of the norm.

Floyd thus sets pursuit of "The True" as a "task, not a foundation," that journalists must undertake with each assignment. Zeynep Soysal similarly sees truth-telling as an aspect of professional role conceptions, but not the entirety of their work. She sets forth three goals that journalists may simultaneously but not necessarily equally pursue: providing useful information that is newsworthy; conveying news stories in a way that makes the information shared actionable; and correcting prevalent falsehoods believed by audiences.

The various goals of journalists are exactly why Floyd characterizes "The True" as an attainable but difficult aim. She allows, too, that in some cases journalists may not hit the target of "The True" but insists that journalists must be aware of the aim and the fact that a particular work is off the mark, perhaps due to the other competing goals elucidated by Soysal, Schiappa, and many others in this book. Journalism is a complex endeavor, situated as economic, cultural, democratic (or political), and moral enterprises. To add, the current context is one of intense political polarization, in which those being reported on denigrate coverage they don't like as fake news. The proliferation of competing claims among various news outlets renders even more difficult the task of conveying a reality with "The True" to audiences.

Given the complexity, Krause and colleagues decline to define fake news as something related to an objective reality; instead, they frame fake news as that which "deviates from those journalistic conventions that have governed the presentation of truth-claims as 'news'" (p. 60) Using this definition, we can see other forms of fake news that have existed long before social media (e.g., in the form of propaganda), and these may take on different definitions:

- Fake news that was never intended to be news (e.g., satire).
- Paid content as news (e.g., native ads).
- Journalistic mistakes (e.g., sloppy journalism).
- Intentionally fake news (e.g., suspect news sites that originated as blogs or opinion sites).

Bucy and Newhagen similarly present a "continuum" of fake news that separates "real news labeled as fake"—which includes factually accurate content that is dismissed as fake because it is damaging, or content that contained errors and must be corrected or retracted—from "fake news made to look real," which is employed to manipulate real news stories (e.g., conspiracy theories from real events) or is fabricated. Fabricated news may be seen as motivated primarily by profit, while manipulated news mostly aims to persuade. Whether imaginary fake news or real fake news, all of these instances may confuse readers, muddying their conceptions of what they can trust and what they should approach with more skepticism. Most of our authors reject the idea that we are in a new and different "post-truth" era from previous points in history, but, per Schudson:

> The conditions under which we learn and can confirm truths or disconfirm falsehoods has grown complicated in ways we have not yet socially and politically assimilated. Knowing the truth is harder because propaganda, profits, prejudices, and pranks travel more quickly and are empowered by new means of cloaking themselves in the garb of truthfulness. (P. 27)

Within the vortex of these turbulent information flows, though, it is important to keep in mind the basic functions of journalism in society. Schiappa lays out two fundamental questions that encompass journalistic role conceptions across the diversity of media outlets that now exist: *whether* to tell a story and *how* to tell a story (with shared definitions, framing, and the storyteller's subjective point of view). Communication scholars might recognize the alignment with first- and second-level agenda setting in these questions. In answering these questions, Schiappa lays out the "two poles" that journalists must navigate, which align with Swartz's description of the economic and cultural poles in the journalistic field. The economic pole is driven by a profit motive that is concerned primarily with maximizing audience attention, and the cultural pole is driven more by journalistic judgment of newsworthiness, that is, "what consumers should and need to hear about" (p. 83). At their extremes:

> The first choice leads to pandering and sensationalism, while the second choice promotes a kind of paternalistic elitism that leads many people to distrust "the media" altogether. We need to recognize that there is no absolute solution this dilemma. It is one that every journalist and editor constantly must navigate, and hopefully does so with humility. (P. 83)

To that end, Schiappa highlights the waning of the "Myth of Objectivity" that we see in journalism and other aspects of civil society. This is not to double-down on relativism and equivalency but rather to "stress other values of good communication—are journalists being fair? Are their accounts trustworthy? Whose interests are they serving? And yes, are they telling us the truth?" (p. 84) Of course, technology may complicate the clarity of these answers: "First, the sheer volume of messages and conflicting sources means that the traditional epistemological role of journalists as information gatekeepers and hypothesis testers is challenged. Second, the cacophony of voices amplifies the problem of conflicting definitions" (p. 82). We turn now to more directly address these technological features, as they present unique challenges to both the producers and consumers of news.

Technology

Two main threads about technology's influence on journalism run throughout the chapters assembled in this volume. The first relates to journalists and their audiences, and the second focuses on journalism as a profession. Journalism exists in a media ecosystem that is pulled in two oppositional directions, as Swartz reminds us, one that emphasizes profit and revenue streams and another that privileges quality reporting and story construction—the pursuit of "The True," as Floyd puts it. In this way, too, technology challenges journalism on these same fronts. The assemblage of audiences for advertisers—on both mass media and social media platforms—may be more related to the economic pole, but there is some crossover in how technology enables the "audience" to contribute to the cultural pole of journalists' work.

Technology and the Economics of Audience

It is clear, and now somewhat cliché, to observe that social media has disrupted the business and revenue models of traditional and legacy media outlets. However, Krause and colleagues point out that the fake news we see on social media today are really "new media [forms] shaped by older [economic] trends" (p. 58), including the economically motivated decisions that elevated the *canards* and spectacular hoaxes of 19th-century Paris, trumped up sensationalist and "yellow" news stories of the late 19th century, and segmented viewers and audiences by niche channels in the cable network proliferation in the late 20th century. Which is to say: while there is an economic incentive for fake news today, it flows from historical precedent.

What is new today, according to Krause and colleagues, is how technology enables "new levels of precision and sophistication" in how online entities can "collect, combine, and analyze complex data sets about their users' characteristics, preferences, and behaviors" (p. 64). This increased capacity for data collection and analysis has created the potential for filter bubbles (online "echo chambers" in which one is exposed to limited viewpoints that reiterate already held beliefs) and content targeting (exposing individuals to narrowly tailored content based on their specific characteristics and behaviors).[1]

Tandoc reviews how these enhanced-feedback mechanisms online, whether direct (e.g., reader comments) or indirect (e.g., behavioral metrics that track what is clicked on and shared), result in ever-finer content tailoring. The proliferation of channels through which content can be shared amplifies the audience's influence in determining the reach of various news items, and these platforms also provide outlets for user-generated content, which alters the balance of gatekeeping power away from the legacy media institutions.

These changes have also been found to alter newsroom culture and journalistic practices: editors and reporters now have to keep an eye on trending topics and engage in self-promotion of their work (a trend that has spilled over to the academic realm). The danger here, according to Tandoc, is that audience metrics may supersede editorial decision-making, shifting priorities for what gets covered and emphasized: "Knowing what audiences want, and giving them what they want, might get in the way of providing what audiences need" (p. 228). Further, the capabilities for user-generated content and news content dissemination through social media enable users to break news and/or boost certain news stories for journalists, raising the possibility of a "reverse agenda-setting" process, wherein the audience determines what is newsworthy and influences what journalists cover. The optimistic take on this is that news developments that otherwise would be overlooked, because they occur outside of the traditional times, places, and sources that journalists usually look to for stories, start receiving more attention; a potential threat flowing from this transformed process is to weaken editorial norms, which have been established and honed over time. Journalists are now competing not only with their professional colleagues but also with their audiences to break news.

Speed thus becomes paramount and may outweigh verification. Beyond the time needed for fact verification, the emphasis on speed in the new, never-ending news cycle also leaves little time for reporters to reflect on editorial prioritizing or to cover certain issues substantively. In the case of foreign correspondence, Hamilton and Tworek discuss how technology has forced a trade-off between speed (stories can be reported from anywhere in the world, instantly) and superficiality (because stories can be reported as events unfold, it leaves less time for in-depth reporting, reflection, and fact-checking).

Another major challenge to journalists and their audiences is the individual fallibility of people as imperfect information processors. Regardless of how thorough and unimpeachable a journalist's report may be, readers are still prone to emotional influence (Weeks and Garrett's observation), potentially biased by personal motivations (as Krause and colleagues discuss), and have cognitive limitations against the sheer volume and velocity of online information in today's era of big data (as described by Bucy and Newhagen). Because of this, Krause and colleagues express skepticism of technological or educational (e.g., media literacy) solutions to fix the problem of fake news. Beyond any potential inability to notice fake news, a larger problem appears to be an "*unwillingness* among audiences to expose themselves to information that is inconsistent with firmly held prior values or beliefs" (p. 58), from which audiences fall prey to selective exposure, cognitive dissonance, and motivated reasoning biases. Weeks and Garret, among others, provide evidence that individual reasoning, in particular, contributes to the misinformation problem.

Aside from being merely unwilling, Bucy and Newhagen show how, through the ways people process information—first by accepting it at face value and then reflecting on it and determining its truth value—they may be more susceptible to believing false news as it typically presents on social media as highly partisan because "information processing shifts to conform to pre-existing feelings and beliefs" (p. 208). To add, Weeks and Garret contend that, particularly if the content on social media platforms angers people, they will be more likely to revert to existing attitudes and beliefs to evaluate the information. Further, while social media is a place for news creation and dissemination, it is also a place of *convergence*—where people intersect their personal, professional, and political lives and interests. This convergence of social media makes it an emotionally charged space, Weeks and Garrett argue; therefore, when encountering political information on social media, it is likely to be emotionally framed, influencing the manner in which users process the information—and making journalistic neutrality more difficult and problematic.

All of these information-processing complications are compounded by the technological affordances of social media spaces, which obscure the "traditional signposts" we have used in the past to discern credibility. As Bucy and Newhagen soberly observe: "Add this to the growing list of reasons

why separating the editorial wheat from the fake news chaff for users of social media, particularly on smartphones, remains a daunting task" (p. 213).

Producing Journalism

Technology also impinges on numerous discrete tasks of producing
news: searching for information, finding interesting stories, and tracking
down sources. The social online environment has created new tasks for
journalists, like disseminating news content and drumming up interest in
stories. The specter of artificial intelligence lays just around the corner and
is already having a nascent impact on news generation. New information
gathering, story assembly, and dissemination tools are arguably benefiting
the journalistic enterprise, but there is a wariness that should perhaps ac-
company their use: search algorithms, new sourcing channels (e.g., chat
apps), trend trackers, social listening programs, and platforms that enable direct communication with the audience to name just a few. Sophie
Lecheler, Sanne Kruikemeier, and Yael de Haan discuss how the top results
of a journalist's search on Google or another engine may be what is popular but not necessarily accurate—a problem for individual users that
metastasizes when used as a tool for reporting. And Maria Molina and
S. Shyam Sundar warn of a "similarity" heuristic (content that aligns with
one's objective appears more credible), which may be triggered by the personalized search results characteristic of many algorithms. The trouble, of
course, is opaqueness: because most algorithms are proprietary, one cannot
be certain which mechanisms and data sources they utilize and to what
extent, depending on how simplistic and/or transparent an algorithm is.
Therefore, it is important for journalists to approach information searches
with a degree of skepticism.

Importantly, Lecheler, Kruikemeier, and Haan contend that information
from online and social media sources has not supplanted information from
"traditional" and offline sources. Journalists, they find, mostly rely on online
information when other sources are not available. This electronic "vox pop"
strategy may be used in the initial stages of information gathering or for inspiration; a point also made by Tandoc in terms of everyday users finding stories
outside of journalists' conventional purview, such as eyewitness accounts
of police brutality caught on video and shared widely online. Of course,
journalists may rely on social media for sourcing to varying degrees, and the
extent to which their reporting consists of reposting content found online
depends greatly on the type of publication—Huffington Post and Breitbart

on the left and right sides of the spectrum come to mind as examples of news outlets that are more embedded in the social sharing ecology.

However, in this platform-assisted search for information, there are technological pitfalls to which journalists' and their subsequent reporting may fall prey. Molina and Sundar review the heuristics that certain technological affordances may trigger: within the MAIN model, these affordances lie in wait in various platforms' modality (e.g., media's content presentation), agency (e.g., media's content source), interactivity (e.g., back-and-forth activity between the user and interface), and navigability (e.g., movement across an online environment). As such, Colin Agur and Valerie Belair-Gagnon make the case that verification is a critical task for journalism today. In their chapter, chat apps are discussed as opening a rich opportunity for reporting, as journalists may gain access to people's more personal, small-group discussions about events. However, chat apps also present new challenges to verification, as posts' origins can be difficult to discern and sources' reliability and credibility are harder to suss out.

Concerns about verification in closed-group contexts is echoed as well by Lecheler, Kruikemeier, and Haan in cases of verifying (virtual) sources on messaging apps. Hamilton and Tworek similarly acknowledge that social media offers an abundance of information that is potentially useful for foreign correspondents, but they also warn of ever-sophisticated techniques for doctoring images and videos (a practice even pursued by the Trump White House). The rise of "citizen journalists" has been leveraged by newsrooms as they experience mounting cutbacks to their foreign bureaus, but this reliance on independent contributors leaves news organizations open to fakes and scams. Hamilton and Tworek argue that foreign correspondents, with their access to "elite" institutional and personal sources out of reach of the citizen journalist, "can remain invaluable if they bring the skills to deduce whether a report, photo, or tweet is 'true' or not" (p. 144). Previously, journalists had editors, who served as a check on their work; now, anyone can be a content creator, and so journalists must take on a new role—not just to root out the truth but also to *verify* the truth others have unearthed and exposed.

In Sum

As our authors have demonstrated, the pursuit of truth is a difficult task. Even with today's live-streaming tools that would seem to present an accurate portrayal of events and comments in real time, it is not possible to fully relate any experience via the tools of journalism (prioritized images and words) in a way that represents an *identical* and full conveyance of the original experience. Even with the arrival of 360-degree panning cameras, the context of the psychology of an event continues to elude. This point was raised decades ago by social constructionists such as Gaye Tuchman (1978) and Herbert Gans (1979). Tuchman observed that journalists "make" the news, and, as such, the news is a "window on the world." It provides a particular view of reality that is necessarily constructed and contingent on numerous factors. Drawing on the window metaphor, conditions such as how large or small the window is, where it faces, and whether the glass is clear or opaque largely determine what one can see (Tuchman 1978). Short of reviewing the history of philosophy and the deep epistemological foundations of what constitutes The True, we would state simply that, although our instruments and records can convey what is generally agreed on as truth, even that agreement is based on social construction.

Take the simple example of the outcome of a baseball game. The "true" score or outcome varies as a function of the umpires' judgment calls. Usually, this expert reliance provides a straightforward and satisfactory solution. But consider the case where an umpire calls a runner out on home base when the player was actually safe. That declaration may have made the home team lose when they would have otherwise won. So what is the truth in this case? According to the record book, the game was a loss for the home team. This is playing by the rules and results in one form of truth. But due to an error in judgment, to many the game is not "truly" a loss. Rather, to them it is an arbitrary win due to the imperfect social process (i.e., respecting the authority and judgment of the umpire) that produces the outcome. From a pragmatic viewpoint it was a loss, but from a cosmic viewpoint it was a win. So even what is true in this case is arguable. Yet it is rare that we ever invoke absolute truth in our daily lives. Quite rationally and pragmatically, we accept a reasonable approximation.

While extreme examples of fake news are easy to define and characterize, there is a great middle ground where it becomes difficult to determine whether a story, narrative, or piece of information is "fake news" because the parameters around the concept are nebulous. Is a press release by a company or labor union (which are at times reprinted verbatim in news outlets) fake news? Do news reports that extol the virtues of a leader while completely ignoring that leader's recent scandals or failures constitute fake news? How should we conceive of false equivalencies between two sides made in the name of "impartiality" and "objectivity"?

There are numerous attempts to pin down what fake news is, and it seems that some of these definitions are aimed at politicians who are disliked by the categorizers so that they can be easily categorized as fake news generators, while exculpating the claims of those they favor. Suffice it to say that some definitions are offered at the book's outset (pages vii–viii), so there's no need to repeat them here. Instead our larger point is that any categorical scheme highlights some aspects and obscures others. While this claim should not be understood as saying that definition creation is not worthwhile, it does suggest that there is much complexity in many such definitions and categorization processes, and that the ideological premises of the system deserve careful scrutiny.

This situation is no more pronounced than in the area of political spin, which—depending on one's preferences—can range from fair exaggeration for the sake of emphasis to the accusation of disseminating false information. Even most fact-checking organizations rely on shades of truth (e.g., determinations that a statement is mostly true) rather than drawing sharp definitional lines. Thus, they classify certain pieces of information as probably true, which in some sense is contradictory as statements theoretically are either true or not. "Mostly true" technically means "not true," that is, false. Such gradations are not acceptable in US courtrooms. Witnesses are instructed to speak the whole truth and are not indulged if they give answers that are "mostly true"; anything that is a partial truth is considered a lie. However, such rigorous and formal use of logic and unyielding use of language would cause a lot of confusion among the public (i.e., by declaring things considered "mostly true" in the everyday sense would be declared a lie) and also cause a lot of hurt feelings among speakers so categorized, so we and the fact-checkers carry on with our gradations of truth.

Moving from the conceptual complications of truth as a concept to the technological complications, clearly ever-more refined technologies for manipulating the news are looming: beyond text and pictures, easy video fakery is on the horizon, with what is being termed "deep fake videos." These videos can show someone doing and saying something they've never done and said; the technology takes numerous images of a person, learns from these visuals how they look, and incorporates that machine learning to project the person in a video (Scoles 2018). There are researchers working to devise methods that can detect and catch this fake content, which in turn evolves (Scoles 2018). The potential for how this technology might further degrade our trust in evidence in general, and especially in journalism, is frightening. Though we should note that video documentation of politicians lying seems to have minimal consequences currently, buffered by people's loyalties and ideologies.

Hope springs eternal for an algorithmic solution, and in some cases they may be successful. But even as we develop new and improved systems, it is unlikely that any such system will be spoof-proof. Despite our various tools of verification, we see that the odds are that we will be left, as we are today: with contested versions of facts, selection of facts in arguments that pass each other by, and injections of false information by both malicious and ignorant actors.

Yet this pessimistic view needs to be tempered by optimism. Just as people have always been fooled by wrong information, there are now many new sources which allow them to get the kinds of information they want and more easily debunk bad information. Their skepticism has value in discounting official sources that have too often taken advantage of their positions of authority to give people wrong or misleading information. Nowadays correct information is more readily available than ever before, and the situation on this front is likely to continue to improve. Despite the dangers it entails of fomenting bad health practices, inter-group hate, and a host of other risks, having new sources at hand for the public that expand people's choices and give them the freedom to decide must generally be considered quite a positive development.

To close, the contributors to this volume aim to dislocate the discussion of "fake news" from the current political climate sufficiently enough to reveal the underlying mechanisms that have troubled and continue to upset the relationship between social media, the truth, and news. The idea that we can eliminate all fake news is chimerical, and as bad as the problem has been, and continues to be, the prospects of a dramatic improvement in the situation are dim. Certainly the efforts of fact-checkers, greater transparency on the part of journalists, algorithms, and consumer education can all work to staunch the flow of untruth. Yet the tools to produce fake news, and blunt verification routines, are likely to advance yet faster. Of course we can reduce it, and we should certainly try, but individuals must rely on their own judgment. Perhaps the best solution is in the hands of professional journalists, who have the opportunity to restore the faith of their audience and turn away from fake and misleading news sources. To do this, journalists must adhere to their professional norms of news collection and analysis. Yet they should also consider new norms that may be required in this digital age, while keeping their efforts to get as close as possible to "The True," regardless of whether they are operating in the economic or cultural pole.

Note

1. Krause and colleagues also take care not to overemphasize social media technology as the main contributor to today's polarization, pointing to recent research that shows the most political divergence has occurred among older Americans, who generally speaking rarely or never use social media but are heavy consumers of traditional media, particularly television.

References

Boxell, Levi, Matthew Gentzkow, and Jesse Shapiro. 2018. "A Note on Internet Use and the 2016 U.S. Presidential Election Outcome." *PLoS One* 13, no. 7: E0199571.

Carson, James. 2018. "Fake News: What Exactly Is It—and How Can You Spot It?" *The Telegraph*, September 28. https://www.telegraph.co.uk/technology/0/fake-news-exactly-has-really-had-influence/.

Hindman, Matthew, and Vlad Barash. 2018. "Disinformation, 'Fake News' and Influence Campaigns on Twitter." Knight Foundation, October. https://s3.amazonaws.com/kf-site-legacy-media/feature_assets/www/misinfo/kf-disinformation-report.0cdbb232.pdf.

Gans, Herbert J. 1979. *Deciding What's News: A Study of* CBS Evening News, NBC Nightly News, Newsweek, *and* Time. New York: Pantheon Books.

Jefferson, Thomas. 1807. Amendment I (Speech and Press). http://press-pubs.uchicago.edu/founders/documents/amendI_speechs29.html.

Scoles, Sarah. 2018. "These New Tricks Can Outsmart Deepfake Videos—For Now." *TechCrunch*, October 17. https://www.wired.com/story/these-new-tricks-can-outsmart-deepfake-videosfor-now/.

Tuchman, Gaye. 1978. *Making News: A Study in the Construction of Reality*. New York: Free Press.

Index

Printed in the USA/Agawam, MA
February 12, 2020

749980.002